FIVE
PATHS
OF STUDENT
ENGAGEMENT

*Blazing the Trail to
Learning and Success*

Dennis Shirley   Andy Hargreaves

Solution Tree | Press

a division of
Solution Tree

555 North Morton Street
Bloomington, IN 47404
800.733.6786 (toll free) / 812.336.7700
FAX: 812.336.7790

email: info@SolutionTree.com
SolutionTree.com

Visit **go.SolutionTree.com/studentengagement** to access materials related to this book.

Printed in the United States of America

Library of Congress Cataloging-in-Publication Data

Names: Shirley, Dennis, 1955- author. | Hargreaves, Andy, author.
Title: Five paths of student engagement : blazing the trail to learning and
  success / Dennis Shirley, Andy Hargreaves.
Description: Bloomington, IN : Solution Tree Press, 2021. | Includes
  bibliographical references and index.
Identifiers: LCCN 2021014249 (print) | LCCN 2021014250 (ebook) | ISBN
  9781942496687 (paperback) | ISBN 9781942496694 (ebook)
Subjects: LCSH: Motivation in education. | Academic achievement. | Holistic
  education.
Classification: LCC LB1065 .S5354 2021 (print) | LCC LB1065 (ebook) | DDC
  370.15/4--dc23
LC record available at https://lccn.loc.gov/2021014249
LC ebook record available at https://lccn.loc.gov/2021014250

Acknowledgments

Many people have played a part in bringing our work on student engagement to fruition. We are grateful to Danette Parsley, Mike Siebersma, Matt Eide, and other members of the management team on the Northwest Rural Innovation and Student Engagement (NW RISE) project for inviting us to work with them on improving education for students in remote rural communities in the Pacific Northwest. Our incredible research team members on this project comprised, at different points, Elizabeth Cox, Michael O'Connor, and Minjung Kim. Cynthia Johnston, Chris Spriggs, Karen and Mark Martin, Rob Coulson, and Jay Derting are just some of the many outstanding NW RISE educators who participated in this project, and we are pleased to have been able to feature elements of their work here.

The CODE Consortium for System Leadership and Innovation in Ontario was the brainchild of Michelle Forge and Michael O'Keefe, who directed it and invited us to work with them in it. Without their leadership, the insight afforded by the many examples of Ontario educators' innovative work would never have become available to be shared with this book's readership. Our thanks go to Shaneé Washington-Wangia, Chris Chang-Bacon, and Mark D'Angelo, for their participation in our Boston College team that conducted the field research and collaborated with us in writing up the CODE Consortium report.[1]

One sub-theme in our analysis of student engagement is technology. Dennis would like to thank his colleagues at the Bosch Foundation in Germany, for their award of a Richard von Weizsäcker Fellowship to study the many ways in which the digitization of learning is impacting student engagement. Sandra Breka, Jannik Rust, and Madeleine Schneider provided excellent hospitality and vital support. As Director of CHENINE (Change, Engagement, and Innovation in Education) at the University of Ottawa Faculty of Education, Andy has experienced the best spirit of intellectual community from his colleagues Amal Boultif, Phyllis Dalley, Megan Cotnam-Kappel, Michelle Hagerman, Joel Westheimer, and Jessica Whitley, who are also codevelopers of the CHENINE Charter that appears, in adapted form, in chapter 3.

This book has been several years in the making and draws on other bodies of research that we have published together and alone. Some of our writing here draws directly on these sources and we acknowledge their permission for reuse.[2]

We would also like to thank our Solution Tree editor, Laurel Hecker, for her outstanding job reviewing our manuscript, collaborating on the final revisions, and as a fellow Appalachian Trail hiker, sharing our passion for the book's quest-like narrative.

Our final thanks go to our wives, Shelley and Pauline, whose patience, good humor, and love have sustained us for decades now, going all the way back to our engagements to be married, of course. This is the third book that the two of us have coauthored together, and we know that we're not always the easiest people to live with when the writing gets tough. Their kind words of encouragement and willingness to listen to us while we sort out just what we're trying to say, and why it matters so much, have made all of the difference.

Solution Tree Press would like to thank the following reviewers:

Katie Brittain
Principal
Rose Haggar Elementary School
Dallas, Texas

Hallie Edgerly
Science Teacher
Adel DeSoto Minburn Middle
  School
Adel, Iowa

Adam Kent
Assistant Principal
Fort Dodge Senior High
Fort Dodge, Iowa

Danette Parsley
CEO
Marzano Research
Denver, Colorado, and Portland,
  Oregon

Neil Plotnick
Special Education and Computer
  Science Teacher
Everett High School
Everett, Massachusetts

Pasi Sahlberg
Professor of Education
University of New South
  Wales—Gonski Institute for
  Education
Sydney, Australia

Darby Tobolka
Instructional Coach
Akin Elementary School
Leander, Texas

Keri Van Vleet
Kindergarten Teacher
Tomé Elementary School
Los Lunas, New Mexico

Table of Contents

About the Authors

Dennis Shirley, EdD, is Duganne Faculty Fellow and professor at the Lynch School of Education and Human Development, Boston College. Among his awards and achievements, he has been a Richard von Weizsäcker Fellow of the Bosch Foundation, a German Chancellor Fellow of the Alexander von Humboldt Foundation, and a C. J. Koh Chair from the National Institute of Education in Singapore. He was principal investigator of the Massachusetts Coalition for Teacher Quality and Student Achievement and has guided and worked with leaders of educational change in many countries. Along with his Lynch School colleagues Deoksoon Kim and Stanton Wortham, he is now conducting an in-depth study of a school innovation network in Seoul, South Korea. His most recent book is *The New Imperatives of Educational Change: Achievement With Integrity* (2017). He holds a doctorate from Harvard University.

To learn more about Dennis's work, visit www.dennisshirley.com or follow him @dennisshirley on Twitter.

Andy Hargreaves, PhD, is a research professor at the Lynch School of Education and Human Development, Boston College, and Director of CHENINE—Change, Engagement, and Innovation in Education—at the University of Ottawa in Canada. He is president of the ARC Education Project—a global network of education policymakers and professional association leaders committed to advancing humanitarian goals in education. Andy is formerly Adviser in Education to the Premier of Ontario (2015–2018) and currently to the First Minister of Scotland, Nicola Sturgeon. He has published more than thirty books and over one hundred peer-reviewed articles. Andy's eight outstanding writing awards include the prestigious $100,000 Grawemeyer Award in Education for *Professional Capital* (2015) with Michael Fullan. He has been honored in the United States and United Kingdom for services to public education and is ranked by *Education Week* among the top scholars with most influence on U.S. education policy debate. Professor Hargreaves is an outstanding keynote speaker and workshop leader and has delivered invited addresses in more than fifty countries, forty-seven U.S. states, and all Australian and Canadian states and provinces. His most recent book is *Moving: A Memoir of Education and Social Mobility* (2020). He holds a doctorate in sociology from the University of Leeds in England.

To learn more about Andy's work, visit www.andyhargreaves.com or follow him @HargreavesBC on Twitter.

To book Dennis Shirley or Andy Hargreaves for professional development, contact pd@SolutionTree.com.

Introduction

This is a book about student engagement. It says so on the cover! We are not the first to study and write about the topic, nor will we be the last. Many articles and books have already addressed how to increase student engagement from a practical or psychological perspective. These texts raise important issues and offer hands-on advice concerning how to improve students' motivation, increase their involvement, and get their attention in order to advance their learning and achievement.

Why do we need yet another book on the subject, then? Well, despite all the well-founded advice that draws on decades of psychological research on motivation and engagement, levels of student engagement don't seem to be improving. Indeed, as we show in this book, engagement levels are at best plateauing and at worst plummeting. This is happening even when test scores have risen. Achievement and engagement are headed in opposite directions. It's a dismal trajectory.

Too many educators and policymakers have adopted a narrow view of achievement. They have associated it with test scores. They have limited it to traditional basic skills like literacy and mathematics. They have elevated achievement above learning in a way that often does injustice to the learning. They have raised tested achievement scores by getting students to memorize things that they barely understand and quickly forget. This kind of achievement involves little learning that actually leads to new knowledge. It is often accomplished without much understanding. Instead of addressing engagement as a way to get genuine achievement, education systems have promoted superficial kinds of achievement, at the cost of engagement.

The Missing Link

There is a missing link in explanations of engagement and disengagement, and of what's responsible for them. This missing link is the social side of student engagement. This neglect has led to strategies that are insufficient for the scale of the problem. Research on student engagement has been dominated by the discipline of psychology—and especially by what is known as *positive psychology*. This has promoted individual and small-scale solutions to what are often social and systemic problems of disengagement.

We review key psychological perspectives in this book because they help us understand the interpersonal dynamics of motivation and engagement. They cover the cognitive, behavioral, and emotional factors that bring about greater or lesser engagement in our classrooms and our schools. The strength of positive psychology is that it suggests practical approaches and strategies that teachers and schools can use immediately. These include things like boosting intrinsic motivation, providing positive feedback, and creating experiences of flow in students' learning. The limitation of positive psychology, though, is that it *only* examines the small-scale factors in individual classrooms and schools that can be manipulated to secure improvement. The problem with the prevailing influence of psychological perspectives is not that they are wrong. They are just not enough.

There is no shortage of well-known, psychologically informed strategies that, in principle, any teacher can use to enhance their students' engagement—from adopting growth mindsets, to introducing interdisciplinary projects, to using formative assessments, for example. The evidence base has increased, the books are numerous, and the professional development has been plentiful. Yet, overall, engagement levels don't seem to be getting better. So, what's the problem? Are teachers simply reluctant to take risks and try new practices that the evidence suggests work well? Or is something else getting in the way?

The distinctive contribution of this book is that it comes to terms with what is obstructing optimum engagement, and with what needs to be done as a result. To do this, we develop a complementary *sociological* perspective on understanding student engagement and dis-engagement. Teachers want to engage their students. That's why most of them came into teaching. But many things impede their efforts. Teachers know them all too well: principals who micromanage teachers' judgments, tests that take away time from learning, and overcrowded curricula that rush everyone through memorizing uninteresting content. Helicopter parents, oversized classes, bureaucratic demands, and insufficient supports are just some of the barriers that teachers encounter when they try to increase their students' engagement with learning.

A sociological perspective helps us acknowledge the existence of and reasons for these barriers. It enables us to see that there are institutional and societal (not just interpersonal) barriers, and to confront the fact that, alongside the solutions suggested by positive psychology, increasing engagement for all students will require institutional and educa-

> *Teachers want to engage their students. That's why most of them came into teaching. But many things impede their efforts.*

tional policy solutions, too. A sociological perspective helps us realize that teachers and school leaders are responsible for increasing student engagement, but also that they are not *solely* responsible. If student engagement isn't improving, it's not *only* or *always* the teacher's fault. It's often also the fault of misguided testing policies, underfunded public education systems, overloaded reform agendas, distorted power relationships, and hasty introductions of digital technologies.

Sociology, like psychology, can suggest practical strategies for change. In fact, by integrating sociological perspectives into the literature on student engagement, we can do so much more than make teachers feel guilty about disappointing student engagement survey results, for example. We can also avoid implying or insisting that teachers alone are responsible for putting things right even when systems of standardized testing and top-down control are working against them.

The positive side of sociological perspectives is that they help us to see not just that bureaucratic testing undermines student engagement, for example, but also that such testing doesn't exist in all school systems and can therefore be changed. Sociological perspectives can reveal how many systems disempower their teachers as well as their students. Yet, they can also highlight how high-performing systems succeed in empowering their teachers and students through proactive government policies. The COVID-19 pandemic also showed that the funding and flexibility that had been withheld from public education for so long (and their capacity to increase student achievement and engagement) could suddenly be granted. We only needed a crisis to release them.

Like an engagement in romance, this book makes a promise. It promises to wed psychological and sociological perspectives to create a deep understanding of student engagement.

If engagement is a problem in your school or your system, our book asks you to change both the system and yourself. If we want our students to get engaged, we must all get engaged too—with the big questions of system change, as well as with the practical and immediate changes in our classrooms.

Our Evidence

Educators first brought the issue of student engagement to our attention when we collaborated on a development project in the U.S. Pacific Northwest. In 2012, we were invited to serve as advisors on what came to be called the Northwest Rural Innovation and Student Engagement (NW RISE) network. The purpose of this federally funded initiative was to build a network of remote rural schools in order to improve student achievement. When we set about designing the network together with state education representatives and leaders from schools and districts in the five participating states, participants decided that they wanted the new network to increase student engagement.

Engagement, they felt, was the pathway to achievement. It was also a way to develop students' sense of belonging in their own schools and communities, as well as increase their attachment to schools and communities like their own, elsewhere. As we introduced participating schools to other networks with which we had worked so they could design a network of their own, their chosen focus on engagement meant we needed to get acquainted with the relevant research and to familiarize ourselves with participants' efforts to improve student engagement in their own schools.

Between 2012 and 2019, we met with our NW RISE colleagues in two face-to-face convenings per year, with an expanding number of schools, teachers, and leaders. They worked with us to develop the network through its different phases of growth and collaborated in what they called "job-alike" groups to create engaging units of learning together. These job-alike groups were sometimes defined in terms of their subject areas, such as mathematics or social studies teachers. Sometimes they organized themselves by age level, as in an early childhood education group. In other cases, they came together on the basis of their roles, as counselors, school principals, or special education support teachers, for example. Between convenings, participants interacted on virtual platforms to plan curricula, share examples of what they had tried in their own schools, and begin to connect their students with each other, too.

We observed, helped facilitate, and participated in these face-to-face and virtual meetings, and we engaged in monthly meetings with a project steering group consisting of representatives from the five states. Our observations, interviews, and online interactions in the NW RISE project provide the basis for many of the examples of student engagement we set out in this book.

Our book also draws on a project we have conducted together in ten of the seventy-two school districts in Ontario, Canada, over many years. On large-scale international assessments, Canada consistently ranks in the top dozen countries. Ontario scored sixth in the world in reading in the 2019 Programme for International Student Assessment (PISA) results of the Organisation for Economic Co-operation and Development (OECD). Ontario and three other Canadian provinces are among the highest performers of all English- and French-speaking systems in the world.[3]

Ontario is a sizeable system. It may be only one of ten Canadian provinces and three territories, but its population of over 14.5 million exceeds that of many countries, and it has almost five thousand schools. Its internationally recognized high performance has attracted educational visitors from all over the world.

We have strong connections with Ontario. Andy worked and researched there for fifteen years until 2002 and relocated there again in 2018. From 2014 to 2018, he also served as one of six advisors to Premier Kathleen Wynne and her education ministers. Even when he shifted his residence to the United States and began working with Dennis and other colleagues at Boston College, senior educators in the province sought his advice and engagement. Together, we took up one of these invitations, from the Council of Ontario Directors of Education (CODE; *directors* being equivalent to superintendents in the United States) to help them form and then collaborate with a Consortium of ten school districts.

Many educators in the Consortium participated in the project that provided data for this book. They opened up their schools, volunteered their insights, and gave us vital feedback that, in the best spirit of collaborative professionalism, was also critical when it needed to be. We visited all ten districts and interviewed over two hundred educators to determine how they were implementing the four pillars of the government's reform agenda.

1. Broadly defined excellence that included the arts

2. Increased equity, understood as inclusion of students and their identities

3. Student well-being

4. Public confidence

The emphases on inclusion, identity, and well-being, especially, meant that much of what we witnessed cast considerable light on the nature of student engagement. We include examples of this at a number of points in our argument. When educators volunteered their perceptions of Ontario's standardized testing system, this also yielded significant data on the existence and manifestations of student disengagement, too.

We ourselves are also unavoidably part of what we study. We have experienced engagement and disengagement as students, as teachers earlier in our careers, and as university professors now. Andy has encountered them while being an occasional stand-in teacher for three of his grandchildren during the coronavirus pandemic, and Dennis manages them while teaching online courses for students from all over the world.

It's a common practice for social science authors to make an opening statement about their own *positionality* of identity, privilege, or marginalization in their work and their lives, and then to show how this might affect their analyses of other people's experiences. We take up this idea and then go further with it in this book, by explicitly weaving in how different aspects of engagement and disengagement have been experienced by and impacted each of us in positive and negative respects. We hope that this will encourage you to reflect on your own experiences as we take up the challenge of improving engagement for all students, whatever their backgrounds or identities.

The Narrative of This Book

This book is a kind of quest in which engagement is both a journey and a destination. We're not advocating student engagement just for its own sake. It should lead to

> *Engagement is both a journey and a destination.*

the improved learning and well-being of students, their educators, and the broader community. A single path will not get us to full engagement, either. There are many ways to get engaged. We can and will need to take more than one path. Of course, it's much better to be engaged than not engaged. But getting engaged is a big step on the way to learning and success within and beyond school.

The engagement journey we describe in this book is a quest to attain these ultimate goals of learning and success. In fictional and historical narratives, imperiled peoples often embark on arduous and dangerous journeys together. Similarly, this book will track the quest for engagement along sinuous trails, where adversaries and adversity are often lying in wait. If educators persevere and stay the course, resist being led astray, and confront and overcome their enemies, then the engagement journey will take them to their promised goal of learning and success for all their students.

This book will track the quest for engagement along sinuous trails, where adversaries and adversity are often lying in wait.

The journey begins with a historic moment in education, when we are emerging from one age to another in which student engagement plays a prominent role. The opening chapter of this book sets the scene for understanding student engagement by describing how we are moving into a new era of educational change. This is a time of transition from an age that has been defined by individual effort and tested achievement, to one that is more focused on engagement, well-being, and identity. This chapter asks what is happening to levels of student engagement and wonders why student engagement decreases from elementary school through high school. We then examine how students' engagement with learning and with their schools came under the spotlight during the coronavirus pandemic and consider the consequences of what has been learned as a result.

As any adventurer knows, the first step in a successful journey is preparation. Chapter 2 introduces the knowledge that educators will need to bring along for their quest. We discuss some of the major psychological theories of engagement and motivation to achieve a more precise fix on what engagement might be and what factors bring it about. These theories of human development, intrinsic motivation, full engagement, mastery, and expectancy value have had a considerable influence on practice in schools. We then briefly introduce our sociologically informed standpoint on student engagement as a complement to the more commonly used psychological approach.

Educators who embark on this journey must be wary of three seductive myths or misleading ideas that may drag them off course or lure them away from achieving their true purpose of getting their students engaged with learning and with life. Chapter 3 identifies, then deconstructs, these three common misunderstandings about engagement and how to increase it. The first myth is that everything students learn has to be of immediate relevance to their interests or real-world problems. The second is that technology alone will eliminate disengagement. The third myth is that making all learning fun will be enough to keep students engaged. We show that engagement is more complicated than any or all of these myths. Avoiding getting waylaid by simple and seductive solutions is essential if optimum and widespread engagement is to be secured.

There are many enemies of engagement. We must learn what they are, be prepared to confront them, and know how to defeat them. Chapter 4 explores the types of disengagement that educators must battle against. This is where sociological perspectives take the stage, blending classical sociological theory with contemporary studies of schools and society. Disengagement, we argue, can adopt five different forms that often intersect.

1. Disenchantment with standardized learning and testing
2. Disconnection from an irrelevant and uninspiring curriculum
3. Disassociation from the school as a community
4. Disempowerment in relation to teaching and learning
5. Distraction by digital technologies

In the quest for greater learning and well-being, educators will have to confront some or all of these formidable adversaries.

In chapter 5, these perspectives and understandings are then applied to an archenemy of engagement. This archenemy embodies all five separate enemies of engagement in a single phenomenon: large-scale standardized testing. This chapter examines Ontario's testing system and its effects as a key example. We propose a fundamental reconceptualization of student assessment and provide examples of how this is already occurring in many school systems.

Having resisted tempting diversions and having defeated our enemies, we will finally be on the right track to engagement. Chapter 6 integrates the psychological and sociological perspectives to set out five paths of student engagement, which mirror the five enemies.

1. **Intrinsic value:** Teachers should harness students' intrinsic motivation concerning existing and new interests that arouse their curiosity and build their senses of passion and purpose.

2. **Importance:** Students should be encouraged and supported to work hard on topics that have importance for them, the world, or both.

3. **Association:** Feeling included in and belonging to the school and community should not be left to chance. Every part of the school should build belonging for everyone.

4. **Empowerment:** Schools must not feel like places of random adult impositions, even if they are well meant. Students must have a voice in the curriculum, assessment, ways of learning, and policies that define the life of the school.

5. **Mastery:** Hard-earned accomplishment provides more lasting fulfillment and continuous engagement than fleeting moments of fun.

These five paths of student engagement are illustrated with detailed examples drawn from our research in the U.S. Pacific Northwest.

The book closes with a short epilogue that reflects back on the nature of the engagement journey. It issues a call to action in our schools and systems to achieve the goal of ensuring engagement, and therefore learning and well-being, for all students everywhere. We make a promise about the future of student engagement. It is a promise to draw on every psychological and sociological aspect of student engagement so we can wed young people to their learning and success.

At first sight, increasing engagement among our students may seem deceptively easy—upping the levels of inspiration, insisting on more focused attention, or making school fun. After digging deeper into the theories and the evidence concerning student engagement, though, the topic gets more complicated. Engagement is no longer obvious. It's an enigma. But as we journey through the arguments and examples in this book, and down the five paths, we hope you will not only develop a deeper understanding of what student engagement is and what causes it, but also begin to see practical ways to increase engagement for all students, in your classroom, your school, and your whole educational system.

CHAPTER 1

From Achievement to Engagement: Two Ages of Educational Change

Since the turn of the millennium, there have been countless books and articles about inadequate student achievement and falling standards.[4] How many times have we heard about wide achievement gaps, worrisome test results, and students getting left behind? Too many of our school systems have been all about racing to the top, beating the competition, and being best in class.

An equally important but frequently overlooked problem is the lack of student engagement. It's not a trivial matter. According to a 2018 Gallup survey report, only 47 percent of U.S. students are engaged with school, with just over a quarter "not engaged" and the remainder "actively disengaged."[5] Around half the students surveyed by the Association for Supervision and Curriculum Development (ASCD)—one of the leading organizations for school administrators in the United States—say that they are bored every day.[6] The numbers fluctuate across ages and disciplines, but a lot of students report that they have no idea *why* they are learning what their teachers ask them to learn. For them, school is a long, tedious ordeal.

As they move from elementary school to high school, students become more and more disengaged. The Gallup survey results show that "engagement is strong at the end of elementary school, with nearly three-quarters of fifth-graders (74%) reporting high levels of engagement," but other surveys, Gallup points out, show steep declines in student engagement through middle school and then high school.[7]

School attendance is compulsory in almost every country. As COVID-19 has made clear, one reason that young people have to go to school is so their parents can go to work. There's no getting around it. For too many students, especially by the time they leave elementary grades, the experience of school is reduced to sitting and suffering in silence.

Student disengagement is a worldwide problem. Two decades ago, the OECD undertook the first of many international studies of student achievement. The PISA assessment that it devised measured student achievement at age fifteen in reading, mathematics, and science across the OECD group of developed economies. We'll say more about this assessment and its impact later. For now, it's important to understand that the OECD's tests, undertaken every three years, are also accompanied by surveys of students' experiences of school. In 2000, these questions addressed students' senses of participation and belonging in school.

According to the OECD's measures "between a fifth and a quarter of 15-year-olds [had a] low sense of belonging in the majority of OECD countries."[8] The scores were similar across countries, although the range extended from 17 percent in the United Kingdom, to 21 percent in Canada, to 25 percent in the United States, and to more than a third in Japan, South Korea, and Poland. The OECD report also noted "wide between-school differences" in senses of belonging— meaning that what happens inside individual schools, from class to class, significantly affects student engagement.[9]

All types of students are affected by these experiences of disengagement. Low-performing students from poorer socioeconomic backgrounds are the most prone to experience failure and to drop out of school as a result. At the same time, higher-achieving students in nations like Japan and South Korea become so disillusioned with traditional schooling in super-competitive environments driven by examination success that when they subsequently move on to university, they indulge in what Japanese professor Manabu Sato describes as an "escape from learning."[10] This entails "opting out of the educational race" by "spending no time learning outside of school," and instead falling prey to "egocentric nationalism."[11]

The OECD report notes that students who are disengaged at school are more likely to experience poor academic outcomes and to drop out. Disengaged students create classroom management problems for their teachers, and they don't acquire the social skills necessary to do well at work or in higher education, either. Student disengagement matters not just because it affects achievement, sometimes, but also, as the OECD puts it, because it is an "outcome in its own right . . . that will affect students' futures as adults."[12]

By the time the OECD reported its results for PISA in 2018, it incorporated many new measures of *What School Life Means for Students' Lives*. These in turn also presented new findings on students' sense of belonging. According to the OECD, "a sense of belonging at school reflects how accepted, respected and supported students feel."[13] Although 71 percent of students surveyed in 2018 "agreed or strongly agreed that they feel they belong at school," "a considerable number of students do not feel socially connected."[14] The report continued: "About one in four disagreed that they make friends easily at school; about one in five students feels like an outsider at school; and about one in six feels lonely at school."[15]

The 2018 PISA report also gives some indications of how students' engagement in their learning, as well as in their relationships, affects their achievement. "Teacher enthusiasm and teachers' stimulation of reading engagement were the teaching practices most strongly (and positively) associated with students' enjoyment of reading," the report found.[16] Students thrived the most in a learning environment that "facilitates and supports students' active engagement in learning, encourages co-operation, and promotes behavior that benefits other people."[17]

Other research supports the OECD's findings. One 2019 U.K. survey, for example, points out that 27 percent of young people believe that life has no meaning or purpose.[18] In *The Path to Purpose: How Young People Find Their Calling in Life*, Stanford University professor William Damon conducted extensive interviews with young Americans and found that only about one in five of them could "express a clear vision of where they want to go, and what they want to accomplish in life, and why."[19] Although about 60 percent had taken part in "potentially purposeful activities," they did "not have any real commitment to such activities or realistic plans for pursuing their aspirations."[20] Worse still, about a quarter "express no aspirations *at all*," and in some cases, "they see no point in acquiring any."[21]

With around a quarter to over a half of students feeling disengaged, depending on the measures used in different surveys, disengagement isn't yet an epidemic. You could even say that, given all the distractions available to young people these days, keeping up to three-quarters of them engaged in school is something of an accomplishment. Still, no society can lose a quarter of its students and expect to fare well in the future.

Two Ages of Change

Student engagement has been under the radar in many countries' educational policies for a long time. However, by around 2015— even before the coronavirus pandemic provided new insights into how young people experienced learning at school and at home— educational goals that look beyond academic achievement alone were already moving to the forefront of global policy agendas. In effect, we have begun to witness a transition between two major ages of educational change. We are moving from an Age of Achievement and Effort to an Age of Engagement, Well-Being, and Identity. In many ways, this shift has been accelerated by the global pandemic.

> *We are moving from an* Age of Achievement and Effort *to an* Age of Engagement, Well-Being, and Identity.

The Age of Achievement and Effort

Since the early 1990s, increasing student achievement, especially for subgroups perceived to be underperforming, was among the most prominent policy priorities for educators around the world. This was an Age of Achievement and Effort. In this age, cyclical reviews of performance data drove teachers to engage in intensive interactions focused on short-term problem solving. These interactions led, in turn, to rapid interventions to improve performance and close achievement gaps. Teachers and leaders worked hard to measure and accelerate the progress of every student, in every class, and in every school. The Age of Achievement and Effort was a golden age for testing, data teams, and teaching to prespecified standards.

For those who felt that previous reforms had been too wishy-washy, and too subject to the whims of individual teachers, principals, or system leaders, the Age of Achievement and Effort had its merits.

Educational reform in this period was driven by four questions.

1. How are we doing?

2. How do we know?

3. How can we improve?

4. How can this benefit everyone?

In the best-case scenarios, these questions led teachers and leaders to pay attention to performance, measurement, improvement, and equity. They made educators focus on helping *all* students, especially those who struggled the most, rather than on raising the overall or average levels of attainment.

The assumptions and motivations behind the Age of Achievement and Effort were sometimes far from virtuous, though. The age first emerged in the English-speaking world in the United Kingdom in the 1980s when Prime Minister Margaret Thatcher believed that the path to economic prosperity was to open up markets, roll back the state, pare back government support for the vulnerable, and replace manufacturing with finance and services. Her government fomented mass distrust of public institutions, especially public education, for being ineffective, obstructive, and unwieldy. By the early 1990s, the United Kingdom had created a highly prescriptive national curriculum that was accompanied by standardized testing and a toughened-up school inspection system.[22]

Meanwhile, in the United States, President Ronald Reagan, who was also inspired by free-market ideology, commissioned an elite task force that wrote a report on *A Nation at Risk.*[23] This report likened alleged declines in educational standards and results to an insidious war being waged against the United States as a nation, in which the teaching profession itself was a big part of the problem. By the late 1990s, a growing drive to develop state standards had led to more testing and standardization as the response. In upstate New York, for example, Andy's research on secondary schools' experiences of educational change found:

> Increased examination credit requirements led to losses of curriculum choice, standardization of content, and diminished capability among teachers to respond to student diversity.[24] Students became more test conscious and teachers found it harder to connect with students' interests and lives. Teachers felt that students with special needs and language learning difficulties were especially disadvantaged when they were required to take the tests. The resulting effect on teachers was widespread demoralization and burnout.[25]

The legislation of President George W. Bush's 2002 No Child Left Behind (NCLB) Act took the standards movement that had begun in states like New York to a national level.[26] NCLB began as a bipartisan initiative led by Senator Edward Kennedy of Massachusetts to combine heightened attention to equity with top-down accountability as measured by standardized tests. But as the implementation of NCLB progressed, schools eventually had to meet ultimately unattainable targets for *adequate yearly progress,* where 100 percent of schools were expected to be proficient or better with 100 percent of their students. When schools struggled, they were closed down. There were also epidemics of systemwide cheating.

Promising efforts to promote engaging educational innovations were sidelined as educators placed exclusive emphasis on driving up achievement results. Dennis encountered this in the early 2000s, when he led the federally funded Massachusetts Coalition for Teacher Quality and Student Achievement to improve student learning by developing teachers' professional skills.[27] Teachers complained bitterly when curriculum innovations they had taken years to develop—on art history, music appreciation, or the history of the Civil Rights Movement, for example—were undermined by the state's and the nation's relentless obsession with testing. President Barack Obama's Race to the Top strategy offered no easing up on NCLB's approach.[28] It granted funding only if states used the federal government's own test-based growth measures in their accountability strategies.

Meanwhile, the U.K. government, led by Prime Minister Tony Blair, set out a similar agenda of national large-scale reform strategies by instituting a National Literacy and Numeracy Strategy from 1997 for literacy and 1998 for numeracy.[29] The strategy provided prescribed and paced instructional materials, exercised relentless surveillance over implementation through the use of coaching and other strategies, retained the tough and even punitive approach of the existing inspection service, and imposed high-stakes consequences for schools that failed to improve on "key stage" achievement tests.[30]

Despite the government's claims of success based on its own data that showed increasing proficiency rates between 1995 and 2000, a report by the independent Statistics Commission contradicted these claims.[31] It concluded that the almost identical year-by-year growth rates in two different subjects were statistically highly improbable. Other large-scale research found that the government's claims about improved reading scores were "illusory" and "exaggerated," and represented very small effect sizes that "could easily result from test practice."[32]

This and other independent evidence demonstrated that the standardized achievement tests had inflicted huge collateral damage: a narrowed curriculum, loss of classroom creativity, teaching to the test, and diminished opportunities for what is now known as deep learning. "Whole class teaching . . . was a traditional teacher-directed style," researchers found.[33] "Teachers asked closed questions, pupils supplied brief answers which were not probed further, generalized praise rather than specific feedback was given, and there was an emphasis on factual recall."[34]

The Age of Achievement and Effort became a global phenomenon, promoted by transnational organizations like the World Bank, the OECD, and the National Center on Education and the Economy (NCEE) in the United States. For instance, when the OECD published its national rankings on its first international PISA test in 2000, governments like those in the economic powerhouse of Germany were shocked to discover that they were mediocre in the league tables, rather than strong performers.[35] In the United States, as each cycle of PISA results was released, the NCEE and the media wrung their hands in despair over the merely middling performance of a country struggling to maintain its reputation as the world's only super-power.[36] This was despite the fact that some states, such as Massachusetts, performed as well as the highest-ranked countries, and that the whole country had an average score similar to that of the European Union.[37]

Instead of developing visions for their educational systems related to what they wanted their students and societies to be like, country after country started setting goals in terms of the international rankings for PISA. Australia's government proclaimed its intention to rank in the top five by 2025.[38] Meanwhile, when Andy went to Wales in 2013 with an OECD policy review team (independent from the branch that administers the PISA assessments), the Welsh Department for Education and Skills stated that it wanted to be in the top twenty by 2015 (which would have placed it higher than England).[39]

More and more educational policies boiled down to how far the countries in question could ascend up the PISA rankings. But PISA metrics and the inferences made from them were flawed. For one thing, when each new cycle of results was published, the OECD added in new systems that ranked near the top, such as Shanghai and Macau. This created the false impression that Western countries below these newly included systems were actually getting worse, even when their actual scores had not declined. Moreover, the apparently exceptional performance of many students in Asia was at least partly explained by a vast *shadow system* of private after-school tutoring and cramming schools to prepare students for university entrance examinations.[40] According to the OECD's own 2019 data on student quality of life, these super-competitive Asian nations, where achievement goals eclipsed all others, actually had the most dissatisfied students in the world.[41]

The Age of Achievement and Effort narrowed learning to what is easily measured, concentrated undue attention on "bubble kids" just below the threshold of measured proficiency at the expense of students with more profound learning needs, and sacrificed engagement in learning for performance in testing. No wonder that super-strict and quasi-militaristic classroom and school behavior programs have flourished in the United States and England.[42] The popularity of these programs is a sure sign that these national systems have sacrificed lasting student engagement with broad and deep learning for short-term compliance with an antiquated educational order.

Though stuck-in-their-ways teachers and out-of-date schools are often blamed for failing to engage their students, in the Age of Achievement and Effort, it was actually top-down government accountability policies that were primarily at fault.

The Age of Engagement, Well-Being, and Identity

Large-scale change happens when old solutions become exhausted and new, more pressing challenges emerge. In the second decade of the 21st century, these problems came thick and fast. In the United States, the strategies of privatization, testing, and charter school development began to run out of steam. Results were showing no large-scale improvement, and people got tired of the constant attacks on teachers. Wildcat strikes by teachers in some of the most conservative states were supported by broad sectors of the public.[43] Republican governments as well as Democratic ones started to raise taxes so they could increase teachers' salaries. Parents and the mainstream media realized how disgraceful it was to be in one of the world's most advanced economies, yet still have school systems where teachers worked second or third jobs on evenings and weekends simply to support their families.[44]

In England, parents also began to side with teachers in opposing the standardized tests that they felt were sucking the joy out of children's learning.[45] Meanwhile, Scotland and Wales divorced themselves from England's educational policies altogether, including the policies on testing.

By December 2019, the international PISA results received very little coverage at all. Everyone, including the media, had gotten wise to the game. If a country went up or down a few places or points, did it really mean all that much? Why should anybody really care? Only a few diehard zealots still echoed Chicken Little and said that the sky was falling. The Age of Achievement and Effort, it seemed, had run its course.

Two decades into the new century, there were new, far more important things for the world to worry about than test scores. There was a global surge of mental health problems among young people, who were experiencing rising rates of anxiety and depression.[46] Technological change enticed a new generation into establishing online identities that often distracted them from more fundamental engagements with their learning, and from developing face-to-face relationships with each other.[47] The greatest global refugee crisis in fifty years propelled millions of youngsters into unfamiliar schools around the world along with accompanying challenges for their new teachers.[48] Racial injustice, climate change, economic inequality, political polarization, and threats to democracy created a growing sense that the world was taking a dangerous turn for the worse.

Meanwhile, although many countries had started to come to grips with educational inequalities in urban areas by harnessing partnerships with foundations, universities, and businesses, inequalities in the hinterlands of the United States, Australia, and elsewhere persisted and grew.[49] Securing improvement in communities that had lost their industries and livelihoods called for different strategies than ones that had worked in the world's great cities.[50]

With increasing consistency, educational systems have begun to enter a new Age of Engagement, Well-Being, and Identity. The defining questions for schools are no longer concerned with achievement, opportunity, and competitiveness. They cut to the very core of what Irish poet William Butler Yeats called the "marrow-bone" of who we are.[51] These questions are more personal, cultural, and existential than the ones that had defined the Age of Achievement and Effort.

1. Who are we?

2. What will become of us?

3. Who will decide?

In the Age of Achievement and Effort, policy priorities for many states, provinces, and systems had been based on three simple, specific, and easily measurable priorities. These were raising achievement in literacy and mathematics and increasing rates of high school graduation.[52] In the Age of Engagement, Well-Being, and Identity, though, policymakers have started to draw attention to the importance of new capacities and competencies. In Norway, for example, these include developing the skills of learning and metacognition; the abilities to communicate, collaborate, and participate; and the capacities to explore, inquire, and create.[53] Scotland's Curriculum for Excellence defines four desired capacities for its students: becoming successful learners, developing as confident individuals, being effective contributors, and becoming responsible citizens.[54] Drawing on the results of the OECD policy review to which Andy contributed, Wales aspires to create ambitious, capable learners; enterprising, creative contributors; ethical, informed citizens; and healthy, confident individuals.[55] In the United States, the Every

> *The defining questions for schools are no longer concerned with achievement, opportunity, and competitiveness. They cut to the very core of who we are.*

Student Succeeds Act of 2015 also promoted alternative measures of student achievement other than standardized tests. Almost everywhere, change has been coming.[56]

Even in the highly tested Asian educational systems, the tide has started to turn. For example, the Gyeonggi Provincial Office of Education—South Korea's largest school district surrounding the capital city of Seoul—has built a network of over eight hundred innovative schools (a third of all its schools) committed to developing dignity, peace, and social justice.[57] Singapore, meanwhile, has placed increasing emphasis on making learning more joyful, meaningful, and values-based.[58] It has reduced the amount of testing in primary schools. It has also introduced a national plan for outdoor adventure learning.[59] In the United States, ASCD has mobilized its resources to support a *Whole Child for the Whole World* campaign.[60] The OECD itself has significantly expanded its portfolio beyond PISA to encompass evidence on students' well-being and has led a global effort to create a vision for Education 2030 that includes over thirty competencies such as compassion, creativity, curiosity, meta-learning skills, mindfulness, and gratitude.[61]

This shift from one educational age to another has also been evident in the Canadian province of Ontario that is one of the two key sources of first-hand evidence about both engagement and disengagement in this book. In 2003, Ontario was squarely within the Age of Achievement and Effort. The province's priorities were to "raise the bar" and "narrow the gap" in measured achievement in literacy and numeracy. In addition, there was a determination to improve high school graduation rates and restore public confidence in education.[62] We will see more of how Ontario's Age of Achievement and Effort affected student engagement in chapter 5 (page 159).

In 2014, though, under new Premier Kathleen Wynne, the Ontario Ministry of Education set out four fresh priorities in its *Achieving Excellence* report.[63] One was to maintain public confidence in the education system, which had gained support by improving student performance 17 percentage points over the previous decade. Second, excellence was now defined more broadly beyond literacy and mathematics to include other areas of learning like science, technology, engineering, the arts, and mathematics (STEAM). A third priority was equity, which was no longer interpreted solely as narrowing measured achievement gaps in literacy and mathematics. Now, it also encompassed inclusion of diverse students and their identities, so they could see themselves, their communities, and their needs reflected in the life and learning of their schools. The final pillar of Ontario education reform was developing children's physical, cognitive, emotional, and spiritual well-being.[64]

Elsewhere, we examine what these new questions and priorities have meant for students' and teachers' well-being and identity.[65] This book focuses specifically on the *engagement* dimension of the Age of Engagement, Well-Being, and Identity.

What are the challenges for fostering student engagement in this newly unfolding world? How will we engage students in rural areas and small former manufacturing towns, as well as in our urban metropolises? How will we engage and motivate students from different backgrounds, cultures, and identities, and with a range of abilities and disabilities? How, in this new age, can we engage children and teenagers not just with their learning, but also with feeling like they belong in their communities and have a sense of meaning and purpose in their lives?

More and more people are realizing that we cannot keep on pushing up achievement with more testing, pressure, resilience, and grit. These approaches can work for a few students, to be sure. For others, however, who foresee bleak job prospects and are rethinking what their purpose in life might be in the uncertain years ahead, calls to buckle down and force themselves through an alienating curriculum just to bump up test scores make little sense.

It's time to get back to the big questions that face all educators. What can be done that will not just make our students clever test takers but also enable them to become deeper learners and better citizens? What role can our schools play in helping them become more

What role can our schools play in helping them become more fulfilled and productive human beings?

fulfilled and productive human beings? Can we find new ways to improve student learning and success by increasing students' experience of engagement? How do we create more of it? It is against the backdrop of these questions and the transition from one age to the next that we set out on our quest for engagement.

The Quest for Engagement

It shouldn't be so hard to get students engaged with being at school. Most people pick teaching as a career because they have a passion for what they want to do. They hope to get children excited about learning in general or fascinated with the particular subject they teach. People become teachers because they want to make a difference in the lives of their students. You'd be hard-pressed to find a teacher anywhere who comes to school every day just waiting to bore students rigid! Teachers no more want to have disengaged students than architects want to design ugly buildings or health professionals want to make their patients sick.

Engagement is almost the natural order of childhood. Leave children alone to play in the yard, on the beach, or just in their own rooms, and they don't appear to have any problem getting engaged at all. But ask them to mow the lawn, rake the leaves, or tidy up, and engagement is the last thing on their minds.

In between these extremes of indulgent pleasures and unwanted chores are the thousand or so hours a year that young people spend in school. In school, you don't always get to do what you want. You have to sit in a circle, line up, take your turn, and learn things that aren't always immediately appealing—from basic number sense to irregular verbs. There's a curriculum to study and skills to be learned, and students aren't always sure they want them.

When we look at school in this way, engagement starts to seem like only a means to an end. It becomes a way to secure achievement in material that schools and school systems have decided in advance is important. This is a big part of our problem in education today. We need to consider not just how we can get students engaged with predetermined curriculum content, but also how that content itself might be selected in relation to its inherent potential for engagement. If we don't consider what material or topics might be engaging, as well as how to make any content engaging, getting students engaged in our lesson plans and assessments can quickly turn into an uphill task.

To some people, engagement seems obvious. Students are absent or present, smiling or frowning, awake or asleep, looking at the teacher or letting their eyes wander elsewhere. But in truth, engagement is an enigma. An apparent smile may actually be a grimace. A frown can signify that a student is fully absorbed in intense problem solving. Engagement has many faces. It can be evident in the raised eyebrows of delight and surprise or the furrowed brows of intense concentration. It can express the joy of excitement about learning something new, and also the sorrow and compassion involved in understanding something important but troubling, such as the history of genocide. It might appear as an outpouring of creativity when students' minds are allowed to wander. Charismatic teachers can hold students in the palms of their hands. Quiet coaches and facilitators can use a different kind of hand-holding with their students as they guide them toward new levels of understanding. Engagement can occur with the assistance of digital technology, but it can happen without digital technology, too.

Recognizing engagement when we see or hear it and *actually getting students engaged* are far from obvious processes. The point of our book is to get beyond superficial signs of engagement, like not gazing out of the window, appearing to be attentive, or simply showing up. We also want to avoid any rush toward simplistic and seductive solutions that work for some students but not for all of them, like following students' transient interests, tinkering around

> *Engagement has many faces. It can be evident in the raised eyebrows of delight and surprise or the furrowed brows of intense concentration.*

with technology, or just having lots of fun. Students can be deeply engaged with ideas they've never heard of and that are presented to them in ways that make no use of technology at all. Students can eagerly engage with all kinds of material, including esoteric topics and darker aspects of life that can hardly be called "fun." Take a closer look at engagement, and its nature and appearance can be surprising, unexpected, counterintuitive, and anything but self-evident. It's not enough to tick a few boxes for engagement on a checklist, or move descriptors of engagement from level to level on a rubric. If we want to do something useful and powerful with engagement, we can't gloss over it or whiz past it. We need to get fully engaged with what engagement actually is ourselves.

The key point is that engagement and disengagement are not just inner psychological states. They are results of what our schools are like and what they do to children's inherent interests in and curiosity about learning. Given that babies and toddlers are naturally engaged with just about everything, we have to think hard about what our schools do to children and teenagers that actively creates disengagement.[66] We will see that disengagement is not the product of thoughtless and uncaring teachers who trudge through tedious material in dull monotones from the front of the class. Rather, it's a consequence of how we design learning and teaching in a diverse and rapidly changing world.

These were big enough challenges in the early months of 2020. Then along came the most disruptive change in schools for at least a century: the global COVID-19 crisis. This unprecedented pandemic led us to question practically everything we knew about teaching, learning, and student engagement.

The Coronavirus Pandemic

Once the pandemic hit, all across the world, children stopped going to school—90 percent of all children, 1.6 billion of them, in 195 countries.[67] Nothing like it had happened since the long-forgotten H1N1 influenza virus had raced across the globe more than a century before. Because of the coronavirus, millions of families were sequestered in their homes and had to follow shelter-in-place rules. In Italy and Spain, Canada and the United States, Hong Kong and South Korea, schools were shut down and playgrounds were taped off. Streets everywhere were emptied of laughter and joy.

Suddenly, educators were running real-life experiments with some of the most extreme educational innovations that had ever been devised. For decades, politicians, business leaders, and media pundits had criticized schools and their teachers.[68] They complained that lessons were boring and that teachers were trapped in a rigid, old industrial model of education.[69] Some claimed that students could be liberated with project-based inquiry, "personalized" learning, and greater uses of digital technology.[70] Right-wing think tanks sometimes wanted to dispense with teachers and with schools as we knew them altogether, and replace them with online learning.[71]

Former Assistant Secretary of Education Diane Ravitch condemned the technophiles as harmful "disrupters" who were motivated by greed.[72] The criticisms of traditional education weren't entirely original, however. Ever since the 1970s, influential gurus like the Austrian-Croatian philosopher Ivan Illich had called for people to commit to *deschooling society*. Brazilian activist Paulo Freire wanted to put an end to the *banking model of education* that deposited knowledge in people's brains as if they were vaults.[73] At both ends of the political spectrum, there seemed to be plenty of agreement that traditional schools were more of a curse than a blessing. The simple remedy seemed to be to abolish them once and for all.

In 2020, all of a sudden, the novel coronavirus *did* temporarily abolish schools. Homeschooling—which had previously catered to just 3.5 percent of Americans and 1.5 percent of Canadians—became the near-universal state of learning for practically everyone. In the most expensive private schools and some of the best-funded suburban schools, teachers received support to flip their classrooms online, and students were able to keep up with their lessons. For many highly motivated students who were already able to learn independently, and ones who were well supported at home, the transition to online learning was manageable. But these were exceptions. Now, for the first time in history, we got to see what learning would look like with hardly any schools functioning in the traditional sense at all.

Learning at Home

When COVID-19 closed schools, advocates of educational transformation, especially through technology, became practically euphoric about the possibilities. For them, the coronavirus pandemic was a miraculous opportunity to transform education in ways they had been advocating for more than two decades. Often generously, but sometimes disingenuously, many publishing and technology companies flooded parents, teachers, school districts, and education ministries with websites, applications, content, and links, all free of charge (at first) so students and teachers could access their learning platforms.

New relationships were being established between students and devices, teachers and machines, and ministries and companies. A new baseline for a post-coronavirus future was being put in place. Much of this was benign, as teachers, students, and entrepreneurs began posting all kinds of innovative materials online. When Dennis asked undergraduates in his classes at Boston College to retrieve and discuss new curricula that were emerging online as a consequence of the pandemic, they discovered a plethora of fascinatingly creative homespun innovations that teachers were devising.

Other aspects were more troublesome. In May 2020, Governor Andrew Cuomo of New York wondered at a press conference why, "with all the technology you have," there was even any need for "all these physical classrooms" anymore. Announcing a major partnership with the Gates Foundation to "reimagine education" on these lines in the post-coronavirus future, Cuomo overlooked the foundation's consistently negative track record with school-improvement interventions—to which prominent critics immediately drew attention.[74]

Everything got a lot messier for everyone. Teachers turned into contortionists as they strove to engage and support their students in any way they could, no matter how unusual it was. While many elite private school teachers just taught their usual classes online, confident in the knowledge that their students had access to the necessary technology, that the students' home environments would likely be supportive, and that the sizes of classes they had to manage on a digital platform were small, the results elsewhere were a lot more mixed. Teachers and school districts scrambled to get resources out to young people and their families.[75]

Some teachers were trusted to use their professional judgment and contact their families within a couple of days. Others, in systems that were worried about students with inequitable access to resources, or even fearful about being sued by parents of children with special educational needs, had to wait up to two and even four weeks before their districts and states would permit them to get started.[76] Some teachers tried to do part of their teaching online. In many systems all around the world, it was teachers who had to go to school, where they taught, while the students remained at home, using virtual platforms.[77] However, unable to see their students face-to-face or respond to their intellectual and emotional struggles in real time, teaching online was far from easy.[78]

In Canada, when the kindergarten teacher of Andy's twin grandchildren held her first online class with seven or eight students, one of the twins lay sideways across her Nanna, the other did a full-frontal grimace in front of her iPad screen to show off her missing tooth (without explaining what she was doing), and their older brother periodically walked by enunciating a Greek chorus of ironic commentary. Meanwhile, another student's dad could be heard prompting him from the side about what to say! With kindergarteners, these moments can seem cute or funny. With truculent and argumentative teenagers, they are anything but.

Students like these were fortunate. At least they had access to technology and parents who knew how to use it. Yet, the Canadian province of Nova Scotia was not alone in discovering that more than 30 percent of its students had no digital devices or internet access at all.[79]

The percentage was roughly the same in the United States, impacting between fifteen and sixteen million K–12 public school students.[80] Even Finland, internationally acclaimed for its high-performing students, had to cope with one in five families having no technology access.[81] A survey of teachers in South Carolina reported that over 40 percent of teachers said students did not have access to digital tools or did not feel comfortable using them: "One family had internet access through only mom's cell phone—which had to be shared among 6 children."[82] Teachers and families also experienced the opposite problem, as they tried to drag their kids away from excess screen use to try out other ways of learning.[83]

Some school districts purchased digital tablets in bulk,[84] although shortages of hardware in the face of surging demand meant that this wasn't always a feasible option.[85] Others turned on the Wi-Fi in their empty schools so that people could drive their kids to the school parking lots to download materials onto their devices, which they could work on back home.[86]

Poor families with few resources, and with no internet connections, struggled even to acquire pencils, coloring pens, Play-Doh, glue, paper, Scotch tape, books, or magazines. School districts did things like having teachers deliver learning resources in plastic or wooden boxes on families' doorsteps.[87] They used school buses to drop off stashes of materials,[88] or contracted with the newspaper or postal services to have worksheets delivered by them.[89] Even then, and even when students had access to technology, roughly three million young people in the United States alone simply stopped attending school by any definition.[90] A survey spanning 150 countries conducted by UNICEF, UNESCO, and the World Bank between June and October 2020 reported that not only were 290 million children still out of school worldwide, but "schoolchildren in low- and lower-middle-income countries [had] already lost nearly four months of schooling since the start of the pandemic, compared to six weeks of loss in high-income countries."[91] Without the care, protection, and compensation that in-person public schools typically provide for young people whose home circumstances are especially challenging, older siblings suddenly found that they were now responsible for childcare for their sisters or brothers because the parents, grandparents, or other caregivers had to work, were unavailable, or were sick, for example.[92]

Meanwhile, parents and other caregivers who *were* able to stay at home with their kids all day started climbing the walls with frustration, especially if their kids couldn't self-regulate. For example, Shiri Kenigsberg Levi, a mother in Israel, delivered a rant that went viral on YouTube. "Listen. It's not working, this distance-learning thing," she said. "Seriously, it's impossible! It's crazy!" With four kids, she was overwhelmed trying to manage their learning: "Just imagine how many WhatsApps, how many teachers for each child, how many subjects per child." Her family only had two computers, so these had to be shared. "All morning they're fighting over the computers," she despaired.[93]

In *The Washington Post*, a mother in Iowa shared her disgust that her child's school could think it was appropriate to give the third grader a C– in the middle of a pandemic.[94] In *The New York Times*, another parent, at her wits' end with being unable to manage her children's misbehavior, consulted a nightclub bouncer, a hockey coach, a child psychologist, and a member of the Los Angeles Police Department for practical advice.[95]

Like a volcanic ring of fire, problems erupted everywhere. *Everybody* was out of their depth. Teachers and families were making everything up as they went along. All of those who had asserted that schools had had their day, that they were relics of the industrial age, and that learning could be delivered in flexible, personalized ways, in online environments, often at home, were suddenly eating massive portions of humble pie.[96] Teachers who had been taken for granted for years earned new respect overnight. If any of us thought schools had been a bad idea, we soon discovered what life would be like without them: an educational, psychological, and economic apocalypse.

> *Like a volcanic ring of fire, problems erupted everywhere.* Everybody *was out of their depth.*

The U.S. magazine *Education Week* surveyed 908 teachers and district leaders in the first week in May 2020 about their perceptions regarding the effects of learning at home. Forty-two percent of teachers said student engagement was much lower than it had been before the coronavirus—worse than a month previously. Sixty percent of educators said there had been a drop-off in engagement over the preceding two weeks.[97]

And yet, we should beware of idealizing the schools we temporarily left behind. Teachers are scarcely going to tell national survey takers that their kids are more engaged at home than they are in the teachers' own classes. What would that say about the teachers' professionalism and their abilities to capture and keep their students' interests?[98]

Writing in *The New York Times*, eighth-grade student Veronique Mintz informed her readers that she was grateful to be learning online, at her own pace, away from her school. She decried her classmates, who were always "talking out of turn. Destroying classroom materials. Disrespecting teachers. Blurting out answers during tests. Students pushing, kicking, hitting one another and even rolling on the ground. This is what happens in my school every single day," she wrote.[99]

University of Ottawa professor Jess Whitley drew attention to how the families of students with special needs coped with the pandemic.[100] Some couldn't fathom what to do with the assistive technologies that the schools had previously been using to help their kids to learn. Others were distraught about why they couldn't explain to their children why they just couldn't go to school, be with their friends, and enjoy their regular routines anymore. However, other parents felt that their children with special needs had been liberated at home because their kids could wiggle around and go outside to let off steam whenever they wanted, instead of having to sit still all the time. Children's play advocates William Doyle and Pasi Sahlberg pointed out that many children had more chances to play outside and enjoy the proven benefits to their well-being that COVID-19 provided, rather than being trapped indoors doing endless hours of test preparation that many systems would otherwise have been preoccupied with at the time the pandemic hit.[101]

Then there are Andy's twin granddaughters and his grandson. When he asked them to draw what they missed about school, none of them drew things that depicted their learning or even their teachers. Andy's grandson drew a picture of digging up worms with his friends. One of the twins drew a slide out in the yard. Then the other one sketched an image of herself, with two figures, that represented what she was *not* missing at school. "Who are they?" Andy asked. "My two enemies," she said. Life in school isn't always all that it's cracked up to be.[102]

When everyone returns to school, then, it's not necessarily going to be a glorious reunion with engaging and innovative learning. Nor will it mark a reluctant abandonment of superior home-based alternatives, either. For many students, teachers, and parents, when the health conditions are sufficiently safe, going back to school is mainly just a blessed relief—a return to some semblance of normality, being part of a community, getting back together with friends.

Back to School—But Not as We Knew It

As the COVID-19 lockdown stretched through into the fall and winter of 2020, pressure mounted to get children back to school. Once safety considerations have been ensured, getting children back to school really does matter. Schools play a vital role in smoothing out the extreme peaks and troughs that define the differences between family circumstances. When privileged families get more and more exclusively involved in their children's education, educational inequalities increase. Richard Rothstein, Senior Fellow at the Haas Institute at the University of California, Berkeley School of Law, wrote an article, which appeared in *The Washington Post*, on "Why Covid-19 Will 'Explode' Existing Academic Achievement Gaps."[103] He pointed to research findings predating COVID-19 that indicated how "children whose parents can more effectively help with homework gain more [academically] than children whose parents can do so less well."

These differences extend into summer learning opportunities. "The educational gap is wider when children return after summer vacation than it was in the spring, because middle-class children frequently have summer enrichment that reinforces knowledge and experience." When almost everybody is confined to "learning at home," these inequalities are magnified many times over, he pointed out.

People like us, who have advised parents and teachers on public media to steer clear of dreary worksheets and to get children engaged with natural learning opportunities in their home environment like baking, gardening, playing music, knitting, skipping, bird-watching, writing postcards to grandparents, and so on, have been speaking mainly to middle-class parents, who already have time, space, knowledge, and resources to support their children's learning in this way. Children in these families may have managed to more than keep up with the curriculum. Many middle-class parents, already used to inundating their children with extra activities to keep them ahead of the pack, actually helped their children surge even further ahead during the pandemic.[104] Indeed, a few elite parents added their children's awesome learning accomplishments to other pandemic boasts on social media about sourdough baking and epic home-gym workouts.[105] Helicopter parents took advantage of the new digital learning environments to hover on Zoom, in front of the virtual teacher, their own children, the whole class, and each other—creating a kind of hyper-engagement that stressed everybody out beyond belief.[106]

Meanwhile, children in many working-class families, especially ones who were already in poverty or who had been thrust into it by the virus, where parents don't have the financial or cultural capital of their middle-class counterparts, have often struggled to find a time and place to study. Millions stayed at home all alone with no one to look after them while their parents went out to work in hazardous situations with no personal protective equipment.[107] These children have had to struggle to get the academic help they need whenever and however they can. For many of these families, issues like buying groceries and paying the rent became new and persistent problems. According to *The Washington Post*, the surge of people living in poverty in the United States in 2020 was "the biggest single jump since the government began tracking poverty 60 years ago."[108] By January 2021, nearly 11 million U.S. children—roughly one out of every seven—were poor.[109] These problems were not specific to the United States. In the United Kingdom, by the end of 2020, and despite government programs of substantial financial support, 700,000 people had still fallen into poverty because of COVID-19—120,000 of them being children.[110] In Europe, the collapse of the tourism industry was a major contributor to rapidly rising poverty levels across the continent.[111]

In many countries, issues of social class inequality are compounded by racial and ethnic marginalization. In the United States, the pre-existing poverty gaps between groups "have widened during the pandemic." While "before the pandemic, the monthly poverty rate for White individuals was 11 percent, versus 24 percent for Black and Hispanic individuals," by October 2020 the rate had climbed to 26.3 percent for African Americans, 26.9 percent for Hispanics, and 12.3 percent for Whites.[112] Meanwhile, the aggregate child poverty rate in the United States had almost reached 20 percent, or one out of every five children.[113] Like the United States, the United Kingdom and other countries also displayed unequal COVID-19 death rates along racial and social class lines, and especially at the intersections of the two. This was due to a number of factors, including poor and racially marginalized populations having a greater likelihood of holding high-risk occupations as essential workers, having a greater frequency of living in multifamily and densely populated dwellings, having to resort to crowded public transportation to get to work and back, or other life circumstances.[114]

Out-of-school factors normally make by far the largest contribution to social inequality.[115] If anything, despite all their problems, public schools actually *decrease* inequality.[116] In spite of everything that critics of so-called factory schools claim, one of the best predictors of longevity and occupational mobility is the number of years spent in school.[117] What the natural experiment of COVID-19 has revealed is that when we eject young people from in-person schooling, in the overwhelming majority of cases, we remove the counterbalancing forces that schools provide for vulnerable students. It exacerbates the problems that many children and teenagers from poor and racially marginalized backgrounds experience, by leaving them at the mercy of the unequal environments outside of their schools.

We have schools for many reasons. One of the most important of them is to flatten out the extremes of difference between children from opposite ends of the social class scale, to offer all children the same opportunities, with extra help for those who need it, and to enable children to learn to live together, and even make friends with peers who are different from them, as well as ones who are similar.

Having children in school is a public priority and a human necessity. Young people's quality of life depends on it. But as countries, states, and provinces moved toward reopening their schools, a brutal reality imposed itself: Schools aren't always or only about learning. One reason for the existence of public schools is, quite frankly, to enable parents to go to work. Without schools, economies cannot function, because those schools look after the young. Postindustrial societies have rightly chosen to put children in school, rather than in warehouses, workhouses, or prisons. But at the end of the day, it's still somewhere for them to be when they can't be left on their own at home.

Some systems during the pandemic wanted to get children back in school with almost indecent haste. They were driven more by the economic imperative to protect jobs and make money than by wanting children to engage with learning. Former U.S. President Donald Trump threatened to withhold funding from districts if they didn't reopen their schools, even in places where infection rates were high.[118] England's Education Secretary, Gavin Williamson, at one point declared he would introduce punitive fines for parents who didn't ensure their children returned to school.[119] These leaders may have shed crocodile tears for disadvantaged students and how much they were falling behind every day they were not in school. But in truth, their concern was less for the loss of learning than for a down-turned economy.

But what did going back to school, with physical distancing and face masks, look like in practice? For the sake of putting parents back to work, has it been better or worse, more or less engaging, than learning at home?

Canada's *Globe and Mail* education reporter, Caroline Alphonso, described the Quebec government's plans to reopen schools earlier than any other province, even as coronavirus infection and death rates in the province remained the highest in Canada.[120] Quebec's plan, she pointed out, involved students sitting apart, in individual desks, without physical education, group work, arts, or play. In student engagement terms, this was like dialing schools back a century from the digital 2020s to the analog 1920s. When Andy shared this story on Twitter, there were outraged responses from educators. They described the move as "devastating" and "shameful." It reduced schools to little more than "a babysitting service."[121]

Physical distancing needn't mean that education has to be this disengaging, though. Many countries are finding ways for children to gather in small pods where they can interact internally with each other but not outside their pods. A number of systems are following the lead of Denmark and other Scandinavian nations by organizing learning outdoors wherever possible, so that being back in school can actually enhance children's well-being, rather than damage it.[122] Perhaps this temporary innovation may turn into a permanent form of increased engagement for students in the future.

Even where physical distancing means that students can no longer sit together in small groups and chat with their friends while they are working, this is not the only way to cooperate. Paper "snowball" tossing activities, for example, involve students in a socially spaced circle throwing problems, answers, and insights to each other by tossing paper that has been crumpled up into balls.[123] Likewise, students' patterns of belief can be mapped out on a gymnasium floor for a real-life scattergram of human opinions that are physically embodied and geometrically represented where the students actually stand. Digital platforms can gather together students' opinions in real time and reflect them back to each other. And skipping together is one of the oldest games of modern times. These are only a few of the ways that youngsters can engage with their learning in and out of school.

Rethinking Engagement After the Coronavirus

The big questions in the end concern how we can apply the lessons of this pandemic to make our schools more engaging places for students. Can we redesign schools so that no student dreads the daily confrontation with his or her enemies? Can we create safe environments that help all students to engage with their learning without being disrupted by their peers? Can we get all teachers to move beyond arbitrary and insensitive grading practices? And can we access and use technology to enhance and enrich teaching and learning in school, rather than undermining or replacing it?[124]

Perhaps the most important question for this book is, What can we learn of lasting value from this pandemic about student engagement? Some children have savored their time at home with their parents. Many parents have gained new appreciation for their children's teachers, as they have discovered how hard it is to keep their children focused on their schoolwork when they are restless, easily distracted, frustrated with their downloads and apps, and annoyed by their siblings. Technology at home has sometimes been a blessing for opening access to learning resources, but it has also been a curse of malfunctions and distractions. Schools have been spotlighted as places we cannot do without. Hour after hour, day by day, over weeks and then months, in all but a few places, we have been reminded that the rich social environment that schools and their teachers can provide offers more enduring engagement for children than many locked-down families or any digital devices ever can.

The most important question for this book is, What can we learn of lasting value from this pandemic about student engagement?

The monumental natural experiment of COVID-19 has brought to all our attention just why it is that we need schools in the first place. In many ways, we see how the precious legacy of free public education for all has been taken for granted. We understand now that we can't do without physical schools, not just as places for children to be while their parents are at work, but also as places where children are part of a community—and as places to learn, explore their interests, and succeed with the support of certified professionals. Capitalizing on what we have learned from this epoch-defining moment will be key to making learning more engaging, with and without technology, for all students, of all backgrounds—rich and poor, successful or struggling, newcomers or long-standing residents—so that they can be fulfilled and make their own unique contributions to their communities.

After the coronavirus, all of us hopefully will still be thinking a lot more about the value of our essential workers who clean our hospitals, stock shelves in the grocery store, and care for our elderly and infirm citizens. We should be thinking more about the children of these workers, too—about them having as many opportunities as anyone else to enjoy school and be successful there. How can we ensure that all young people, especially those who are most disadvantaged and marginalized, are truly engaged with their learning and with the world around them? How can learning be more fulfilling in the short term and also have lasting value for students in the world and in their lives beyond schools?

To answer these questions, we not only need to advocate for more engagement in schools—we also need to know what engagement truly is and isn't. We need to know when engagement is being reduced to a distracting process of superficial entertainment, and how, on the other hand, engagement with complex problems can lead to empowerment of oneself and others to build a better world together.

If we are wise, the pandemic will not be an interruption to or departure from the Age of Engagement, Well-Being, and Identity. Coronavirus challenges have spotlighted the paramount importance of well-being, the inequities of access to technology and to learning opportunities in general, and the human dignity of all members of society—including the families of essential workers. All these insights must strengthen our resolve to fulfill the promises of this fledgling age that include greater and better engagement with learning and life, for all young people, whatever their family circumstances.

CHAPTER 2

Theories of Engagement and Motivation: From Maslow to Flow

When you think of the word *engagement*, what's the first thing that comes to mind? We've put this question to a lot of educators at conferences and on webinars, and one of their most common answers is *marriage*. Indeed, that's where one of the earliest definitions of engagement can be found. In the 18th century, engagement was defined as "a state of having entered a contract of marriage."[125] Engagement here is about a commitment, a relationship, a promise sealed with a ring and a kiss, for better or worse, in sickness and in health.

This is not the very first definition of *engagement*, though. A century earlier, engagement meant "a battle or fight between armies or fleets."[126] This is what we mean when we talk about engaging an enemy. On the surface, this kind of engagement doesn't seem to have much to do with marriage at all. Or perhaps it does—after all, you only need to switch two letters to turn *marital* into *martial*!

The point, though, is that in both cases—amorous relationships or armies in conflict—engagement is about intense involvement with another individual or group. Like engaging a gear wheel, it locks us in. Indeed, another meaning of *engagement* is simply an arrangement to meet or be present at a specified time and place. It's a meeting of two or more people or groups that requires commitment to each other.[127] These definitions might seem overly simplistic, but it's important to grasp the basics before setting out on a quest.

Whenever you head out on a journey, you need to be fully equipped with a sense of where you're headed and how to get there. Adventures require persistence and fortitude for when the going gets tough and surprises happen, as they inevitably will. If you're hiking straight uphill, you need courage as well as resourcefulness to be ready when danger threatens and accidents occur. There's also something else you'll need when you're undertaking a big adventure: the right gear.

When we're not being professors, one thing we love to do is hike multiday sections of the 2,000-mile-long Appalachian Trail on the East Coast of the United States. In 2018, we decided to tackle the reputedly hardest five days of the trail on the border of New Hampshire and Maine. After one day of torrential rain, summiting several peaks over four thousand feet, and making a perilous descent by headlamps in pitch darkness, which took us until nearly midnight, the next day seemed like a walk in the park. On a perfect summer morning, we set out on the next, far less grueling section. And then, in one careless moment, as he was hiking quickly, Andy took his eye off the trail to look for moose on the opposite side of a mountain pond and trapped his foot under a tree stump. His body kept barreling forward, his leg stayed where it was, and he crashed down to earth, fracturing his ankle on both sides.

It took many volunteers from the New Hampshire Fish and Game Department over nine hours to reach him and bring him down. They immobilized his ankle and carried him on their backs, one volunteer after another, in the dead of night, on a route they had bushwhacked through the forest. Then they spent the next two or three hours maneuvering an all-terrain vehicle down a precipitous trail to a waiting ambulance. It was a complicated, time-consuming, and expensive extraction.

As Andy was receiving treatment at the nearest hospital, a law enforcement officer arrived, took out a pen and paper, and asked Andy a series of questions. Did he have a map? Was he carrying a compass? What about a whistle? It was a hot summer's day, but had he thought to take extra layers of clothing, gloves, and a warm hat, just in case?

And did he have a decent first-aid kit? The questions went on and on. The officer filled in his checklist. After receiving positive responses on every item, he thanked Andy for his planning and diligence, and got up to leave.

"Before you go," Andy inquired, "what if my answers to your questions had been mainly negative?" "If your answers are positive," the officer replied, "*we* pay for the rescue. If they're mainly negative, *you* pay for the rescue." That's about as succinct an explanation of the importance of both the collective responsibility of the rescuers and the personal responsibility of the individual that we've ever heard.

When you set out on any journey, it's not enough to hope that there'll be no adversity, or that you'll be able to muddle your way through it when there is. It's not enough to set out with a goal in mind, some good intentions, and an inclination to follow your intuition or improvise your approach along the way. This rule also applies to a professional journey—in this case, transforming students' learning, engagement, and well-being. You have to pack enough gear for this kind of journey too. And a big part of that gear is the collective knowledge and wisdom, the theories and research, of all the experts who have passed this way before. This chapter packs our bags with what leading thinkers in the fields of engagement and motivation have found in the past. Like maps, food, water, and sunscreen, getting acquainted with and packing in this theoretical knowledge is an essential prerequisite for this expedition, even before we take a single step.

Achievement Through Engagement

What do you do when your strategies to improve results in the Age of Achievement and Effort hit a ceiling? What's next, once you've exhausted all the test preparation, allocated more time for learning after school, and given up recess for reviewing assignments? What can be done after you've developed more grit and resilience in your students, delivered more precise and explicit teaching, and analyzed data in endless meetings to see where interventions can be made? One deceptively simple answer is this:

If you want more achievement, get more engagement!

Surely, students are more likely to learn if they're interested in what they're studying. Pedro Noguera, Dean of the Rossier School of Education at the University of Southern California, understands this. Noguera is a national advocate for public education and regularly appears in mainstream media like *The Wall Street Journal* and *The Washington Post*. Working with tough schools like South Philadelphia High School, Noguera argues, it's important to get African American and Latino boys engaged with learning and success at school. Otherwise, they will be drawn into all the other things that await them on the street that can engage them all too easily instead. If we're disengaged from one thing, it usually means we're engaged with something else. "The path to higher achievement is through engagement," says Noguera.[128]

In the Age of Achievement and Effort, the theory of improvement was that with more and more testing—in some cases, of every student in every grade—results would drive teachers to work harder, focus more intensely, identify gaps precisely, make interventions swiftly, lift performance, and reduce inequities. In this way, results would improve, and students would learn more. As we saw earlier (page 17), though, testing entire cohorts of students rarely leads to genuine achievement gains. Even when it does, test-focused education comes at the expense of many kinds of learning that are not tested, such as critical thinking, physical education, or the arts.

Noguera's theory of improvement reverses the traditional testing formula. It argues that we must first improve learning by increasing student engagement. Only then will we be able to raise achievement. Engagement is a complicated thing. As Noguera points out, it is multidimensional. "It's not simply about whether the kids are present, doing the work; that's the *behavioral* part," he says. It's also a matter of whether they are *cognitively* connected to their learning—understanding it, being curious about knowledge, and investing in their projects. Then, "there's the *emotional* part. How much do they actually care about what they're doing? How invested are they?"[129] For these reasons, getting to grips with engagement means making learning interesting and accessible, as well as working hard to develop senses of emotional attachment to the school as a community through things like extracurricular activities.

Psychologists contributing to the 840-page *Handbook of Research on Student Engagement* agree with Noguera that *all three* dimensions of student engagement—behavioral, cognitive, and emotional—have to be addressed by teachers when preparing their lesson plans.[130] Students can be trained to be physically present with regard to their *behavior*—awake, alert, and fixing all eyes on the teacher. But they may still be bored to tears with the subject matter. If a student is confronted with a complex problem or difficult concept that has no meaning or relevance for them given their personal *cognitive* dispositions, they may never truly grasp it. An assignment may be *emotionally* enjoyable and fun, but this doesn't mean the work demands a high level of thinking. In a noisy, poorly managed class, students may be too distracted to concentrate on what could otherwise be very interesting projects and ideas. The interaction of these three dimensions is shown in figure 2.1.

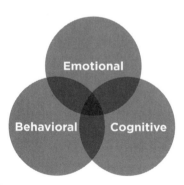

FIGURE 2.1: Three psychological dimensions of student engagement.

Relying on one dimension of engagement alone is rarely sufficient to maintain students' attention for long. Even when it does, it may not deliver much in the way of learning that matters and lasts. It's essential to address all three dimensions of student engagement at one point or another in your lessons, then. You can't leave out one of them without leaving some or maybe even most of your students behind.

But how do all of these components hang together? What does a coherent theory of engagement and its associated concept of motivation look like, and what have leading scholars offered in terms of engagement and motivation theory? Last, what do we offer in this book that is different from, and yet complementary to, this existing body of psychological theory? These are the issues we explore in the remainder of this chapter.

Engagement and Motivation

Engagement is closely connected to motivation. There are more classic and long-standing theories of motivation than there are of engagement, but the two are tightly connected nonetheless. The consensus is that "motivation can be seen as the underlying psychological state that sets the stage for engagement."[131] This sequential relationship between motivation, engagement, and achievement is a development of Noguera's position and is expressed in figure 2.2.

FIGURE 2.2: From motivation to engagement to achievement.

Essentially, *motivation* sparks our interests and initially moves us. *Engagement* grabs our attention and sustains our involvement, even in the face of obstacles or difficulties. *Achievement* reflects the attainment of an essential goal or an aim that is perceived to be beneficial for the individual, the group, or the society as a whole.

This is not always the case, though. For example, while students could be highly motivated to learn physics, they nonetheless might fail to get engaged with the way in which concepts like gravity, magnetism, and atomic particles are actually taught in their schools. Conversely, though, it's hard to see how, in most cases, engagement can occur without there being at least some underlying motivation in the first place.

Let's see what some leading thinkers in the field have to say about motivation and engagement issues, and then consider their implications for teaching and learning.

> **Motivation** *sparks our interests and initially moves us.* **Engagement** *grabs our attention and sustains our involvement, even in the face of obstacles or difficulties.*

Abraham Maslow's Theory of Human Motivation

Psychologist Abraham Maslow set out the first comprehensive theory of human motivation.[132] Maslow argued that motivation springs from the drive to satisfy basic human needs. These needs, he proposed, are arranged in a hierarchy of human development, with five (and later, six) levels. Originally, Maslow contended that each need had to be satisfied before the next in the hierarchy, so that they proceeded in a sequential order from one to another. The general view today is that while one need may be dominant at a given time, they can and do often overlap.

The needs underpinning human motivation, according to Maslow, are as follows.

1. **Physiological:** These are the basic survival needs for food, shelter, and sleep. In schools, it's essential to ensure that children are fed, are properly clothed, and have had sufficient sleep if they are going to learn once they get to school. In this way, Maslow's hierarchy of needs precedes and supersedes Benjamin Bloom's famed taxonomy of learning. In other words, the guiding principle is to *put Maslow before Bloom*!

2. **Safety:** This refers to protection from violence, abuse, and disease. All children need to go to a school that has a safe environment, free from bullying, mindful of child protection, and caring toward all students and adults.

3. **Belonging and love:** This level covers needs for affection and attachment to social groups and communities as protections against loneliness, anxiety, and depression. Belonging is a big part of what it means to be engaged. Conversely, disassociation or lack of belonging is a prime reason for young people's experience of disengagement.

4. **Esteem:** Esteem means acceptance, recognition, and being valued by others in the community. This is a fundamental issue of inclusion in diverse schools. We would also now say that there are risks in school not just from insufficient self-esteem that comes from being excluded or ignored, but also from egocentrism, narcissism, and levels of self-esteem that are excessive. This points to the importance of basing self-esteem on real accomplishment rather than mere participation or sheer existence.

5. **Self-actualization:** This is realization of personal potential, fulfillment, and a sense of worth through quests for accomplishment as a learner, athlete, creative artist, gardener, or parent, for example. Here motivation and engagement become intertwined. Once other basic needs have been satisfied, motivation and engagement alike are about inquiry, discovery, learning, self-fulfillment, and achieving mastery. Self-actualization is the opposite of alienation.

6. **Transcendence:** At the end of his career, Maslow added a final level of commitment and contribution to something greater beyond oneself in spiritual or social terms. He became fascinated with "peak experiences," in which "striving, willing, straining, tend to disappear" and the person becomes "utterly lost in the present."[133] Maslow came to believe that psychology had become too preoccupied with pathologies and needed to study what he called "the farther reaches of human nature" as well.[134] Motivation and engagement are, in this respect, about pursuing a life of meaning and purpose beyond oneself.

Maslow's hierarchy of needs is represented in figure 2.3. Like all developmental frameworks, Maslow's is not as neat and tidy as it first appears. People go up and also down through the levels, so there is no easy developmental progression from one stage to the next. It's also possible to be on several levels at once.

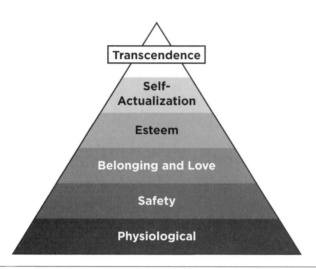

FIGURE 2.3: Abraham Maslow's hierarchy of needs.

Not all cultures value the same kind of progression, either. In East Asian cultures influenced by Confucianism, for example, supporting one's family and serving the nation, as well as making sacrifices for the benefit of others, have more value than the individual's self-actualization, or they might even be a different kind of self-actualization.[135] Still, especially at the higher developmental levels, Maslow's framework helps us understand how motivation and engagement are both integral to the more sophisticated forms of learning and human development.

Intrinsic and Extrinsic Motivation Theory

Harry Harlow, a psychology professor at the University of Wisconsin from the 1940s, was, for a brief time, a supervisor of Abraham Maslow. Harlow became famous, indeed notorious, for his laboratory experiments with rhesus monkeys. By raising his monkeys in a nursery, then experimenting with surrogate mothers made of wire, with and without cloth coverings, Harlow made a significant but controversial contribution to theories of maternal attachment and deprivation.[136] He also designed experiments to inflict protracted isolation on young monkeys, which are now regarded as animal cruelty.

Along the way, Harlow got interested in how monkeys learn, and invented the modern idea of *learning to learn*.[137] He set up puzzles for his monkeys to solve to determine whether rewards would stimulate performance. In the process, he discovered that the monkeys became interested and proficient in solving the puzzles for their own sake. This made him come up with the idea of *intrinsic motivation* to do something for its inherent interest or satisfaction, versus *extrinsic motivation*, where something is done for external rewards.[138]

The two kinds of motivation are all around us. Examples of intrinsic motivation include volunteering to help people (rather than to add it to your résumé); learning the guitar for the love of music (rather than to attract a love interest); cleaning up to be responsible (rather than to avoid your parent's wrath); and writing a book to the best of your ability to achieve craftsman-like quality and beauty (rather than to appease your coauthor or pick up a prize). In school, intrinsic motivation is about learning for its own sake, for personal interest, or to pursue an important purpose (rather than to attract the teacher's approval or get a higher grade).

The modern masters of intrinsic motivation theory are University of Rochester professors Edward Deci and Richard Ryan.[139] Deci and then Ryan set out a theory of *self-determination* that examines people's motivations for doing inherently interesting tasks and the effects that this has on their performance. Their greatest contribution has been to show, through a series of experiments with human subjects, that while small payments for task completion can boost short-term performance, in the long run, external rewards fail to improve performance in many activities. Against all expectations and against the way most organizations are structured, Deci and Ryan found that external rewards actually make performance worse.

Once again, though, things are a bit more complicated than this. For example, learning the periodic table may not be inherently interesting for many students. However, if these students can be convinced that acquiring this knowledge will pay off in terms of a subsequent career in science, then, with their teachers' help, they may transform this extrinsic motivation into a process of inner determination on the grounds that engaging with this part of the curriculum will ultimately be worth the effort. The intrinsic motivation argument can take us a long way in figuring out how to engage our students, but there are important exceptions, where extrinsic motivation also has value. We shouldn't dismiss them too swiftly.

While some kinds of extrinsic motivation do have their place, it's really intrinsic motivation that drives lasting engagement and achievement. But what, in practical terms, can educators do to increase intrinsic motivation? Deci and Ryan argue that students need three things for intrinsic motivation.[140]

1. **Autonomy** in terms of choice and control over activities. Extrinsic rewards reduce this autonomy—or sense of *empowerment*, we should add—and lead to decreases in intrinsic motivation.

2. **Competence** and a sense of growing *mastery* that can benefit from authentic positive feedback.

3. **Relatedness** to others—what we refer to later as a sense of *association* or belonging—in and through the performance of tasks.

In his best-selling book *Drive: The Surprising Truth About What Motivates Us*, Daniel Pink takes readers through the classic experimental work of Harlow, Deci and Ryan, and others. He then adds two additional elements to motivation theory.[141] First, he affirms the first two elements of Deci and Ryan's theory of self-determination: *autonomy* and *competence*. But in place of the third element of *relatedness*, he advocates for having and pursuing a sense of *meaning and purpose* in any particular activity.

Cultivating a sense of meaning and purpose, we have seen, is also a vital ingredient in students' and teachers' well-being. Making sure that students view their schoolwork as purposeful, rather than pointless or irrelevant, is far more likely to motivate students and engage them with their studies. For this reason, teachers should always try to be what Pink calls "purpose maximizers" who encourage their students to learn to act "in the service of a larger social mission."[142]

Pink's findings represent a major transformation for the study of motivation—and a huge opportunity for schools: educators increase students' motivation by helping them to identify an overarching sense of meaning and purpose for their lives. This is much broader than career training, because for some students, their sense of purpose may go beyond what they hope to accomplish through work. It could encompass public service, spiritual or religious callings, or dedication to family and friends, for example.

Second, Pink says, while extrinsic rewards like performance-related pay can work for simple, uninteresting, and even unpleasant tasks, especially over short time periods, they actually worsen performance in more complex, ambiguous, or creative tasks. This is because people lower their intrinsic investment in the work, since the extrinsic rewards have already communicated to them that the work is inherently unpleasant. They get distracted from exercising high-level professional judgment. In these circumstances, people often indulge in learning how to get rewards and meet performance targets by cutting back on quality, manipulating their customers to give positive reviews, teaching to the test, and so on.

Pink summarizes the practical implications of this finding: "For artists, scientists, inventors, schoolchildren, and the rest of us," he says, "intrinsic motivation—the drive to do something because it is interesting, challenging and absorbing—is essential for high levels of creativity. But," he continues, "the 'if-then' motivators that are the staple of most businesses often stifle rather than stir creative thinking."[143]

One of the most important things to cultivate in students, therefore, is being able to know and articulate what they are learning and why they are learning it. This is part of not feeling alienated or disconnected from the experience of learning. This means that educators need to take the time to get to know all their students well, so they can help them develop that indispensable sense of meaning and purpose.

Flow and Full Engagement

In the mid-1970s, one of the most significant contributions to the study of human engagement was by a Hungarian-born psychologist, Mihaly Csikszentmihalyi. Csikszentmihalyi is a Distinguished Professor of Psychology and Management at Claremont Graduate University in California. Along with Martin Seligman at the University of Pennsylvania, he is credited with being one of the creators of the booming field of positive psychology.

Csikszentmihalyi's unique and lasting contribution to the discipline of psychology is expressed in one word and a single idea: *flow*.[144] When people feel that they are in flow, Csikszentmihalyi says, they are totally immersed in what they are doing, and experience immense happiness as every aspect of their being is wrapped up in their chosen activity. Observing artists and people in other fields of activity, Csikszentmihalyi found that they became pleasurably lost in and at one with their work when the activity was at the boundary of their capability. This occurred when they were being challenged and stretched in something of importance to them, and when they were achieving a sense of accomplishment in mastering something difficult. This is similar, in some ways, to Maslow's concept of the peak experience, though it tends to be more active than Maslow's more receptive and contemplative approach.

In his popular 2004 TED Talk, Csikszentmihalyi describes flow as that moment or process when "you know that what you need to do is possible to do, even though difficult, and sense of time disappears. You forget yourself. You feel part of something larger."[145] States of flow can occur in high-performance and high-energy activities like sports—which is one reason why this concept has become influential in sports psychology—but also in low-energy activities, like meditation, silent reading, or prayer.[146]

Flow can occur in many ways in education. When Dennis was in sixth grade at Keene Mill Elementary School in Springfield, Virginia, his teacher, Mr. Levine, showed his class a film about Albert Einstein's theory of relativity. Mr. Levine then asked students to imagine that time could speed up and slow down. This wasn't so hard for Dennis to do. He knew that time always sped up during recess and slowed down on Friday afternoons before the weekend!

Mr. Levine went on to ask the students if they could imagine that time could slow down so much that it could stop. Dennis protested. He said that time always had to go on. Mr. Levine asked him why he was so sure—*and he let Dennis argue with him.* Dennis enjoyed the exchange so much that he argued with Mr. Levine for a full hour after school. Dennis had completely lost track of time, all the while arguing that time couldn't stop!

The problem with many schools is that they give their students (and their teachers) insufficient opportunities for the flow that Dennis experienced. The late Ken Robinson, a global expert on creativity and human potential, was not alone in arguing that the constant quest for increased achievement in test scores and examination results is narrowing the curriculum.[147] The Age of Achievement and Effort deleted or downgraded much of the attention to dance, the arts, physical education, outdoor activities, engagements with nature, and the sheer opportunity to play—the very activities that have high potential for creating experiences of flow.

Does Csikszentmihalyi's convincing case for flow and its importance for student engagement mean that we need more flow, more often, for more students? Is this even possible, most of or at least some of the time? Though it's tempting to want as much flow as we can get, for ourselves and others, achieving a never-ending sense of flow seems like a big ask for students and teachers alike. The answer from Jim Loehr and Tony Schwartz in their book *The Power of Full Engagement* is paradoxical. Drawing on their expertise and experience as consultants and coaches with top-performing athletes, Loehr and

Schwartz argue that engagement is about managing and releasing people's energy, and *not* about being full-on all the time. Full engagement, they say, means that:

> We must be physically engaged, emotionally connected, mentally focused and spiritually aligned with a purpose beyond our immediate self-interest. [Full engagement] means being able to immerse yourself in the mission you are on, whether that is grappling with a creative challenge at work, managing a group of people on a project, spending time with loved ones, or simply having fun.[148]

Full engagement, compared to disengagement, then, is about managing energy. Counterintuitively, it is about actively seeking stress rather than avoiding it or just trying to "keep calm and carry on," as the popular motivational poster advises.[149] It is about treating life as a series of thrilling sprints that keep you alert, rather than as a grueling marathon that wears you down. It is also about putting an intrinsic purpose before extrinsic rewards, even in competitive sports, so that the pursuit of personal excellence prevails over the desire to beat others, for example.

The power of full engagement comes down to four basic principles.

1. **Draw on and combine four sources of energy:** They are physical, mental, emotional (aligned with the behavioral, cognitive, and emotional components of engagement), and spiritual (a sense of awe, reverence, or wonder). At their best, activities as varied as adventure sports, writing, public speaking, restoring antique furniture, and teaching embody all of these. There are few things more uplifting for us than teaching a group of part-time master's-degree students at 4:30 or 7:00 p.m., who come to class exhausted from working in some of the city's most challenging schools, and then, if everything is organized well, find that the next two and a half hours absolutely fly by, and that they leave with more energy than when they came in.

2. **Push beyond normal limits:** Like top athletes, learn to push beyond normal limits, in a disciplined and

deliberate way. When we write together, for example, this means trying out better ways to write, and experimenting with new narrative structures, like in a novel, or dumping conventional transition sentences and paragraphs, for example.

3. **Practice routines for generating and managing energy:** Dennis practices mindful, deep breathing when he has writer's block and is discouraged. At other times he will shout and wave his arms about until it becomes clear to him just what he is trying to say. Andy will often do yoga stretches just before a keynote presentation and try to focus on two or three members of the audience to imagine what they might have given up, or what they are hoping for, when they come to hear him.

4. **Renew energy:** Renew energy as well as expend it by taking time out, relaxing, and doing something else. When our email inboxes are overflowing, instead of deluding ourselves into believing that happiness is to be found in an empty inbox, we try to take up a creative activity. Sometimes we literally walk away from our tasks altogether by heading into nearby woods or meadows.

The last of these four principles—about renewing energy as well as expending it—is perhaps the most interesting from the standpoint of full engagement. Full engagement doesn't mean full-on and relentless engagement with no let-up, ever. It shouldn't be a recipe for burnout. If we're always in flow, eventually we'll drown! None of us can or should be constantly exhilarated, or always lost in our work, oblivious to our families and friends.

Someone who did not comprehend the need for renewal is Dominic Cummings, former senior aide to British Prime Minister Boris Johnson. In a controversial and much-criticized blog in January 2020, Cummings advertised for people to come work with the government, claiming he was looking for "weirdos" and "misfits" who think differently.[150] True to his word, his job specs for a young personal assistant who would do a mixture of creative and grindingly dull routine work took the form of a warning: "You will not have weekday date nights, you will sacrifice many weekends—frankly it will be hard having a boy/girlfriend at all."[151] This is a man who doesn't understand how to renew people's energy—only how to burn them out, then replace them with someone else. No matter how interesting the work, the learning, or any other activity is, we should still take time out

Full engagement doesn't mean full-on and relentless engagement with no let-up, ever. It shouldn't be a recipe for burnout. If we're always in flow, eventually we'll drown!

to recharge our batteries. Some of the best ideas can come to us when we walk away from thinking about them too much and stop trying too hard. Sometimes it's wisest simply to "sleep on it."

In his book that compares teaching in the United States and Finland, Timothy Walker, a U.S. teacher who moved to Finland, describes his experience of going to the Finnish teaching staff lounge. He felt guilty at first, because in America, with so much to do for the students, chatting away at leisure in the staff lounge several times a day would be regarded as a frivolous luxury and a waste of valuable time.[152] In Finland, though, Tim came to realize, time spent with colleagues in this way was an investment. It was time to build trust and understanding so that problems could be solved quickly together later on. Test preparation and devoting more and more time to formal learning in literacy and mathematics have reduced physical activity and break times in U.S. schools to disturbingly low levels. By contrast, Scandinavian schools typically give their children an outdoor exercise break every fifty minutes or so. In this way, most U.S. schools deplete their students' energy through relentless work. Nordic schools renew it through play.

Whether you are a teacher or a student, it's good to experience flow and full engagement more than occasionally—at least once or twice a week, for sure—and schools and teachers should do a lot more to make that happen. But students, indeed all of us, cannot and should not work flat out all the time. That's not full engagement—it's total derangement!

Mastery Learning

The psychological theories of engagement and motivation we have reviewed so far follow the line of much of the business and self-help literature. They are inspirational and uplifting as they extol the virtues of intrinsic interest, the power of flow, and the value of attaining states of self-actualization and transcendence. These theories are, to some extent, existential and even romantic in nature. They appeal to the idea of releasing the natural qualities of the human spirit.

But other theories cast engagement and motivation in a different light. These allude to and activate less romantic, and more industrious, stoic, and even self-sacrificial dispositions in the pursuit of human development. One such set of theories addresses the quest for *mastery* as a source of, and spur to, motivation and engagement.

The term *mastery* comes from the noun *master* and the verb *to master*. One origin of the word is the Latin *magister*—meaning *teacher*.[153] There are some unfortunate and even offensive origins of and associations with *masters* who exercise power over servants, slaves, or members of a household. But to master or have mastery in relation to a skill or topic rather than over other people can have more positive connotations. Universities offer master's degrees. A master class is delivered by a master of an art, craft, or profession whose expertise has been hard won and is widely recognized. A masterpiece is a "supreme artistic or intellectual achievement."[154] Master bakers, master brewers, and all master craftspeople are at the top of their trade or profession.

The idea of *mastery* is associated with this latter usage. It refers to having command of knowledge, possession of great skill, or capacity to exercise positive self-control even in the face of obstacles and setbacks.[155] The notion of mastery appears in a number of fields such as sports, coaching, health, and leadership. It also occupies a prominent place in the learning sciences.

Benjamin Bloom was an educational psychologist at the University of Chicago and developed what he called *mastery learning* in the 1960s.[156] When he had been a graduate student at Pennsylvania State University, Bloom recalled, he was given an assistantship that required him to classify "various types of standardized tests."[157] He soon found himself "disgusted with this job" because of "the highly predictable quality of all these tests."[158] Without exception, Bloom found, "the standardized achievement tests sampled only the students' recall on the informational content of each of the school subjects."[159] There must be more to education than this, Bloom thought.

Bloom came to realize that something was amiss with how student learning was measured in most schools. He observed that when a traditional bell curve is applied in grading, for example, an unintended consequence is that of reduced "motivation for learning in students," because of a "self-fulfilling prophecy," in which only a limited number of students can demonstrate expertise.[160]

In his 1968 paper *Learning for Mastery*, Bloom proposed that up to 90 percent of all students should be able to demonstrate complete and thorough understanding of academic content, provided that they receive adequate time and support to do so.[161] If the pressure of completing a task punctually to keep up with the pacing of a lesson was removed, he held, many students with no apparent academic inclinations or aptitudes would be able to demonstrate mastery of the content with the right support.[162] As Tom Guskey points out in his review of research on mastery learning, appropriate adaptations to instruction contribute to increased learning outcomes and to a more engaging school day for students.[163]

Today, Bloom's invention of mastery learning endures in school networks like the Mastery Transcript Consortium (MTC).[164] Schools in the MTC identify key goals or learning outcomes they are striving toward. They then work together to use software platforms that enable students to demonstrate progress on a range of activities. As with some of the engaging digital assessment tools we describe later, students can show their strengths in a wide range of areas, including traditionally marginalized disciplines like the visual and performing arts, and teachers can map their students' progress in them. Schools can also factor in cross-curricular themes like global citizenship that they want their students to promote. Through networks like the MTC, Bloom's concept of mastery learning has been reinvented to accommodate a much broader range of global competencies in the Age of Engagement, Well-Being, and Identity.

For all its originality and its positive impact on how many educators now view students and their learning, Bloom's theory of mastery learning nonetheless misses something. The cognitive processes of attaining command over knowledge and learning by progressing upward through hierarchies of understanding and proficiency represent only one aspect of engagement. What Bloom didn't really grasp is the emotional and even spiritual intensity of mastering a new discipline or skill to an exceptionally high rather than merely proficient level.

Mastering something—playing a musical instrument, riding a bicycle, becoming a fluent reader, or acquiring a difficult sports skill—involves much more than ascending a cognitive hierarchy.

Mastering something—playing a musical instrument, riding a bicycle, becoming a fluent reader, or acquiring a difficult sports skill—is no mean feat. It involves much more than ascending a cognitive hierarchy. It may require grueling practice, endless repetition, tireless dedication, sacrifice, challenge, frustration, failure, moments of self-doubt or even fear, setbacks, pain, suffering, and much more besides. When a significant new level of accomplishment or dexterity has been achieved, mastery can also involve pride, joy, exhilaration, senses of flow, and new levels of self-awareness and self-regard that can feel almost like epiphanies. As Daniel Pink points out, mastery and flow are closely interconnected. If you've ever felt you were performing at the height of your powers as a teacher, school leader, or athlete, or in any other activity, you know just what this feels like.

The knowledge or skill being mastered may be socially or morally profound. But it does not have to be. Mastery may also be found in the immense pleasure of baking a perfect cake without looking at the recipe, hitting all the right notes together in a gospel choir, or bending a soccer ball in a precise arc around a defensive wall. In all these cases, it is the prospect of attaining peak performance, like that of a true maestro, that keeps many learners going.

Somehow, as a cognitive psychologist, Bloom never quite got to these more intense aspects of the human condition, and of the process of learning that the fullest sense of mastery could capture. The learning sciences in general have been dominated by cognitive psychology and have tended to view progression toward mastery in incremental steps, with students being supported to move gradually and steadily upward from one level to the next. This can make learning and teaching tedious and tortuous, rather than inspiring and engaging.

Authors in other fields have approached mastery differently, however. For them, learning to master something sometimes occurs in leaps and bounds. Even the incremental aspects are not just rational and linear in nature. They have emotional, moral, and even spiritual dimensions too.

One area of practice that can open up our minds to the wider meanings of mastery is sports coaching. Among the most popular approaches to coaching is *mastery coaching*. In sports psychology, mastery coaching is typically opposed to ego-centered or performance-driven coaching.[165] An ego-centered or performance-driven climate created by coaches, or by parents of players, is organized around extrinsic rewards, individual contributions, and winning at all costs. This individually competitive approach engages and affirms elite athletes and winners. However, like the bell-curve grading systems of which Bloom disapproved, it has dispiriting consequences for the rest, who either come to see themselves as losers or burn out in their frantic attempts to succeed.[166]

> *Mastery may also be found in the immense pleasure of baking a perfect cake without looking at the recipe, hitting all the right notes together in a gospel choir, or bending a soccer ball in a precise arc around a defensive wall.*

Mastery coaching, by contrast, provides positive reinforcement to athletes who work hard and put in their best effort, continually strive to improve rather than become complacent about their success, and assist others to contribute to the overall team performance. Mastery-oriented coaching climates are not only ethically preferable; they are also more likely to develop better sportsmanship, positive attitudes toward other players, improved moral reasoning, team satisfaction, persistence through challenges and failures, and collective efficacy or self-belief among all players and participants.[167]

Carole Ames, emeritus professor of psychology at Michigan State University, has significantly influenced the mastery approach to sports coaching. Drawing on the foundational research on *achievement motivation* of David McClelland, to which we will return in the next section, Ames's highly cited research in the 1980s and 1990s distinguished between students with *mastery* orientations who focus on improving themselves and deepening their understanding, and students with a *performance* orientation who are more intent on out-performing others.[168] Ames's research led her to draw on and develop a framework known as the *TARGET* model of effective motivation, first proposed by Joyce Epstein in a book that Ames co-edited.[169] TARGET is now widely used in mastery coaching, a field to which Ames has contributed directly.[170]

- **Task:** Its value in terms of its importance, intrinsic interest, utility to the student, and costs of time and effort (issues we will explore in the next section)

- **Autonomy:** In terms of belief in one's self and self-determination (a factor also identified in different ways by both Maslow and Pink)[171]

- **Recognition:** Praise that is appropriate and specific, rather than gratuitous and generalized (to encourage further improvement, while avoiding inflated self-esteem and narcissism)

- **Grouping:** According to cooperative principles, as Bloom advised

- **Evaluation:** That balances individual and cooperative contributions and achievements

- **Time:** And support to meet expectations, as Bloom also recommended

The TARGET framework has been evaluated in a number of studies in sports psychology. In one study, 283 student athletes were divided into an experimental group that received a TARGET intervention with five specially trained coaches, and a control group that experienced a similar training regime, but without the addition of the TARGET aspects. The TARGET intervention "had a significant positive effect on the athletes' perceptions of cooperative learning, improvement, decision/election, social relations, competence, autonomy, self-determined motivation, persistence, effort and boredom" that, in most cases, persisted after six months.[172] A small-scale intervention that used Ames's mastery-oriented version of TARGET in physical education classes showed an almost 10 percent increase in moderate and vigorous physical activity during lessons in the mastery group, compared to the control group.[173] A meta-analysis of twenty-two studies using TARGET interventions found modest positive overall effects of the interventions compared to control groups in all three of the usual domains of motivation and engagement—behavioral, affective, and cognitive.[174]

Even in the fields of athletics and corporate competitiveness, the research literature has raised questions about the value of ego orientations, where winning and winners are at a premium. Ego goals can be even more harmful in classroom learning. Classrooms in which ego goals predominate diminish students' sense of belonging. They lead students to attribute failure to an innate lack of ability, rather than to a breakdown in the ways in which teaching and learning are organized. Morale also suffers because students consider classes where ego goals predominate to be unfair.

When schools are driven by an ego orientation to increase test scores, rise up the rankings, receive more external awards, or outperform and be seen to outperform others, then students who have a more intrinsic interest in learning tasks get discouraged. Signs of status and recognition that are often favored by affluent or high-achieving parents don't motivate these students. Rather, they have dispiriting effects that lead to disengagement. Win-lose and ego-driven achievement motivations can have negative effects on deeper learning and on the prospects for inspirational teaching. Mastery orientations, by contrast, promote and recognize collective efforts to keep improving, whether this applies to players on a team, learners in a class, or schools in a system.

When we contrast the work of Ames with that of Bloom, it becomes clear that mastery orientations to motivation and engagement involve emotional management and moral development, as well as cognitive progress and processing. Mastery is a personal process, as well as a technical one. There is probably no author who has argued this more effectively than Peter Senge, senior lecturer in leadership at MIT's Sloan School of Management. In 1987, in the midst of his daily meditation practice, Senge came up with the idea of a management book that would focus on the importance of organizations having the capacity to improve through processes of continuous learning. The book that resulted from this flash of insight, *The Fifth Discipline*, has sold over four million copies.[175] It has been listed among the top ten business books of all time by *Time* magazine and the *Financial Times*. Senge's ideas are now used extensively in many fields as well as business, especially in education.

Senge argues that "organizations where people continually expand their capacities to create the results they truly desire" and "where collective aspiration is set free" practice certain disciplines.[176] Disciplines, he says, are "a series of practices and principles that must be applied to be useful."[177] One of the five essential disciplines of what he calls learning organizations is *personal mastery*.

For Senge, personal mastery is not about "gaining dominance over people or things."[178] Rather, it is about approaching life like an artist, to determine what really matters and to achieve the related results or impacts that are truly desired. Personal mastery "goes beyond competence and skills . . . It means approaching one's life as a creative work."[179] But those who practice personal mastery are not merely dreamers, Senge points out. They constantly juxtapose and live with the tension of managing their vision in relation to the current reality. Personal mastery is not just about mastering this thing or that thing. It is about becoming highly proficient as a human being, in work and in life.

Personal mastery, Senge argues, involves a number of basic characteristics. One's vision is a calling, not just a fantasy or a daydream. Reality presents constant opportunities, rather than only frustrating obstacles. People pursuing personal mastery are "deeply inquisitive. They feel connected to others and to life itself." They are always learning. They never "arrive." For them, personal mastery is something they constantly pursue and never completely possess.[180]

What might personal mastery look like as part of engaging students in the quest for mastery in a classroom? The most important insight is that learning and mastery shouldn't be treated as strictly cognitive in nature. Growing up and developing mastery of knowledge and skills and of oneself is a process of human development, and not just of learning. For Senge, personal mastery is about acquiring a sense of purpose that connects you to the wider world, to the whole, and to compassion for and connectedness to other human beings. Mastery is about the asymptotic progress toward ever-elusive perfection rather than merely reaching levels of greater proficiency. It's also about students' developing their sense of a vision or purpose beyond medals, successes, or peak performances for their own sake, because of the pleasure they will give to others. It's about the purpose of making a positive difference in the world, and the spiritual quest to become a better human being.

Mastery is the capacity to prevail over setbacks, disappointments, frustration, and adversity, in order to achieve a higher standard and greater purpose. Part of the problem of disengagement is being without meaning and purpose. Personal mastery is about recovering and developing that purpose and both pursuing and fulfilling your personal vision of who you want to be. Although mastery in learning is often incremental in the Bloom-like sense, ultimately, when it reaches its peak, after all the struggle and the sacrifice, it can be truly inspirational.

Expectancy-Value Theory

It's a common human flaw in leadership and in life to lose sight of what's important or to fail to keep your mind on the job. Both these things are expressions of disengagement among people who have, in some way, simply lost the plot. They are so common that they define dominant narratives in Greek mythology, modern Disney fantasies, and ruined marriages. There is a theory that addresses these twin phenomena of losing sight of your purpose and taking your mind off the job (and their opposites). It is known as *expectancy-value theory*.[181]

Have you ever wondered why you return to some particularly challenging task, over and over again? Why do you keep at it, even when it makes you miserable? Conversely, why do activities that are easy to excel at sometimes fail to hold your interest, even when others congratulate you on your effortless accomplishment? Expectancy-value theory provides one approach to addressing these kinds of questions.

It's rarely easy to identify one source point of an idea or a theory, but expectancy-value theory seems to have its origins in research by John William Atkinson, professor at the University of Michigan, in the 1950s and 1960s. Atkinson was a doctoral student of Harvard University psychologist David McClelland, and, later, also a coauthor with him. In psychology and in business management, McClelland became famous for his theory of *achievement motivation*. This identified three basic motivational drives—for power, for affiliation, and for achievement. His concept of need for achievement, and an associated set of psychological assessment tools for human resource management, had a huge impact in educational and business fields and established a prominent career for him as an organizational consultant.[182]

Atkinson built on McClelland's research and his own to develop a new conceptual framework in order to explore and explain "individual differences in the strength of achievement motivation."[183] While Atkinson confirmed McClelland's contribution that individuals vary in their need for achievement, he also found that, for many people, a sense of pride in accomplishment was at least as strong a source of human motivation as the quest for extrinsic, material rewards. This double insight has given rise to two interacting components of expectancy-value theory.[184] On the one hand are people's hopes for, or expectancy of, success in some activity or other. On the other hand are their subjective task values, which refer to how much people value the activities at which they hope to be successful.

Perhaps the best explanation is an example: Have you ever seen young people spending hours on the basketball court practicing three-point shots, even though their chances of building careers as professional athletes are slim? The basketball activity has high subjective task value even if there is little prospect of success. What about students who will do anything to avoid science and mathematics classes even though modest performance in these disciplines can open up a host of lucrative career options? Here, we are witnessing the opposite phenomenon, in which activities with good prospects of success are assigned a low subjective task value by students.

Once again, what we discover here is the extraordinary complexity of human motivation. What expectancy-value theorists argue for is to have a healthy dose of realism that will acknowledge the full range of drives that motivate people. They want to be able to study and recognize everyday phenomena such as the importance of extrinsic rewards like good grades or a paycheck, along with down-to-earth cost-benefit analyses. They believe that these kinds of motivations can and should be measured—and can even be used to predict some learning outcomes.

In 1977, a young scholar named Jacquelynne Eccles joined Atkinson at the University of Michigan. Unlike McClelland or Atkinson, Eccles was interested in applying the expectancy-value model to students and schools. In her early work, she took the "expectancy-value theoretical model, and applied it to students' course-taking decisions," she later wrote.[185] This helped her to understand that girls typically shied away from curricular offerings in science and mathematics because they doubted their abilities to succeed in these disciplines and saw few reasons to value them as well. The equity implications of this kind of research were profound. Educators saw that they needed to boost students' confidence and also to help them to assign value to disciplines that they had considered to be of little significance for their futures. Eccles's influence has become so prominent in student engagement that her work has been cited over 143,000 times according to Google Scholar.

Eccles followed Atkinson in arguing that motivation can be measured and understood as the interaction between expectations and values. Her additional contribution was to differentiate *subjective task values* into four distinct groups that, she believed, could be even more powerful than *expectancies* in terms of their role for increasing motivation.[186] These are as follows.

1. **Attainment value:** An activity is seen by students as being important or not in terms of whether it encourages them to stick with it in order "to feel that they are doing well on the task."[187] The exact nature of the task can and does vary. It could be a political problem the students are aware of or a topic from popular culture that they care about. What matters most is that students agree that the task is significant, so that they undertake its challenges with all of the persistence it requires until attaining success.

2. **Intrinsic value:** The activity is chosen for its inherent interest or worth, as in the theories of intrinsic motivation we discussed earlier. This may be a puzzle that is intriguing in its own right (as we learned from Harlow's monkeys), or material that is connected to students' interests and passions, for example.

3. **Utility value:** This concerns a task's relationship to "future goals, such as career goals. The individual may

pursue some tasks because they are important for future goals, even if he or she is not that interested in that task for its own sake."[188] This is where extrinsic motivation kicks back in, and it is why teachers tell students about the reasons they need calculus to get into university, no matter how repugnant learning calculus may feel to those students at the time.

4. **Opportunity cost:** This is a question of whether engaging in something is worth the effort or the trade-off compared to the other available opportunities for engaging in something else—doing homework versus holding down a part-time job, working hard versus scrolling through social media images, spending a lot of time in competitive sports at the expense of getting higher grades, and so on.

Eccles's research found that good teachers are skilled at helping students to understand the role that their values play in motivation. Whenever a teacher inquires, "How important is it to you that you do well in class?" a question about attainment value has been posed. If a teacher observes a group of students lingering after class to debate excitedly with one another the best way to solve a problem, then their intrinsic value has been awakened. Teachers who ask students how something that they're learning could be useful to them aren't being misguided, as some theories of intrinsic motivation might suggest. Utility value is entirely appropriate in many situations—for example, for students in a vocational educational program who want to learn a trade to meet their survival needs and contribute to their families. Finally, teachers need to understand that there are many things that students would like to do, and others that they would prefer to avoid, so being realistic about opportunity costs for taking on a challenging task is just as important in education as it is in the world of work.

The big takeaway from Eccles's research is that teachers and counselors should get their students explicitly engaged in discussing *both* their expectations for success *and* the things that have value for them.

These kinds of explicit self-reflection will help students to understand themselves more deeply, and learn just why they are or can become driven to excel in activities that are of paramount importance to them.

Incorporating Sociological Perspectives on Engagement

The world's largest professional association of educational researchers is the American Educational Research Association. Its members number over twenty-five thousand. Every year, the association awards a prize to the highest quality and most influential article in a peer-reviewed scholarly journal. In 2014, this award was given to the father-son team of Michael Lawson and Hal Lawson, for their comprehensive literature review of existing research knowledge on student engagement.[189]

Like many of their predecessors, Lawson and Lawson concluded that the extensive body of psychological research on student engagement had emphasized the interrelated importance of behavioral, cognitive, and emotional engagement. But the added value of their work was a critique of how psychological research had dominated the field at the expense of research into the significant impact of the many sociological factors that affect whether students engage with their learning.

Lawson and Lawson were concerned that research on student engagement and motivation had been largely undertaken from the standpoint of experimental psychology. With its isolation of variables in controlled experiments with monkeys or paid student volunteers in artificial laboratory settings, this research tradition seemed to have little or nothing to do with everyday teaching in ordinary classrooms. They complained that "the majority of quantitative studies on student engagement employ just one dimension of student engagement in their analytical models."[190]

Without any grasp of everyday classroom life where variables come in tangled bunches, not in treatment and control groups, too much psychological research on engagement has become captive to the ordinary ways of doing school, Lawson and Lawson argued. It assumes that students have to fit into the institution and into better or worse ways of teaching as they are. There appears to be little curiosity about exploring how schools themselves might be transformed so they are more engaging, not in this method or that strategy, but in the very nature of how schools might operate differently with diverse student populations.

Lawson and Lawson took direct aim at the *Handbook of Research on Student Engagement*.[191] They argued that the book's exclusively psychological studies focused on in-school specifics, and overlooked important out-of-school factors, such as "population characteristics" and "place-based, social geography" that could "better highlight the engagement-related strengths and needs of vulnerable student populations."[192] Because these kinds of sociological variables are difficult to measure in experimental methodologies, they said, researchers missed many of the important factors that contributed to or got in the way of student engagement. The sorts of factors they had in mind included how literacy programs are or are not responsive to students' cultures, how learning does or does not engage with emotional ways of expression and being in the different communities from which students come, and what experiences students are having with digital technology outside of their schools that can affect their learning potential when they are in the classroom.

Interestingly, the entire *Handbook of Research on Student Engagement*, published in 2012, does not make a single reference to technology! By excluding compelling issues of modern times, like technology or poverty, from the psychologically dominated field of student engagement, the field acquires an air of unreality. A plethora of experimental or quasi-experimental research designs has led to findings that can appear useless to busy teachers, administrators, and school staff. With a few exceptions, such as those we discussed earlier in the chapter, only blind control studies, experimental investigations, or meta-analyses seem to count in studying student engagement.

Many researchers and reformers seem to take the view that nothing of value can be gained from studying teachers and students in their natural, everyday learning environment. The keys to effective teaching and learning seem to exist not in real-life interactions and relationships, but elsewhere, in clinical laboratories, brain scans, or vast clouds of big data. The irony of the preponderance of psychological work in the field of student engagement is that, in the end, most of the research on engagement is just plain boring!

Lawson and Lawson explain that we need to understand issues of engagement in sociological—not just psychological—terms. As a phenomenon that occurs in institutions, schools, and societies, engagement can change depending on how these entities are set up. The authors make a compelling case for frameworks focused on the people involved and on research methods "that attend to relationships among *multiple* variables, events, and systems simultaneously and inclusively."[193] If we want students to be more *engaged*, then, whole schools, teachers, and teaching must become more *engaging* in their totality, not just in relation to one controlled variable or another.

In these respects, our approach to student engagement in this book is more sociologically based than the approaches rooted solely in the psychology of human motivation and development that have mainly informed practice in schools. We want to push the study and practice of student engagement further than minor tweaks to the routines and details of mainstream classroom practice. As we set out on the journey into the Age of Engagement, Well-Being, and Identity, we need to rethink not just how teachers can ask questions differently, change their approaches to grading, or start traditional lessons off in a more interesting way—important though these things are. We also need to examine how we can dramatically increase student engagement by changing the curriculum, deepening the learning, introducing digital technologies where appropriate, or transforming the system of assessment. This is why our book looks at student engagement in its sociological and institutional contexts and asks open yet critical questions that get to the bottom of how our schools are set up and what we need to do to change them.

With the relevant knowledge and theoretical background in our backpacks, we can now continue on our quest for engagement well prepared to face what lies ahead. The first obstacle along the route is a series of branching paths that appear enticing but lead only to dead ends. These wrong turns are marked with the names of three common and frequently over-simplified engagement strategies: relevance, technology, and fun.

CHAPTER 3

Three Myths of Engagement: Relevance, Technology, and Fun

Engagement is a serious business. It involves commitment and intensity. There is nothing frivolous, fun, or merely entertaining about engagement. So, let's hang on to this conceptual baggage as we explore and inspect what engaging with learning may or may not mean today. This will help us to reassess some of the most popular strategies for getting students engaged. These are making learning *relevant*, using *technology*, and having *fun*.

These three strategies all have a larger-than-life, mythological quality. They provide compelling narratives of engagement that inspire and motivate many teachers and leaders in schools. But if they are adopted wholesale, if educators follow any one of them in an uncritical way, then these myths—defined as widely held but somewhat false or completely false beliefs—will draw them away from the true path toward improving learning and success for all young people. University of Toronto professor Steve Anderson warns that one of the greatest dangers to implementation of good ideas in education is not *insufficient* implementation, but *poorly understood* implementation of new practices even and especially when they have been widely adopted.[194] When innovative strategies are misunderstood and misapplied, practice doesn't actually improve, and traditional instruction often persists.[195]

There is a lot of merit in these three approaches to engagement. But taken in isolation and followed to extremes, there are fundamental flaws in each of them. Let's examine them in turn, beginning with their potential, before moving on to the misconceptions and misdirections that are often associated with them in practice.

Relevance

One common approach to engagement is to make learning the opposite of boring: interesting and relevant to young people's lives. In 1967, one of the most influential U.K. education reports of all time heralded the onset of a new age of child-centered education. *Children and Their Primary Schools*, otherwise known as the Plowden Report, memorably stated that the school had "deliberately to devise the right environment for children, to allow them to be themselves and to develop in the way and at the pace appropriate to them." This new kind of school, it went on, "lays special stress on individual discovery, on first-hand experience and on opportunities for creative work."[196]

In 1959, as this progressive educational spirit was gathering momentum in the United Kingdom, Her Majesty's Inspectors of schools visited Andy's primary school while he was a young student there. They praised how "written work is commendably neat and accurate; much of it is related to history, geography and nature study and is linked closely with the children's environment and interests." It was this kind of curriculum, learning, and, in one of his classes especially, inspiring teaching that prompted Andy to want to become a teacher himself one day.[197] Learning was related to the environment and children's interests. It was motivating and engaging because it was relevant.

The professional responsibility to improve engagement through relevance was also an explicit part of the Ontario government's *Achieving Excellence* agenda. "Culturally relevant teachings" that are "undertaken by the whole school community" were upheld as aspirational aims.[198] Teachers who were "creating more relevant, applied, and innovative learning experiences that spark learners' curiosity and inspire them to follow their passions" were held up as exemplars.[199] The Ontario Ministry of Education called for "new measures of student engagement and belonging for all students" with the goal of producing "healthy, active, and engaged citizens."[200] It was in this spirit that the Age of Engagement, Well-Being, and Identity was inaugurated in this Canadian province.

We found widespread evidence of this transition in our ten Consortium districts. Students in one high school studied the Syrian refugee crisis and the enormity of its impacts. They then worked with their teachers to fundraise to bring a refugee family to their region. Although the original concern for this drive "very much came from the students," according to the district's director, the educators knew that they had a prime opportunity for "a teachable moment" that the students would remember for their whole lives. The students learned how to work with local charities and government agencies to raise the money so they could turn their aspirations into reality. They brought their concerns to the community and pushed all the way to the point where a family of seven, from Aleppo, Syria, arrived in Toronto and settled into their new home.[201]

A principal in another district told the story of a seven-year-old Syrian refugee boy who had arrived in Canada only five months before. His grade 2 teacher proposed that the new classmate teach a "word of the day" in Arabic to his fellow students. The principal commented that, from the perspective of the student, this meant that "you know and the class knows I matter—that means something to me." The next day, the rest of the class then asked if they could learn five more words in Arabic. The student in question was "excited that someone cared" about a relevant aspect of his identity that he had not been able to share previously. "For just a minute of the day, that kid is the leader, instead of the one who can't do it," the teacher said.[202]

The push to create a more relevant curriculum led teachers in a district with a large number of Indigenous students to design lessons that integrated students' cultural knowledge and practices into their classes. An outdoor education program held most classes outside. One principal described how his fellow principals said:

> We need to engage these kids. They put in an Indigenous
> case manager to work with them. They brought in an
> outdoor education program where they take them out
> for canoes, dog sledding, all these life skills, so the kids

said, "We'll come." Their attendance has improved. We
actually have more kids in that program than we do in
the music and the drama [programs].[203]

Outdoor education in this district teaches Indigenous life skills such
as fishing, making fires, and building shelters in wilderness settings
to make the curriculum more relevant to students' lives and identities
and to build on their prior knowledge and strengths. A teacher noted,
"There are kids in there and you can't get them to do stuff like writing
and reading. Then you take them outside and they are the first ones
to know how to build a fire and shelter."[204]

One common mistake is to imagine that students can only experience the curriculum as relevant if it speaks to their particular ethnic, linguistic, or cultural group. Students and teachers must not fall
into the traditional trap of relevance that restricts students to what
is immediate and local. Instead, they can learn to bridge their experiences with other cultures while also honing their academic skills
in reading and writing. In a lesson about the children's book *Flat
Stanley*, for example, students in one of our Consortium districts
mailed Flat Stanley photographs and figures to Maori students in
New Zealand.[205] This allowed them to build relationships with other
students, and with different Indigenous heritages, on the other side
of the globe.

In southern Ontario, there are many schools with no Indigenous
students. Leaders in one of those schools were inspired by a national
movement known as the *Red Feather Project*, which sought to raise
awareness about 1,180 missing or murdered Indigenous women in
Canada. All students in this school researched the identity of one of
the missing or murdered women, wrote down their chosen woman's
name on a red feather, and participated in a commemorative outdoor
ceremony to honor and recognize the women's lives. They learned
about the Native Women's Association of Canada and their efforts
to draw attention to the plight of missing women.[206] Students' work
featured music, poetry, and art. They highlighted the injustices these
women experienced and the need for better programs on their behalf.

One of the district's leaders described the value of students' participation in this project:

> They would take a red feather and on each red feather, they would write the name of one of the murdered or missing Indigenous women. That student would write the name and know who that woman was, and put that feather on the tree. The beautiful thing is that everybody was involved in this. Everybody! In the English classes, they were writing essays about it. In drama, they were doing plays. To be there that day was beautiful, because there were so many members of the community there. There were members from the First Nations community and the pastor of the parish really took an interest in the project and what the kids were doing. It was a real coming together of the community.[207]

The Red Feather Project shows how culturally relevant curriculum development can be put in practice at a schoolwide level and can be used to engage students whose own identities don't have direct correspondence with the cultures they are studying. It also has relevance for the United States, where over five thousand Native American girls and women have gone missing or been murdered.[208]

These examples from Ontario are modern reincarnations of what many distinguished traditions of educational theory and practice have advocated for a century and more. American philosopher of education John Dewey, Italy's early childhood expert Maria Montessori, and Brazil's adult literacy educator Paulo Freire all saw relevance as an essential way to engender engagement and achievement—relevance in service of a deeper purpose, not for its own sake.[209]

The *Escuela Nueva* network of twenty-five thousand schools that serve poor children in Colombia, across Latin America, and beyond puts peace, democracy, and students' participation at the center of their learning.[210] Gabriel Cámara, Santiago Rincón-Gallardo, and their colleagues helped build networks of thousands of successful progressive schools across rural Mexico by developing and expressing the practice of freedom through learning a curriculum that is designed to be relevant and engaging for students.[211]

More and more policy frameworks in places as disparate as Scotland, Norway, Singapore, South Korea, Canada, and Uruguay are moving beyond tested basics to emphasize the importance of citizenship, social responsibility, student confidence, innovation, and creativity. The OECD's vision for Education 2030 contains a total of thirty-six competencies along with advocacy of innovative methods such as problem-based or inquiry-based learning to engage students with socially relevant, real-world problems.[212]

What's relevant isn't always relevant to student engagement, though. Automatically associating relevance with engagement can turn out to be quite misleading sometimes. This has become an issue with the popular rebranding of an older concept known as *deep learning*. Many of the modern uses of deep learning do not merely argue that students need deeper experiences of learning at school, but assume that this kind of depth is only found in relevant, real-world problems. For this reason, we will go deeper with deep learning itself in order to figure out where exactly relevance does and doesn't play a part in advancing student engagement.

> *What's relevant isn't always relevant to student engagement.*

More than a thousand schools in the global network New Pedagogies for Deep Learning (NPDL), created and convened by Michael Fullan and his colleagues, support students to engage with what they call *deep learning* about compelling issues and current problems. "Deep learning," they argue, "is about finding our place in a complex, indeed scary world. It is about transforming our reality through learning."[213] Further:

> Deep learning is valuable learning that *sticks.* . . . It situates the learner as someone who acts upon the world (usually with others), thereby transforming her- or himself *and* the world itself. *Engage the world, change the world* is fundamentally a learning proposition. It excites students; it excites teachers and parents; and it is the future.[214]

Fullan and his team contend that deep learning "is especially powerful for those most disconnected from schooling."[215] Among other things, deep learning "increases student engagement" by working consistently "through personalization and ownership." It "connects students to the *real world*, which is often more reflective of their own reality and cultural identity." It builds new relationships with family and branches out to students' communities as well. It "deepens human desire to connect with others to do good."[216] Here, deep learning is relevant, purposeful, and engaging because it connects students to the natural idealism of the young and their aspirations to make a positive difference in the world.

In *Preparing Teachers for Deeper Learning*, professors Linda Darling-Hammond and Jeannie Oakes from Stanford University and the University of California at Los Angeles, respectively, present a similar view of deep learning. Deep learning, they say, is "developmentally grounded and personalized," and is "applied and transferred" from the academic environment of the school to "*real-world* problems and settings." They want deep learning to be "equitable and oriented to social justice," through "an awareness of race, class, gender, and other social characteristics that shape student experiences."[217]

But does all learning that engages students need to be immediately relevant to their lives? The idea of *deep learning* did not originate with these books or their concerns with learning to change the world.[218] The concept of deep learning actually first emerged in the fields of cybernetics, information processing, machine learning, and artificial intelligence, where it referred to how data could be transformed through multiple layers of meaning in artificial neural networks. This idea of deep learning persists in the technological field, where it now encompasses the use of digital algorithms to mimic thinking processes in the development of abstractions.[219]

In the educational field of learning sciences, in the 1970s, two Swedish researchers, Ference Marton and Roger Säljö, distinguished *deep-level* from *surface-level* approaches to learning.[220] University of Edinburgh educational psychologist Noel Entwistle later extended this distinction in his interviews with higher education students. He found that surface approaches emphasized scanning and retention of information, whereas deep approaches entailed "active learning processes that involve relating ideas and looking for patterns and principles . . . and using evidence and examining the logic of the argument." Finally, "the approach also involves monitoring the development of one's own understanding," he added.[221] As university education proceeded into later years, Entwistle found, success with increasingly difficult ideas depended on students making effective use of deeper learning strategies.

None of these uses of deep learning necessarily imply relevance of learning to personal experience or compelling social or environmental problems. In 2006, David Hargreaves (no relation to Andy, although they once team-taught graduate classes together at Oxford University) and his colleague Emma Sims developed a series of pamphlets on deep learning for England's Specialist Schools and Academies Trust—a national organization that coordinated improvement efforts among almost all the secondary schools in the country.[222] They argued that accountability pressures to increase test and examination scores drove schools toward Entwistle's surface approaches to learning, at the cost of deeper approaches. These deeper approaches, they recalled, were characterized "by relating ideas to students' previous or prior knowledge and experience; looking for patterns and underlying principles; checking evidence and relating it to conclusions; and examining arguments carefully and critically."[223] For Hargreaves and Sims, deep learning involves three principles.

1. **Student voice:** Actively involving students in creating their learning with their teacher

2. **Assessment for learning:** Moving away from tests and examinations after the fact of learning, to provide continuous feedback from teachers, peers, and students' own self-assessments to enhance the process of learning, and the success that springs from it

3. **Learning how to learn:** Helping students understand the ways they are learning, and how they might best improve how they learn in general, as a deliberate process— otherwise known as *metacognition*

These principles help engage students more fully with both *why* they are learning a particular piece of subject matter and *how* they are learning it. Note that this kind of deep learning would apply equally well to studying Latin or abstract quantum mechanics in physics as it might to more obviously relevant and immediately compelling issues such as the science, politics, or geography of climate change. It has a universal dimension that goes far beyond students' everyday, real-world environments to engage them with topics that are as far away as the twenty-seven moons of Uranus and as apparently indecipherable as the hieroglyphic symbols of the ancient Egyptian writing system.

Canadian education professor Kieran Egan actually opposes the idea that learners must always be studying serious social issues in their local community or society, such as where their food comes from or what the local water quality is like. In some stages of their development, Egan says, children are looking for other deep ways to think about and engage with their learning. For instance, in what Egan calls a *mythic* phase of development from ages four or five to about nine, children are drawn to ideas, plots, books, and teachers that merge fantasy and reality, elicit intense emotional responses, and play with binary themes like life and death.[224] Certainly, this would explain children's global fascination with the Harry Potter books, *Where the Wild Things Are*, and *Frozen*, which have nothing at all to do with local issues, cultures, or histories. It is the strange and mesmerizing worlds of wizards, monsters, and ice queens that draw them in. These imaginary characters are about as remote from the immediate lives and communities of students as anything could possibly be—and that is precisely what makes them so exciting!

Egan pushes this idea further in his book *Learning in Depth: A Simple Innovation That Can Transform Schooling*.[225] Although many reformers advocate deep learning, he says, their recommendations don't represent real depth at all. Learning *something* in depth, he argues, whatever it might be, has a number of justifications. Engaging with project-based inquiry as a purposeful foundation of democratic life is only one of these. Egan also argues that learning something in depth also builds expertise and mastery through disciplined study. It makes learning for its own sake pleasurable. It stimulates imagination by building it on a platform of rich understanding. It develops both the wisdom that comes from knowing a lot, and the humility of the expert who appreciates how much there is still to be learned.

To make his case, Egan advances a startling proposal. Imagine, he says, a ceremony for children starting school, attended by families and community members as a rite of passage for the children involved. At this ceremony, each child is given a topic he or she will study for part of every week for the rest of his or her school life. The topic should lend itself to interdisciplinary inquiry. Egan gives examples like railways, apples, robots, rubber, and dust (yes, dust!). Students should have no choice over their topics. Their study and progress would be gathered and assessed through portfolios. By the age of eight or nine, most students will know more about their topic than their teachers.

This, says Egan, is true depth. It is not restricted to local or real-world relevance or students' pre-existing interests. Indeed, it may disrupt or transcend these. What matters is sparking the learner's intensity of inquiry into a subject that is inherently fascinating and that all children will become interested in—*if it is approached in the right way*. The subject of dust, for example, can be studied in physics, astronomy, literature, theology, mythology, and geology. Egan describes a girl whose inquiry subject was apples and who was fascinated to discover that there are over 7,500 varieties of this fruit and that people began cultivating apples in Kazakhstan at least four thousand years ago.[226] Such deep learning, Egan says, is student-directed, teacher-supported, and driven by the advancing levels of expertise and mastery that children acquire.

Of course, Egan is deliberately presenting his case in an extreme way for shock value. Indeed, whenever we have set out his model to teachers, they might love it or hate it, but they never respond with indifference. Behind the provocative proposal, though, is a key insight: An engaging teacher doesn't just follow students' existing interests or passions. That teacher also introduces students to *new* interests or timeless subjects that may engage them for the rest of their lives. "The more you know about something, the more interesting it becomes," Egan asserts.[227]

When we strive for greater engagement, it's easy to take the shortcut of appealing to local relevance or immediate connection to students' interests. Sometimes, this is exactly what is needed, of course, when we invite young people to study climate change, the local environment, upcoming Olympics, and so on. However, children don't just need learning that addresses their immediate circumstances, that is socially relevant, or that involves them in a project or two. They also need to have the freedom and the opportunity to explore things in considerable depth that carry them far beyond their everyday lives.

> *An engaging teacher doesn't just follow students' existing interests or passions. That teacher also introduces students to new interests or timeless subjects that may engage them for the rest of their lives.*

Indeed, Howard Gardner, one of the world's most cited psychologists in education, proposes that high school students should develop deep and disciplined understandings of issues that matter but don't always seem immediately relevant by studying things like Mozart's *Marriage of Figaro*, Charles Darwin's theory of evolution, and the Holocaust.[228] When it comes to engagement, what's relevant isn't always deep, and what's deep isn't always immediately relevant, either.

Technology

A second common proposal to secure student engagement is using digital technology. Here, technology companies and experts associated with them have developed a persuasive and popular attack against the existing schooling system. Showing pictures of students sitting in rows, two centuries ago and today, they complain that modern school systems are run on an anachronistic industrial model of factory schools. They say that schools bore students to tears and are blindly and blithely indifferent to how young people use technology in their everyday lives outside of schools. Only by completely disrupting schools as they now exist, and starting from scratch with new technologies as the foundation, will things get better, they say.

There is more than a grain of truth in this argument. Technophiles aren't the first to take on the traditional grammar of teaching and learning—one class, one teacher, graded by age, taught as a whole group, all at the same time, in a standardized way. But technology advocates overstate this critique of traditional schooling. Teachers don't all drone on from the front of the class all the time. Nor do they dish out reams of worksheets with impunity. In places like the United States and England, when they do, it is the pressures of high-stakes testing that are more often to blame, rather than any alleged bad habits among teachers themselves.

Digitally enhanced alternatives aren't nearly as effective as their advocates claim, either. In place of the discredited factory model, and instead of so-called bad old pedagogies of learning, technology companies, U.S. charter schools, political leaders, and a sizeable number of academics now promote alternatives like *online learning, blended or hybrid instruction, personalized learning,* and *disruptive innovation.* Each of these opens up new potentials for learning and student engagement, but also contains significant drawbacks and risks.

Online Learning

Before the coronavirus pandemic, Ontario's conservative government attempted to mandate online learning in high schools—at first, four courses, then two—on the grounds that all students need to benefit from digital learning. Ontario's teachers unions opposed even the reduced two-course proposed requirement and, just before COVID-19 restrictions and home learning were implemented in March 2020, the government offered opportunities for students to opt out if they wished. In effect, the move to wholesale at-home, remote learning beginning in April 2020 put all these negotiations on ice until the end of the pandemic. Nonetheless, the issue of mandatory rather than optional online learning courses for Ontario's high school students remains on the table for negotiation once all these students return to a full-time physical school environment.[229]

Of course, online learning as an option can and does provide benefits sometimes. Students in isolated areas can get access to teachers in subjects that aren't available locally. Students being homeschooled, teenage parents with babies to care for, adolescents who cannot cope with a conventional school environment, and some of the millions under shelter-in-place restrictions during the COVID-19 pandemic have had positive learning experiences with online programs. For example, in one Norwegian study, teachers "were able to facilitate more creative tasks during the home-schooling period" because they had more time for schooling, and students said they "could concentrate better at home."[230] To the surprise of many, "parents/caregivers reported that many vulnerable pupils performed better at home than with the distractions of the classroom."[231]

Andy has seen his grandchildren have more than a few moments of genuine confidence and pleasure during at-home learning led by their teachers online and supported by their Nanna (a former teacher) in person. These have included identifying and reproducing animal tracks recorded on video by outdoor teachers in the local nature reserve, making cardboard cutouts of leprechauns during asynchronous learning time on Saint Patrick's Day, recognizing survivors of Indigenous oppression and their accomplishments in whole-district virtual events, and simply receiving upbeat and affirming emojis when they successfully complete online mathematics practice assignments. These online opportunities are real and a credit to the teachers who design and deliver them. Yet they also rely on vital in-person, at-home support that many families, for many reasons, have been unable to provide.

Higher education has seen massive accelerations of online learning opportunities and options during the pandemic that will likely never be dialed back to in-person-only instruction once the pandemic has passed.[232] For example, Dennis has designed an online master's degree course on global perspectives in education, offered through Boston College, that brings together diverse students from many countries and cultures in synchronous and asynchronous interactions.[233] This creates opportunities for outstanding students from all over the world who ordinarily wouldn't be able to participate in higher education opportunities at all. Examples of people who have benefited include a local mother of four young children who couldn't attend a physical classroom because of childcare costs, and a principal from a remote village in Kenya who used one session to introduce her students to educators from all over the world. Interestingly, some students in this online environment say they feel safer about opening up, sharing their struggles, and being critical of others' ideas than they do in a campus setting where they might come across their classmates on other occasions. All of this also means that Dennis no longer has to make hard choices about getting colleagues to cover his classes when he has to conduct research in schools or present findings at professional and scientific conferences. Not only can his courses be managed from anywhere in the world now, but top international experts can also be beamed in to join class interactions alongside Dennis as the instructor.

To help educators in schools and in higher education who are developing online courses and programs, Andy's colleagues at the University of Ottawa, Michelle Schira Hagerman and Hugh Kellam, have developed an open-access guide to online teaching (www.onlineteaching.ca). The guide was initially developed for preservice teachers who suddenly found themselves confronted with how to teach online, but it has value for many other teachers too. The guide is in six separate modules—(1) relationships, (2) equity and accessibility, (3) planning, (4) assessment, (5) modeling norms, and (6) standards of practice. The online guide is the epitome of a necessary yin-yang approach to digitally connected learning. For instance, it takes on themes, such as relationships and emotional engagement, that others dismiss or even deny as possibilities in the digital world. As Hagerman and Kellam say, "relationships are everything."[234] It's important, they say, for students "to feel safe, supported, and connected to their teacher(s) and their peers."[235]

There are many examples of how this can look. These include a welcome at the time of digital check-in, supplementary visits to students' doorsteps where possible, teacher-designed materials customized for the students rather than off-the-shelf worksheets, and personal photos and videos. Teachers can also hone their skills at moderating good discussions, asking for feedback about the online environment and how to improve it, and providing students with cheeky little online prompts to click this or that button because "you know you want to," so as to lighten up the whole experience.

At the same time, Hagerman and Kellam are upfront about how online learning can quickly become impersonal and overwhelming too. As just one illustration, they include screenshots of Hagerman's own daughter's email inbox (figure 3.1, page 92), which became flooded with "new assignments," "new questions," and daily subject lines ominously proclaiming, "Due tomorrow."[236] Her nine-year-old felt so "disconnected, disengaged, and anxious" that she checked out of online school entirely.[237] "School, which has always been a challenge for her," Hagerman writes, "became even more difficult. She just wanted it to stop."[238]

As the case of Hagerman's daughter vividly demonstrates, mandating online learning as a cure-all isn't just problematic; it can be downright insensitive. Critics of online learning point out that individual support for students with weaker skills often delivers a lot less than is promised.[239] Vulnerable students who lack confidence, who are not already self-directed, or who have other distractions in their lives, like family responsibilities or learning difficulties, often do poorly in an online environment. While economically disadvantaged U.S. high school students who are moved into online credit-recovery courses after failing their regular program may gain a pass at first, the lower standards that are common in these courses jeopardize these students' chances of subsequent success later on.[240] And, despite what teachers and students were able to accomplish against the odds during the

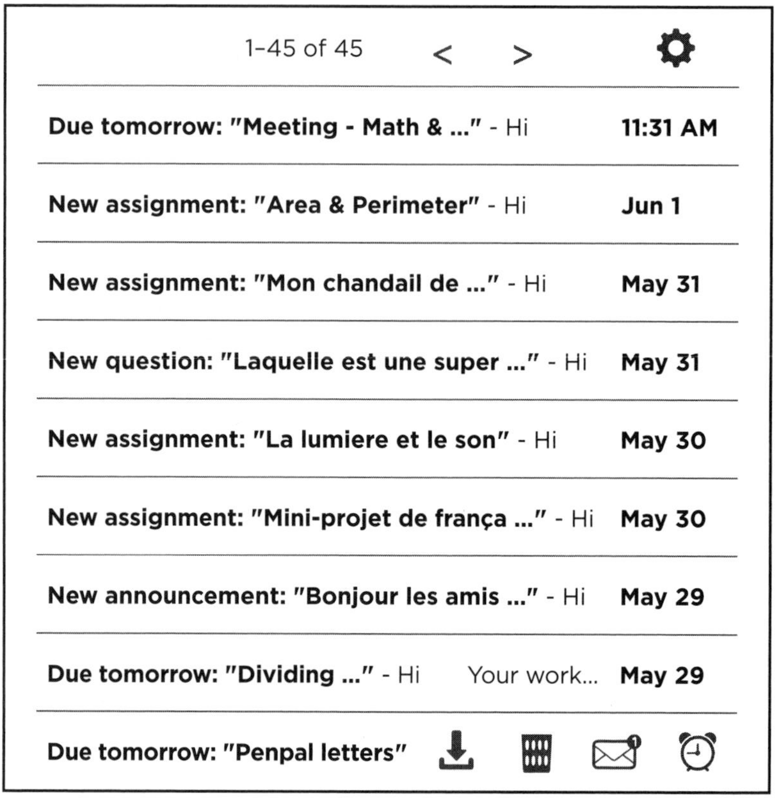

1–45 of 45 < >	⚙
Due tomorrow: "Meeting - Math & ..." - Hi	11:31 AM
New assignment: "Area & Perimeter" - Hi	Jun 1
New assignment: "Mon chandail de ..." - Hi	May 31
New question: "Laquelle est une super ..." - Hi	May 31
New assignment: "La lumiere et le son" - Hi	May 30
New assignment: "Mini-projet de frança ..." - Hi	May 30
New announcement: "Bonjour les amis ..." - Hi	May 29
Due tomorrow: "Dividing ..." - Hi Your work...	May 29
Due tomorrow: "Penpal letters" ⬇ ▦ ✉ ⏰	

Source: © 2020 by Michelle Schira Hagerman. Used with permission.

FIGURE 3.1: A nine-year-old's email inbox during COVID-19.

pandemic, an online survey of students in grades 6–12, conducted by Canada's largest school district, the Toronto District School Board, nonetheless showed that "84 per cent of students said they preferred in-person learning to virtual school."[241]

As Dennis has discovered in his own online teaching, the technical support that is needed to get courses up and running is labor-intensive. It requires a skilled team working over many months to build up the necessary infrastructure, and to respond to inevitable glitches once courses are up and running. COVID-19 has also exposed how hard learning at home with technology can be when children find it hard to concentrate, don't have enough devices in the family, don't have strong Wi-Fi connections, lack the proper space to work, and struggle to make emotional connections with their teachers.[242]

Blended or Hybrid Learning

In contrast to fully online programs, blended or hybrid learning uses an approach of teacher-led and technology-assisted activities. It combines face-to-face interaction with individual and group-based inquiries, designed by expert teachers and mediated by technology. Here, students work on projects that require offline learning as well as digital skills and present those projects to their classmates in school. In the best cases, students pursue their own freely chosen topics, while their teachers move around the class, offering individual assistance or small-group instruction to all those who need it right at the moment that a problem is identified.

Andy's first university job, in 1978, was at the United Kingdom's Open University—a public university that was the first distance-learning university in the world. The Open University was established in 1969 by Prime Minister Harold Wilson, as a university of the second chance for people who had been unable to access higher education earlier in life due to poverty, lack of funding, or other restricted opportunities. Wilson also promoted the Open University as a symbol of how the "white heat" of modern technology could improve learning. Course designs included a mixture of expert-designed study texts with associated readings from existing research, television programs in the afternoons or late at night, multiday residential retreats, and regional classes in the evenings or on weekends with local lecturers whose full-time jobs were with other universities. Andy found himself writing correspondence materials, including exercises that would actively engage students in the texts they were reading—a professional learning skill he has retained for life. He shot BBC television programs that made him famous in his village, because they appeared immediately following children's afternoon TV programs. He also undertook reviews of instructors conducting the occasional face-to-face evening and weekend classes across the regions of Britain. The Open University continues as a "distance learning" institution using blended learning to this day, and has replaced television technology with modern digital alternatives.

Blended ways of delivering higher education remain powerful options for improving people's opportunities for upward social mobility and provide a unique value proposition for some people who cannot fully access in-person, higher learning opportunities in any other way. In K–12 schools, the same possibilities concerning blended and hybrid learning also apply. But the benefits of blended and hybrid options are often overstated and oversold. In particular, *blended* and *hybrid* learning might not even be the best terms to use. They really denote only a form of delivery, and don't make any judgment about quality.

We shouldn't adopt blended or hybrid learning for their own sakes. Whether, how much, and for what purposes we use digital technology, like any other resource, should be determined by the value it adds to other methods of teaching and learning, and whether it makes a unique impact that cannot be offered in any other way. We return to this issue later in this chapter.

Personalized Learning

Personalized learning is a third option often promoted by technology advocates. In principle, personalized learning need not involve digital technology at all. But, 21st century conceptions of personalized learning often amount to getting algorithmic feedback from a computer on progress in developing a skill or learning a concept.

Personalized learning was first introduced in the United Kingdom in the early 2000s under Prime Minister Tony Blair's government, where it was meant to adjust and adapt learning and assessment to the pace, style, and interests of different learners.[243] Distinguished Professor in the School of Education at the University of Kansas Yong Zhao has unpacked what personalization in learning actually means.[244] At its root, he argues, personalization is simply about designing learning so it can address individual differences. Personalization, he says, encompasses students choosing what they learn, how and how fast they learn, and how they express or exhibit the results of that learning in relation to their passions and their strengths. David

Hargreaves, whose ideas we encountered earlier in relation to deep learning, made some of the first intellectual forays into personalization in education. He pitched personalized learning as a way to enrich young people's learning experiences and their capacity to reflect on their own learning, with support that includes digital technology.[245]

Both Zhao and Hargreaves distinguish these kinds of personalization, which are related to human meaning and understanding in learning, from uses of the same term in business and technology, where personalization is equated with digital customization (like the apps on your phone or your preferences on Spotify). Too often, they say, the business understanding of personalization intrudes on the educational one, with dire consequences for student engagement.

Technology and software companies are making big-money investments in these computer-based forms of personalization. Writing in *Forbes* magazine, education contributor Natalie Wexler notes that between 2013 and 2017, the Bill and Melinda Gates Foundation invested over $300 million to support research on personalized learning. The Chan Zuckerberg Initiative has made similar commitments to "provide every student with a customized education" perfectly curated for the student's needs and interests.[246] Wexler counters that, notwithstanding evidence of modest impact on mathematics achievement, results of personalized learning point to reduced student enjoyment, diminished access to caring adults, and temptations for students to choose topics that are trivial and entertaining rather than deep and meaningful. Wexler echoes critics who say this is just one more way to deplete the teaching profession and replace it with profit-making programs and machines.

As if to drive the point home, a 2017 study of forty U.S. schools implementing personalized learning in a project funded by the Gates Foundation found that their performance was not much different from comparable traditional schools'. This was true even though the sample schools were smaller, with better student-teacher ratios, and had charter school status that granted them greater freedom to innovate than their comparison schools.[247] Over time, therefore, the original meaning of personalization as human and responsive inter-action has slipped into a business-driven definition that is more akin to algorithmic and impersonal customization.

Disruptive Innovation

It's easy to be blinded by the digital light: video games; simulations; 3-D printing; online polling; digitally enabled, real-time feedback; YouTube videos; Kahoot quizzes; Google Earth; and the Ngram Viewer. With this cornucopia of digital delights, it's little wonder that students can find learning with technology—be it fully online, blended, hybrid, or algorithmically personalized—far more interest-ing than workbooks, exercises, and teachers talking from the front of the room. The teacher's role in the age of blended learning, personal-ization, and online instruction, advocates say, is now to support stu-dents in their own self-directed learning: to be a facilitator, not a presenter of information anymore.[248]

> *It's easy to be blinded by the digital light.*

In the spirit of technological entrepreneur-ship in the private sector, and following the highly cited and popular work of the late Clayton M. Christensen, what schools need, we're told, is *disruptive innovation.*[249] In *The Innovator's Dilemma*, Christensen describes how established companies become overly loyal to their current line of products and resistant to the idea of innovation that first created these products.[250] Frustrated innovators leave estab-lished companies that don't want to change a winning formula so they can start up on their own. Ultimately, they overtake the original companies when their disruptive alternative secures a mass market.

Christensen says these disruptive processes led to the replacement of the steam shovel by the diesel shovel, the big steel mill by mini-mills, and desktop computers by laptops and then smaller handheld devices (and now, we would add, digital tablets). A familiar example is how Finnish company Nokia became complacent about its domination of many cell-phone markets up to 2007 and thereby failed to catch the technological leap to touch-screen technology and the smartphone market. Its own innovators jumped ship: they took their ideas and expertise to Silicon Valley competitors.[251]

With his associate Michael Horn, Christensen went on to promote disruptive innovation as a digitally driven change strategy for school systems still stuck in the factory age.[252] On the basis of little or no evidence, school systems and even entire countries have now introduced laptops or digital tablets for every child. Yet arguments that traditional schools need the same kind of technological disruption as entrenched businesses are dangerous and ill informed. It's not even a useful analogy. Disrupting a student's or class's learning for a year or more for the sake of a longer-term and far-from-guaranteed innovative gain cannot be equated with the value of disrupting the complacency of a group of corporate executives.

Diane Ravitch is brutally frank in her critique of disrupters, who "say that schools should be run like businesses," making profits or closing down when they don't. These schools generate revenues for their owners, providers of services like professional development, software companies, and hiring agencies. "Disrupters are proponents of privatization. They distrust the public sector. They don't like local control. They like to close public schools. They belittle teachers,"[253] so they can replace them with lower-cost alternatives. They ignore the effects of poverty and race, and "wreak havoc" on schools and school districts, especially those that serve the most vulnerable students.[254] Technology advanced in the name of personalization, blended learning, or increased student engagement should be taken with not just a pinch of salt, but a towering *pillar* of it.

Digitally Enhanced Learning in Action

In schools, as in life, people are quick to take up entrenched and opposed positions about digital technology. Are young people's smartphones as indispensable now as a decent pair of shoes, or should they be completely banned from school property? Should we start teaching coding to infants to give them a head start in learning? Should we follow pediatricians' advice and give young children access to screens for no more than an hour or so a day? Do GPS applications make paper maps redundant, or do they rob us of our ability to read maps at all? If we spend more and more time in virtual worlds, will the physical world look too tiresome whenever we return to it? Some think it's time to empty libraries of books and make them practically paperless. Others cling to book-based cultures with almost religious fervor.

In the abstract, digital technology can divide people into opposing camps. In research and in everyday practice, though, the benefits and limitations of educational technology are less one-sided, and considerably more complicated.

On the one hand, it's important to reiterate that digital technology *can* enrich student learning and enhance student engagement. We will see powerful examples of this in due course. But it's also important to accept that the benefits of learning technologies should not be exaggerated. What we somehow need to do is hold these two positions at the same time, then find a way through them that offers the best opportunities and experiences for students.

As a source of student engagement, technology is as complicated and counterintuitive as deep learning and relevance. Technology does not improve learning by itself. When it is implemented carelessly, it can actually make learning worse by distracting students and their teachers with gimmicks and gadgetry at the expense of truly deep, challenging, and all-engrossing learning.

In our work helping to increase student engagement in rural schools in the U.S. Pacific Northwest, we saw the double-sided character of educational technology all the time. We observed a number of teachers use technology in action with positive results. They planned collaboratively with faraway colleagues in other schools on a range of digital platforms. They had their students make short videos about their local communities and share with their peers in other states. These activities increased students' engagement, the teachers said.

Other examples were not so positive. One school we visited had implemented digital tablets across the school. In many small rural schools, teachers are required to teach a lot of different subjects. This can put overwhelming demands on them to master immense amounts of content and to prepare fully for every class. So understandably, some teachers just weren't always on top of what they were teaching. In one social studies class, for example, the teacher resorted to directing students to the textbook page on the tablet that they all then scrolled through together, just as if it were a traditional text, only worse. The students certainly seemed behaviorally engaged. All eyes were fixed on their screens. They were as quiet as mice. But in truth, they were just soporifically mesmerized by the glow of their devices. Little engagement with learning seemed to be occurring at all. Classrooms, it turns out, can sometimes be even more boring with technology than without it.

One of our Consortium districts in Ontario, Canada, encapsulates both the plusses and minuses of technology in education. A major component of this large urban district's approach to learning and change was driven by a vision of Transforming Learning Everywhere (TLE) that was launched in 2014. The director of the district described TLE as follows:

> Learners are able to own their learning. They are able to work independently and collaboratively to engage real life issues and ideas. Our learners are creative and innovative if we give them the opportunity to be these things. They are champions of social justice and willing to challenge the status quo if we create the conditions for them to do so.[255]

Insisting that TLE was not simply a technology initiative, the director nonetheless pointed out that the vision would "put [digital] tablets in the hands of every teacher and every student in grades 4 to 8 by 2019."[256] He stated that one-to-one technology would support and accelerate the creation of a "personalized, collaborative, inquiry-based learning environment for every student."[257] TLE was supported by significant financial investment from the Ministry of Education's Technology and Learning Fund and from the district's own resources. In the 2015–2016 school year, from an overall expenditure on TLE of almost $1.3 million, more than half was spent on iPad purchasing and leasing.

One group of seven elementary schools supplied all teachers and students in grades 4 and 8 with their own iPads, along with associated support and professional development, to promote inquiry-based learning. An independent evaluation of the second year of implementation of TLE found evidence that progress had been made in securing deep and lasting changes in students' learning.[258] The report credited TLE with securing sustainability in the face of competing pressures and priorities, with making the core beliefs and principles underpinning the innovation widespread, and with moving ownership for the transformation to the schools from the district's central office.

The evaluation found that inquiry-based learning was employed in topics as diverse as wildlife habitat, healthy eating, GarageBand, poetry, letters to government officials, pollution, environmental science, child labor, and advertising. It also reported that many of these projects were related to compelling issues in the local community or the world at large. Depending on their grade level and the nature of each assignment, teachers reported that students spent 30–50 percent of their time working on inquiry-based learning projects. Students, they said, demonstrated greater autonomy and persistence than they had previously. They credited inquiry-based learning with increasing student engagement. "You could hear a pin drop sometimes when they're researching," one teacher said. Another remarked, "I can't tell you enough about the enthusiasm they have, and the focus that they have, and I just really don't ever see anybody look bored or off track when it's inquiry based." The evaluators concluded that the use of iPads "facilitates student research, intrinsically motivates students, and makes learning more visible."[259]

Alongside TLE, the district's other major innovation involved sixteen of its schools in the New Pedagogies for Deep Learning (NPDL) improvement network, in which the accelerating effects of technology on student engagement were also promoted as a key component.

The district was enthusiastic in its support for NPDL, just as it was for TLE.

Our own data revealed a range of views about the value of using iPads as early as grade 1. One principal felt the iPads normalized the presence of technology in school in a positive way that was especially valuable for those students with learning disabilities who needed the support of assistive technologies. A teacher felt the issue was straight-forward: "Being able to have the technology, if you ask the children a question—how would we find that out? You have that right there. 'OK, let's go look at that on the computer, find that information.' In that way it's helped."

However, the same teacher also noted that "We don't do a lot of work on the iPads in our class because I find a lot of kids are already at home playing video games and I'd rather have them interacting with each other and hands-on activities." Digital technology is not always appropriate for younger children, she felt. In this sense, the spread of technology to ever-younger students, while normalizing its use in the learning environment, can distract children and their teachers from other valuable forms of learning and play.

The disruptive pace of implementation also incurred chaos among teachers and students in these schools. The independent evaluation remarked that "the initial rollout of iPads to schools in 2014–15 was quite chaotic."[260] Indeed, the district's subsequent director described to us how, when he went to visit the schools one year after implemen-tation had started, teachers gave him the message that "Last year was hell." "It was brutal," they told him. He became "very worried" by "the chaos we created." The new director determined that far greater support for teachers and students was going to be needed than had originally been anticipated.

This district's experiences with technology mirror those of many other school systems. Initial high expectations have some intended benefits, but also many unintended consequences that can demoralize staff and confuse students. There may or may not be long-term gains, but serious sacrifices in students' learning that last a year or more are an unacceptable face of technological disruption. The use of digital technology's fresh options in the battle for students' attention and engagement must be thoughtful and prudent.

A Charter for Change

Andy and his colleagues at the University of Ottawa have established a research, development, and public advocacy center known as CHENINE (Change, Engagement, and Innovation in Education). It pays particular attention to the thoughtful and ethical development and use of technology in relation to innovation in schools.[261] CHENINE addresses issues such as the following.

- What are the best ways to strengthen student engagement and educational innovation with and without digital technology?

- What can we do about the deep digital divide that is amplifying existing inequities in Canadian education?

- How can we explore the unique innovative potential of digital technologies in schools while developing clear strategies to deal with the proven risks for students of digital addiction and excess screen time?

- What new opportunities do we now have for reshaping teaching, learning, and testing to make schools more engaging and innovative?

CHENINE examines both the opportunities *and* the threats of digital technologies in relation to all students' learning and well-being. The Center has produced a CHENINE Charter to provide itself, as well as schools, school systems, governments, and technology companies, with clear guiding principles for positive technology use in schools.[262] These principles are edited and adapted from the original in the following text.

1. **The primacy of schools and teaching:** Physical schools and teaching are essential for the vast majority of students

and communities. Learning at home during the pandemic taught us that most children and families need physical schools, with in-person teaching and learning. Physical schools promote equity of access. They flatten out the most extreme inequalities by supporting both individual and collective achievement. They provide mutual support and common purpose in a diverse community. They are essential because they enable children and teenagers to gather together as members of a community and develop identities in relationship to others. Most obviously, physical schools are necessary because children's parents need to go to work.

2. **Enriching good teaching:** Educational technology can enrich good teaching, but can't replace poor teaching. Teaching and learning are first and foremost about relationships. The most important relationships are between teachers and students. These relationships cannot be replaced with technological solutions. So, technological innovation must be guided by pedagogical expertise. Digital technology can support, strengthen, and further stimulate the great teaching and learning that is embedded in strong and caring relationships, in understanding how young people think and learn, and in connecting students' learning to the wider world. Technology can enrich good practice. It is not an adequate substitute for the art, science, and craft of inspiring and effective teaching.

3. **Universal public access:** Educational technology access must be public, universal, and free. The COVID-19 pandemic made everyone acutely aware of the need for equal access to computers, high-speed internet service, and educational software. The swift and widespread move to online education laid bare the social, economic, and political inequalities that continue to plague kindergarten

through postsecondary education. Some households have the most advanced personal computers, phones, and other devices. In others, children and teenagers compete with parents and siblings for access to a single device. Some children live in communities with reliable high-speed internet access and distributed Wi-Fi service, while others have access only to slow, very limited, or no services at all. These disparities are magnified by ever-increasing social and economic inequalities. Even when the technology is available, not all families can afford it. Reliance on expensive technologies makes an already unequal playing field in education even worse. Public, universal, free access to suitable technology and internet access for all students and their families is therefore an essential human right.

4. **Unique value proposition:** Educational technology should be adopted when it offers unique value. Technology use within and outside of schools must be guided by determining its unique value proposition. What aspects of learning and well-being can be uniquely provided through digital technology that cannot be provided as effectively or at all in another way? For example, assistive technologies enable many students with special educational needs to access and express learning that they are unable to by any other means. Students in small minority communities can make virtual connections with minority peers elsewhere as part of belonging to a larger world. Teachers in remote rural schools are able to collaborate routinely with their colleagues to plan curriculum, or undertake professional learning through digital platforms more frequently and less expensively compared to in-person collaboration. There is great potential to transform assessment and reporting through technology, especially through digitally assisted self-assessment and peer assessment. Work and

feedback can be shared quickly between students and
their teachers, teachers and colleagues who have students
in common, and schools and families. Educational
technology should be used whenever it uniquely extends,
enhances, and engages students' learning.

5. **Disciplined innovation:** Technology use should be
   evidence-informed, inquiry-driven, and impact-assessed.
   A new innovation paradigm must include, engage, and
   empower teachers and students as design drivers of
   learning. Before schools adopt digital tools, all designers
   and developers must show evidence of impact, established
   through rigorous, impartial research and inquiry that
   includes honest assessments of both students' and
   teachers' needs. Technology designers must be aware not
   only of digital technology's desired effects but also of its
   negative side effects, such as the time and resources it
   redirects from other priorities.

6. **Risk reduction:** Educational technology strategies
   should address risks. Digital technologies and their
   implementation come with considerable risks as well
   as benefits. Risks include the impact of excess screen
   time on young learners, adolescent anxieties arising
   from online identities and interactions, algorithms
   that reinforce existing preferences and prejudices,
   surveillance of student activities, misuse of personal
   data, and digital displacement of other valued activities,
   such as outdoor play and sleep. Another significant
   risk is digital addiction. Many digital technology
   platforms are deliberately designed to stimulate the
   pleasure centers in the brain so that people will be
   unable to resist coming back for more.[263] Additionally,
   the overarching presence of the English language on
   digital platforms can contribute to the marginalization
   of knowledge and participation in other languages and

cultures. The risks involved in digital innovation can be mitigated by bringing learners, education professionals, and community members into critical conversation with one another. This should involve honest, ethical deliberation about all kinds of digital learning issues through technology watchdog groups in schools, districts, governments, and technology companies themselves.

7. **Inclusive design:** Educational technology should foster understanding and collaboration across cultures, identities, and languages. The shift to more virtual ways of connecting offers opportunities for all kinds of groups to share experiences and resources, mobilize advocacy efforts, and develop a sense of belonging. How can we build on these ways of coming together to promote understanding across groups as well as deep connection within them? How can learners of different cultures, languages, and identities participate in learning through digital technology? Building virtual collaborative networks within and across school systems can help students and educators engage with colleagues and partners in different communities than their own.

8. **Teacher professionalism:** Educational technology should value, include, and enrich teachers' professional judgment. Digital technology cannot and should not replace teachers or bypass their professional judgment, expertise, and skill. Algorithms can provide useful digital feedback for some kinds of skills or tasks, but few learners will pour their hearts out for writing assignments that will never be read by another human being, for example. Teacher professionalism means having and being encouraged to develop the valued professional competence and confidence to use all available resources—like books, paints, digital tools, natural environments, and human

interaction—in an integrated and flexible way that benefits all students and their communities.

9. **Public responsibility:** Educational technology companies should pay fair corporate taxes. The coronavirus pandemic has brought the need to rethink national and global economies into focus. Enormous profits have been accrued by many technology companies during this time, as more leisure, work, learning, and consumption activities have migrated online. Socially responsible technology companies, especially those that provide products and services for children and their families, have a responsibility to contribute a share of their profits to the public good through fair taxation.

10. **Social benefit:** Educational technology should aim to improve society. Technological solutions have had a spotty record when it comes to ameliorating stubborn social problems on a large scale, and have in some cases created digital inequalities that parallel and amplify those that already exist. Thoughtful digital engagement, however, offers immense possibilities for the equitable and inclusive development of digital skills and access, democratic participation, and critical engagement with shared and conflicting worldviews in ways that transcend social status or immediate location. Educational technology should strengthen social institutions, increase civic engagement around issues of public concern, and enhance learning and success for all.

Digital technology both attracts and distracts. Traditional teaching is not all awful, and we shouldn't write off teachers and teaching as positive sources of student engagement just yet. Not all new pedagogies are good; nor are old pedagogies all bad either. Instead of having a face-off between overzealous technology boosters and cynical Luddites, we can and should develop a more constructive dialogue. More teachers could open themselves up to the opportunities for student engagement presented by digital technologies, as many have already done during the pandemic. At the same time, advocates for technologically driven innovation in schools could provide greater transparency about the dangers of digital distraction that stalk their own innovations and that lurk in the DNA of some of the tech companies that invest in educational innovation. These are the positions that many educational institutions and socially responsible technology companies are now moving toward, as they become leaders in the field.

Fun

One of the charms of very young children is that they seem to be interested in just about *everything*: pebbles on the seashore, puddles after a summer shower, a line of ants advancing toward a crumb. A few adults are able to sustain this high level of curiosity throughout their lives. Leonardo da Vinci, for example, didn't just paint the *Mona Lisa* and *The Last Supper*. He was also fascinated with designing flying machines and submarines and kept copious notes on observations of nature—like how a woodpecker's tongue works![264] Helen Keller, the famed deafblind protagonist of *The Miracle Worker*, was not only an accomplished writer but also an activist for women's rights and pacifism.[265] The immensely popular Nadiya Jamir Hussain didn't only win *The Great British Bake-Off* TV show in 2015. She then baked Queen Elizabeth II's ninetieth birthday cake. She developed an entirely new skill set and became a highly successful TV presenter. Then she authored best-selling cooking books and children's books in addition to everything else. Finally, through her sheer enthusiasm and apparently endless talent, she became a beacon of a positive, multicultural future that includes everyone. In the opinion of a writer of a U.K. government report on community cohesion, Hussain did

> *One of the charms of very young children is that they seem to be interested in just about* everything: *pebbles on the seashore, puddles after a summer shower, a line of ants advancing toward a crumb.*

"more for British-Muslim relations than 10 years of government policy."[266] Da Vinci, Keller, and Hussain manifest immense breadth as well as depth in their interests.

Extraordinary individuals like these exhibit intense curiosity and creativity. They work intently in their fields but also explore passionately beyond them. They are constantly learning new things throughout their lives. A claim that is commonly though uncertainly attributed to Sigmund Freud is that to work and to love are the two driving forces of life. Whether the attribution is true or false, it still misses a third driving force: the power of play, of doing pleasurable things for their own sake.

Play—the action of indulging the imagination, flipping ideas or objects inside out or upside down to see what they look like, or turning the next corner or page to see what surprises lie in store—is an essential ingredient of innovation and entrepreneurship. It is a big part of creativity. Creativity draws on and also drives a particular kind of engagement that often becomes all engrossing for the people involved. This is what Ken Robinson referred to when he talked about being "in your element."[267] People are in their element, Robinson said, when they are intensely involved in learning and doing something where they have a strong interest and existing or potential talent. It could be art, dance, mathematics, reading fantasy novels, playing sports—anything at all, almost.

> *Play—the action of indulging the imagination, flipping ideas or objects inside out or upside down to see what they look like, or turning the next corner or page to see what surprises lie in store—is an essential ingredient of innovation and entrepreneurship.*

We are both in our element when we're hiking through the mountains together. We share a sense of awe with the power and beauty of nature. When we're on our extended hikes, we find we become alert to subtle yet potentially serious changes in the weather. It is exhilarating to experience our minds feeling totally in tune with our bodies.

Sometimes, when we can get together, side-by-side, writing a book can also feel like this. It's exhilarating to experience the excitement of bouncing off each other's ideas, tearing into each other's misconceptions, striving to find a better word or phrase, or seeing if two or three adjectives look better when arranged in a different order. At moments like these, we feel like we're playing, not working. We lose all track of time. We may forget to eat or sleep. At its best, we know that we are in a state of flow, and we want this glorious feeling to last forever.

In his now legendary TED Talk "Do Schools Kill Creativity?" Ken Robinson claimed that schools drive the creativity out of children.[268] While almost all young children feel they are creative, very few adolescents do. After ten or more years of achievement tests and targets focused on basic skills, he said, young people seem to have little creativity left. The problem with schools, Robinson argued, is that they prevent many children from ever being in their element, because the ways of learning and being that our schools have come to value restrict and exclude many cultures, personalities, and strengths. Standardization, testing, and teachers who seem obsessed with conformity and compliance grind children down. A student may love to dance, but her school makes her sit still. An Indigenous student may feel spiritually part of nature, but the school imprisons him indoors all day. Perhaps you feel in your element when you are exuberant, but emotional self-regulation programs insist you stay calm. Paradoxically, many people who found themselves constantly at odds with their teachers for making wisecracks, fidgeting, and talking too much now find they can make a highly successful living in public speaking, drama, or comedy.[269]

Schools that turn all of this on its head and enable students to be in their element can achieve extraordinary results. In a previous study, Andy and his research collaborators examined leadership in organizations that performed extraordinarily well in very difficult circumstances.[270] One of the factors explaining the ability of these unlikely organizations to attain exceptional results was their capacity to adopt strategies that went against the grain. There were several educational examples.[271]

England, where the study took place, was at that time in the grip of relentless government pressure to drive up examination and testing results that resulted in widespread tendencies to teach to the test, narrow the curriculum, and teach harder rather than better. The schools Andy and his research team studied adopted a contrary approach. One that had narrowly escaped being designated as officially failing reconfigured the curriculum around the artistic strengths of its Bangladeshi-British learners so that, in Robinson's terms, its students could be "in their element." A nearby primary school made students part of the learning by teaching them metacognition or *learning to learn*. Learning was celebrated by a "'wizard learners' reward system. The school put a toy wizard up in the foyer and he became the model learner: a symbol of what learning is."[272] Wizard hats and cloaks were purchased, and wizard learners of the week were dressed up as wizards in assembly to receive a certificate. Right in the middle of England's highly competitive reform environment, a third school committed itself to Spencer Kagan's strategies of cooperative learning and trained all its teachers in the use of the method.[273] All these schools shifted from conformity to creativity and significantly improved their results as a consequence.

What's the moral of these stories? If we want to engage students by putting more emphasis on creativity, does this mean that learning just needs to be a lot more *fun*? Think of all the workbooks that come into classrooms packed with "fun" activities, puzzles, and games for the kids to do! It's hard to argue against making learning a lot more fun in school. But is this always realistic, or even desirable, as a basis for creative engagement?

Climbing a mountain through lashing rain definitely doesn't always feel like fun, although it can be really invigorating. Writing a book alone or together can sometimes feel exhilarating, but as we can attest, for much of the time it's more like the way George Orwell described it: "a horrible exhausting struggle, like a long bout of some painful illness."[274] Creative artists are renowned for expressing their psychic conflicts, struggles, and tensions through their work.

Waiting your turn in a group discussion, or giving way so someone else can speak instead of you, isn't really a fun thing to do, but these are some of the essential skills and dispositions we have to learn in school as part of growing up. And sometimes, as Charles Darwin noted in his book *The Expression of the Emotions in Man and Animals*, when we are learning something hard or solving a difficult puzzle, we furrow our brows to concentrate.[275] We shut out distractions in an expression of intense engagement that is totally different from the raised eyebrows of surprise or delight.

When we're engaged, then, it isn't always fun. We're not always happy. Sometimes we may even have to suffer, for weeks or months at a time. Just ask the exhausted marathon runner, the composer in dogged pursuit of just the right notes, or the actors who repeatedly fluff their lines in rehearsals and have to do numerous retakes as they struggle for the perfect delivery.

In *Let the Children Play*, Sahlberg and Doyle point out that there is no evidence that digital play is better than real-world play. "We should not automatically accept screens as a play substitute," they argue.[276] They quote a 2018 report on play by the American Academy of Pediatrics:

> Media (e.g., television, video games, and smartphone and tablet applications) use often encourages passivity and the consumption of others' creativity rather than active learning and socially interactive play. Most importantly, immersion in electronic media takes away time from real play, either outdoors or indoors.[277]

Play and creativity as paths to engagement cannot be reduced to fun. In *Democracy and Education*, John Dewey argues that fulfilling work should feel like play, and that a lot of play is really hard work.[278] Think of how demanding it is to kayak upstream, solve a Rubik's Cube, or square off against someone who is better than you in a board game or on the basketball court, and you'll appreciate just how strenuous play can be.

In their book *Teaching Creative Thinking*, Bill Lucas and Ellen Spencer describe why coming up with new ways of solving problems can be so hard.[279] They define creative activity as a purposeful thing that "generates something which is to some degree original and of value."[280] Creative individuals, they argue, have five characteristics.

1. **Collaborative:** They work with others, and this collaboration often leads to individual light-bulb moments.

2. **Inquisitive:** They wonder, explore, question, investigate, and challenge.

3. **Imaginative:** They are playful, intuitive, and able to make connections among ideas that may sometimes evade others.

4. **Persistent:** They do not give up easily and move on to something else, even when they are frustrated, unclear, or just plain tired.

5. **Disciplined:** They develop knowledge and techniques in crafting, not merely polishing up, improvements.

Creative engagement, in other words, isn't just about hanging loose, having fun, getting outside the box, or being downright weird. It requires discipline and persistence as well as imagination and playfulness. The discovery of radium by Marie Curie in France and of insulin by Frederick Banting in Canada didn't come instantaneously or easily. Each discovery followed years of professional and financial struggles, intense frustration, and countless setbacks.[281] Likewise, when the Dyson model replaced the traditional vacuum cleaner, it required trialing, testing, and refining over five thousand prototypes before it was ready to go to market.[282]

> *Creative engagement isn't just about hanging loose, having fun, getting outside the box, or being downright weird. It requires discipline and persistence as well as imagination and playfulness.*

What teachers can and should take from lives of real scientists and actual processes of scientific discovery is that they should do something that few books on self-esteem or positive psychology ever mention: They should sometimes make their interactions with students more difficult, at least in the short term. Just like in parenting, the support given by educators needs to be supplemented with a bit of positive pressure, so that students are called on from time to time to challenge themselves to try harder than they might initially have been inclined to.

Teachers still have vital roles to play in making students redo something that is not yet their best effort. They should also acknowledge that different groups of students confront all kinds of obstacles on the path to engagement, and they need extra attention to help them negotiate and overcome them. Perhaps unfashionably, our findings indicate that, like Curie, Banting, and other scientists, students may sometimes even have to be prepared to suffer a bit, as teachers push them to understand or achieve something that those students might have previously thought was beyond them.

Forging the Right Paths

In this chapter, we have learned that engagement entails much more than relevance, technology, and fun. But engagement is not ineffable, and we have detected a few clues about its meaning and importance. Engagement seems essential to most students' achievement and takes us beyond promoting resilience and grit in the face of a boring curriculum or a bad teaching environment.

Relevance is often important for engagement, but it's hard to read off, in a standardized way, what will be most relevant to any given class or group. Many things that fascinate children, like enthralling books and movies, concern completely made-up worlds that are engaging precisely because they *aren't* immediately relevant to their lives. Teachers have to be able to follow children's interests. Yet they also need to ignite new interests in areas about which students previously knew little.

Digital technology can sometimes increase student engagement, but, lacking purpose and guidance, it can addict children to short-term rewards, rather than engage them with longer-term pursuits. Digital technology can also disengage young people from other ways of learning, like outdoor activity, stimulating conversation, or unstructured play. Technology can also be utterly stupefying rather than engaging, as everyone who has ever experienced Zoom fatigue can testify.

Likewise, if we pursue fun as a path to engagement, we could simply end up immersed in superficial entertainment, diverted from engaging with fundamental questions about human existence and the most compelling challenges of our time.

There isn't one best way to secure engagement, and engagement is considerably more complex than it first appears. Beyond knowing and responding to every child in an educationally purposeful way, there is no silver bullet of engagement—relevance, technology, fun, or anything else.

Having identified these wrong turns and the dead ends they can lead to, we can now move forward again along the paths of engagement. But the journey ahead will not be easy. Any traveler on any epic journey will meet formidable foes along the road. Our enemies on this quest for all students' learning and well-being are five forms of disengagement. If we want our students to experience engagement, we must recognize and combat disengagement. To do so, we have to understand what makes it so prominent and prevalent in the first place. This is the subject of our next chapter.

CHAPTER 4

The Five Enemies of Engagement: And How to Defeat Them

The opposite of engagement is *disengagement*: to "release or detach oneself: withdraw";[283] "the action or process of withdrawing from involvement in an activity, situation, or group."[284] Disengagement can mean active opposition to the thing that's supposed to engage you, or just checking out of it physically or mentally by being absent or not caring. In whatever ways it is manifested, disengagement means that people have no purpose, sense of connection, or emotional investment regarding what they are doing.

Anyone who has ever taught or been a parent of an adolescent might think that student disengagement is just part of being a teenager. Haven't we all encountered teenagers in our families or classrooms who convey mostly cynicism or insouciance when it comes to just about anything associated with adults? The signs of this kind of disengagement get worse as students get older. In modern Western culture at least, adolescence means separating yourself from your parents, establishing your own identity, breaking free. It's not cool to get excited or enthusiastic, or to actually *say* you're interested in what your teachers or your parents are saying or doing. If most of us cast our minds back to teaching, raising, or simply being adolescents, those moments of eye-rolling were all too common.

But this doesn't mean adolescents can't be engaged or empowered if they are approached in the right way. How else could we explain the massive global wave of student strikes, initiated by Swedish high school student Greta Thunberg, to pressure governments into taking stronger action in response to climate change?[285] What about the student movement across the United States to dispense with standardized testing to replace it with better assessments?[286] Then we could consider the worldwide outrage expressed mainly by younger protesters of all races and ethnicities about the deaths of George Floyd, Breonna Taylor, Ahmaud Arbery, and others, as well as the systemic and historic neglect of the basic human principle that Black lives matter.[287] In this book, we will see one example after another of how adolescents become energized when the curriculum is meaningful for them.

Think of a student you've taught or are teaching now who seems disengaged a lot of the time. What does that look like? How do you explain it? Now consider your own experiences of disengagement when *you* were a student, or even as an adult sitting in a team meeting, trying to get the hang of online teaching, or participating in a professional learning activity. Are the explanations for your student's and your own disengagement the same or different? Who is responsible for the disengagement—the person who is not getting engaged, or the teacher or leader who seems unable or unwilling to engage that person?

> *Think of a student you've taught or are teaching now who seems disengaged a lot of the time. What does that look like? How do you explain it?*

Disengagement is complicated. It's not a personality disorder, an all-consuming flaw of individual character. Disengagement is a set of actions and thoughts and feelings that vary from moment to moment, task to task, and one relationship to another. Teenagers who seem irritatingly disengaged from their parents can be profoundly engaged with their peers. They may be highly engaged in one subject, but horribly disengaged from another. Disengagement can also vary in its manifestations and intensity, from silent withdrawal and passive resistance to outright hostility and defiance.

Disengagement is often seen as something that is the fault of an individual: the worker or the boss, the student or the teacher, the coach or the athlete. It's regarded as a moral failing, personal deficiency, or psychological blind spot that needs an individual answer—a local fix. Better by far to blame the individual than criticize the system and its hierarchies.

Some young people simply will not put up with insensitive adults and institutions that impose unreasonable demands on them. Walking through the halls in *complete* silence, *always* having to keep their eyes on the teacher, *never* using curse words, *constantly* being bored into submission, and being required to exhibit *total* compliance *all the time* are common rules in thousands of schools around the world. These are things that sane adults would never do unless they were in the military or in prison! Yet we often demand these kinds of behaviors from our young people for years on end.

Psychological problems suggest individual rather than institutional solutions—no more so than in the business field. Writing in the *Harvard Business Review* about "How to Work With Someone Who's Disengaged," industrial-organizational psychologist Tomas Chamorro-Premuzic offers advice on how to work with disengaged colleagues.[288] His suggestions include accepting quirky personalities that don't project enthusiasm, focusing on getting the job done rather than winning hearts and minds, fitting the person to the task, finding out what makes people tick, and resorting to the carrots and sticks of extrinsic rewards. Chamorro-Premuzic concedes that intrinsically engaging work may be the prerogative of the privileged. In the face of technological routinization of other people's work, he wonders "whether there will ever be enough jobs out there to engage the vast majority of the workforce."[289] So it's not surprising that his solutions focus on how to manage disengaged individuals, rather than on questioning the disengaging nature of the work itself or the structure of businesses and organizations that make people feel disengaged.

What Chamorro-Premuzic does not interrogate is how the rise of digital technologies and robotics has concentrated more and more corporate profits within the top 1 percent of wealth holders in society. He doesn't discuss how those profits might be disbursed into public education, public space, and public health to improve everyone's quality of life, and to fund more meaningful work for those outside the elite. He doesn't consider the calamitous consequences for large numbers of employees in the insecure gig economy. These include the healthcare workers during the coronavirus epidemic, who had to move from place to place and job to job every week, just so they could accumulate enough hours to make ends meet, leaving no time for them to engage with any one place or piece of work.[290] What can look like plain disengagement is sometimes an important indication that there is something profoundly wrong with the larger system.

If disengagement were a result of poor teaching or bad planning, the remedies would be simple. Train teachers where to stand in the classroom and how to hand out materials in the right way, so they'll maintain their students' attention. Show them how to hook their students in at the start of a lesson. Help them find interesting materials beyond the textbook, on the internet, or in their own bank of personal resources, so they can make their learning more engaging. If none of this works, conduct some decisive performance evaluations and just replace disengaging teachers with others who have the gift of getting students excited about learning.

However, when upwards of one-third of students are disengaged, there has to be more to it than cumulative shortsightedness or collective lack of effort. When a few students are disengaged in a few classes, it is indeed probably the fault of a few individual teachers. But when a significant proportion of students is disengaged, there's something profoundly wrong with the system that teachers are working in. The truth is that disengagement in schools is more than simple boredom. It is not a problem that can be attributed to individual students or teachers. And combating it will require more than simply being more entertaining, vigilant, or able to pick up the pace.

This chapter identifies five types of disengagement and sets out ways to turn them into something more positive instead. It's going to be a bit of a Magical Misery Tour. But don't worry—we'll develop more positive momentum later. Here are the five enemies of engagement.

1. Disenchantment

2. Disconnection

3. Disassociation

4. Disempowerment

5. Distraction

In line with our integrated theoretical approach to understanding engagement, this chapter complements the psychological theories we described in chapter 2 (page 43) by developing sociological understandings of forms of disengagement and their antidotes. The first three forms of disengagement are elucidated and explained by perspectives first developed by the three "founding fathers" of 19th century thinking in sociology. They are the liberal German sociologist, Max Weber; his fellow countryman, the radical Karl Marx; and the conservative French social theorist, Emile Durkheim. The fourth type is derived from sociopolitical perspectives on how power and associated processes of empowerment and disempowerment operate in organizations. The fifth form of disengagement draws on both sociological and psychological thinking to address how new technologies can distract and therefore disengage students from their learning and success.

Disenchantment

Disengagement can represent young people's disenchantment with schools that offer them play and a love of learning in the early years, only to replace them with an iron cage of bureaucratic standardization and testing later on.

Max Weber is strongly associated with the concept of bureaucracy. He didn't invent the term but was the first to undertake a systematic study of it. Though we usually cast bureaucracy in a negative light as something that is unwieldy, impersonal, and obstructive, for Weber it could be, and often was, a positive thing. "Precision, speed, unambiguity, knowledge of the files, continuity, discretion, unity, strict subordination, reduction of friction and of material and personal costs—these are raised to the optimum point in the strictly bureaucratic administration," he argued.[291] Bureaucracies were cleansed of allegiances, factions, and other nonrational attachments to people in an organization. "The more bureaucracy is dehumanized," he asserted, "the more completely it succeeds in eliminating from official business love, hatred, and all purely personal, irrational and emotional elements which escape calculation."[292]

Weber believed that bureaucracy was efficient and effective. It was also impartial, impersonal (in a good way), and rational. There were clear hierarchies of responsibility and what we would now call accountability. Sets of rules provided clarity about what people should and shouldn't do. Last but not least, job promotion was based on objective merit, not on patronage or favoritism. If they assumed their most perfect form, modern bureaucracies would never have to deal with corruption, sexual harassment, or people being given jobs for which they are not qualified.

Despite its benefits, though, bureaucratic organization could turn into what Weber called an inflexible "iron cage" that took away the nonrational, spiritual aspects of life that make it most meaningful, through a process of *disenchantment* or loss of magic.[293] This iron cage of self-serving bureaucracy, he worried, could turn a person into a "specialist without spirit."[294]

Government education departments, school districts, and even schools themselves are often regarded and experienced as being impersonal and inflexible bureaucracies. Historians David Tyack and Daniel Tobin argue that many of the basic structures and practices of education—with their age-graded classes and desks in rows—are actually a result of public education systems that were designed for educating and managing large numbers of students for the age of industrial manufacturing.[295] These practices became as ingrained as grammar is in language. Once they became routine, it was as hard to imagine organizing schools differently as it was to imagine speaking a new dialect. Public schools were set up not just to give more children access to learning, then, but also to manage and enforce custody and control of lower-class populations in large classes.

U.S. historian Michael Katz went one stage further in *Class, Bureaucracy, and Schools*.[296] He described four ways in which schools were organized in the 19th century—through charities, corporate sponsorship, local control in rural communities, and what he called *incipient bureaucracies* in large cities. Over time, he argued, bureaucracy won out over the alternatives because it kept the children and teachers of the working classes literally as well as figuratively in line. Bureaucracy, and its associated problems of disenchantment, or loss of magic, remains a major feature of what Tyack and Tobin called the *grammar of schooling*.

A central aspect of bureaucracy for Weber was the centralized use of credentials to secure professional entitlements for civil servants. In *Economy and Society*, he points out that examinations were indispensable to bureaucratic institutions. They were the only way to ensure an objective meritocracy of performance and accomplishment. Weber writes:

> If we hear from all sides demands for the introduction of a regulated curricula culminating in specialized examinations, the reason behind this is, of course, not a suddenly awakened "thirst for education," but rather a desire to limit the supply of candidates for these positions and to monopolize them.[297]

For Weber, examinations might impartially select for expertise, but they could have dreadful consequences for people's love of learning, and for the human spirit in general. In many countries, one-time, sit-down, pass-or-fail examinations still control entry into universities and into higher-status secondary schools before that. In the next chapter, we will look at how high-stakes standardized tests used for *accountability* purposes have become an archenemy of student engagement in many countries. But the use of end-of-school examinations as a *selection* device to qualify for higher education has massive consequences for disengagement too.

In countries like the United Kingdom, South Korea, Singapore, Japan, and China, the ruthlessly competitive quest to qualify not just for university in general, but for the most elite group of universities in particular, creates immense pressure, anxiety, depression, and sleep-lessness due to never-ending schedules of studying, practicing, and cramming. This is the result of combining bureaucracies with competitive markets. In the most extreme cases of what South Korean educators call *examination hell*, students—in increasing numbers—have even resorted to suicide.[298]

The life-shaping importance of these selective examinations and tests also exerts negative *backwash effects* on teaching and learning in the grades running up to the examinations.[299] These include failing to address deeper learning outcomes that are not easily examined, diverting teaching and learning time to rehearsing the answers to examination and test questions, and overemphasizing evanescent knowledge that is easily memorized, then quickly forgotten.[300]

Examinations are not the only dispiriting feature of bureaucracies. Standardization is too. Standards are a good idea: students have a right to know what is expected of them and the end goals of their learning. Standards for building codes, water quality, and professions like teaching help ensure that houses stay standing, communities have safe water, and professionals know their material and upgrade their expertise over time. But too often in bureaucracies, standards degenerate into standardization—the same treatment for everyone, without exception.

Every parent knows that their children are different—even if they are twins. Parents respond to their children as human individuals, not genetic clones. And, as far as they are able, teachers do too. Yet, too many modern school systems have turned important standards into inflexible standardization, and the results are depressingly byzantine and bizarre. Many U.S. kindergarten teachers have been required to write standards-aligned lesson goals on the board, not so that kindergarteners can read them (because most of them can't), but because the teachers must comply with standardized rules. By definition, zero tolerance behavior policies accommodate no exceptions, but it is callous to disregard the context of transgressions and the extenuating circumstances behind them. Mandated textbooks that have had all the nuance and controversy edited out of them, along with scripted lesson guides that read like refrigerator repair manuals, make it exceedingly difficult to engage students, given the diversity of languages, identities, and cultures that exist in practically all classrooms.

Mandated textbooks that have had all the nuance and controversy edited out of them, along with scripted lesson guides that read like refrigerator repair manuals, make it exceedingly difficult to engage students.

In education, standards hold out the promise of mastery. Yet standardization inflicts mainly pain and misery. Whenever disengagement is really disenchantment, one answer is to do away with soulless standardization and inject more creativity and innovation back into education. Another is to convert selective examinations from one-time, win-lose events to continuous processes or repeat opportunities. Sophisticated digital technologies can be part of the solution here—allowing assembly of digital portfolios, opportunities for real-time feedback, and accessible sharing of assessment information with families and colleagues. When the coronavirus took students out of schools, most of them missed their friends and their teachers, but two things hardly anybody in school missed were its rituals of examination preparation and its deadening rounds of standardized worksheets. Educators everywhere called for a "new normal" after the pandemic that would include more opportunities for creativity, the arts, outdoor learning, and project-based inquiry across the curriculum.[301]

When the virus has gone, as surely as the birds have been singing more sweetly, and pedestrians have walked more often and more freely, let's let the magic and the love of learning flourish in our schools. Let's not just reimagine education. Let's re-enchant it too.

Let's not just reimagine education. Let's re-enchant it too.

Disconnection

Disengagement can amount to a sense of disconnection, detachment, or alienation from curriculum content and school culture that is elitist and obscure, or standardized and dreary, and unresponsive to students' social class or cultural identity.

Most people probably associate Karl Marx with *The Communist Manifesto* that he wrote with Friedrich Engels. Less well known are Marx's more humanistic ideas, which he expressed in a set of notes known as *The Economic and Philosophic Manuscripts.*[302] In these writings, Marx theorized how human fulfillment was accomplished through meaningful work. If work was not meaningful, he argued, workers experienced *alienation*.

Alienation refers to a sense of estrangement, separation, or detachment from something to which a person should belong.[303] For Marx, though, alienation was an endemic feature of capitalist work organization and represented a lack of fulfillment in it. Marx claimed there were four aspects to alienated labor.

1. **Alienation from the product:** This occurs when workers produce things that have little or no *use value* of their own and that only have *exchange value* for the money that they can bring on the market. It also arises when workers produce things for other people and the profits they make from those things, rather than for themselves. Under alienated labor, workers make things to which they have no sense of connection.

2. **Alienation from the process of producing:** People not only create a product, but also sustain themselves through their labor, Marx said. Yet when "the work is external to the worker," the human being "does not fulfill himself in his work but denies himself, has a feeling of misery rather than well-being," and feels only at home during leisure rather than work. Work is compulsory rather than voluntary and is only "a means for satisfying other needs." In alienated labor, there is no "joy of producing."[304]

3. **Alienation from others:** Laborers work for capitalist owners, not for themselves or their fellow men and

women who work alongside them. They then become estranged from others as well as from themselves.

4. **Alienation from being human:** Because alienated labor is not a source of meaning or fulfillment, it becomes just a means to an end—to merely staying alive, or to earning income that can then be expended on leisure.

Almost all of us have experienced alienated labor at one point or another. When Dennis was an undergraduate and earning money to cover his college expenses, he worked in a factory making sewer pipes. His job was to climb up a ladder about two stories high, with an iron stick in his hand, to push wet concrete about as it poured out of a chute, so it would settle properly into its final form. The noise from the machinery was horrific. It made any kind of conversation other than shouting at the top of one's voice impossible. The work was mind-numbing in its repetitiveness and physically exhausting, too. Only the prospect of a break for coffee or lunch gave the day any measure of relief.

Dennis experienced all four forms of alienated labor in this job. First, he was alienated from the product. He had no say in how it was made and no idea where it would be used. Nothing at all was done to convey a sense of pride in making a social contribution. Second, he was alienated from the process. Not only was there no trace of pleasure in his job, but the cement dust that he breathed in for eight hours a day was also profoundly unhealthy and, he later discovered, actually carcinogenic. Third, he was alienated from his fellow workers. There was almost no chance to communicate with them on the job, and there was no union to represent their interests. Finally, he was alienated from his own humanity. The job was so boring and drain-ing that all he could do was push through each day until the whistle blew at the end!

Although Dennis could quit his job and head back to university, it gave him empathy for other workers who did this labor permanently. He now had a visceral sense of how punishing it is to endure these conditions of alienated labor, day in and day out.

What's the opposite of alienated labor? Andy has a vivid recollection of what nonalienated labor feels like. When he was living in England in the mid-1980s, he did most of his own car repairs. Paying someone else to do it was not financially possible. On one trip to the auto parts store to pick up a windscreen wiper motor, he encountered a worker from the local car manufacturing plant in Oxford who offered to go with him to the wrecker's yard (or junkyard, in American English) to dismantle a used part from an old car at much lower cost. Off they went to spend a couple of hours in the pouring rain, suspended upside down in a greasy, rusty vehicle as they removed its old wiper motor from under the dashboard. This complete stranger would take no money for his pains. He even invited Andy back to his home for a cup of tea.

This experience was the opposite of alienation. The labor was hard, but it had meaning. It had use value for the people doing it. They were experiencing all aspects of the task. They were connected, in working-class solidarity, fixing the car together. They were experiencing and expressing their basic humanity in relation to the work and each other. Every society and organization should find more ways to promote meaningful and purposeful work.[305]

Theories of alienated labor do not only apply to people earning low wages and working in the grueling conditions that Dennis experienced. In the 1960s, Oxford University professor John Goldthorpe and his colleagues found that even well-paid workers were alienated. They would endure repetitive jobs, and even leave behind more intrinsically meaningful ones, for higher wages they could spend in the booming consumer society.[306]

Social psychologists today take a different approach to studying worker alienation than Marx did. They don't regard it as an endemic feature of all capitalism. Instead, they feel, it is a variable condition. You can have more or less of it, depending on the circumstances. Where the work *is* alienating, though, it has all kinds of negative consequences—ones that appear in schools, too, as we will see. Only around a third of workers in the United States say that they are engaged in their occupations.[307] Workers who have no attachment to their work or workplace, for example, might meet only the minimum requirements rather than go the extra mile. They may pilfer small items for their own use. They may even commit industrial sabotage to express their contempt for their employers or to slow down the work process.[308]

Problems of alienation in work bleed into alienated learning in schools. Student disengagement may be the ideal preparation for the alienated world of work where boredom in the workplace is common-place. In an influential study in the 1980s, City University of New York professor Jean Anyon studied elementary schools serving fifth-grade students from different social classes.[309] The affluent professional-class school largely prepared young people for professions involving work in universities, journalism, the arts, and so on. Here, students experienced creativity and independence in their learning. "The students are continually asked to express and apply ideas and concepts," she observed.[310] "Work involves individual thought and expressive-ness, expansion and illustration of ideas, and choice of appropriate method and material."[311] This was meaningful and fulfilling learning.

In the working-class schools, though:

> Work is following the steps of a procedure. The proce-dure is usually mechanical, involving rote behavior and very little decision-making or choice. The teachers rarely explain why the work is being assigned, how it might connect to other assignments, or what the idea is that lies behind the procedure or gives it coherence and per-haps meaning or significance. Available textbooks are not always used, and the teachers often prepare their own dittos or put work examples on the board.[312]

In work and in school, engagement remains more common for privileged members of society, whose children often attend private schools or public schools in well-resourced suburban communities, where learning allows for exploration and independent thought.

Meanwhile, a growing number of schools in England, and entire groups of *no-excuses* charter schools in the United States, subject their lower-class and minority students to highly traditional teaching with disciplinary regimes of strict silence and unquestioning obedience. There may be some evidence that associates these behavior regimes with academic achievement in schools serving low-socioeconomic communities, but critics say that the regimes do little to foster lasting engagement with learning, or to help young people become part of a community and function effectively in society.[313] These all-too-common examples represent what Dennis has called "alienated teaching."[314]

How could something as potentially fulfilling as teaching children be twisted into an activity that teachers and students experience as alienating? Dennis's account of alienated teaching arose out of a partnership between Boston College and a group of teachers in Boston Public Schools. This partnership, which Dennis led with local educator Elizabeth MacDonald, enabled the teachers to articulate their frustrations about structures that alienated them from their work. Imposed standardization and testing in the city and the state, for example, converted the professional learning communities in which they had once thrived into data-driven meetings that neither asked for their judgment nor valued it. Another fad of the moment was *expanded learning time.* This was originally proposed to provide extra time and support for disadvantaged students to accomplish the same levels of mastery as their more privileged peers. In practice, though, it actually meant that both students and teachers spent more hours in school, without changing any other features of how the schools were organized. When it was implemented without additional support, the policy simply meant that teachers had less time than ever at the end of the official school day to plan their lessons or give proper feedback on students' work.

Some of the teachers described how they engaged in elaborate strategies of passive resistance in response to conditions of workplace alienation. For example, they surreptitiously used student messengers to carry secret codes to alert one another when the principal or external evaluators were coming through on misnamed *learning walks* that were actually strategies to enforce compliance. A red card carried by the student messengers meant that administrators were coming through to "clipboard" the teachers—carry out unannounced assessments of them on externally determined protocols. The teachers knew that monitoring learning was just a pretext. What was really happening was a thinly veiled form of command-and-control surveillance, which they intentionally set out to sabotage.[315]

Alienated teaching leads to alienated learning, especially among the most vulnerable students. Alienated or disconnected learning occurs when:

- It has no personal meaning or purpose
- It is produced for someone else, not oneself
- It has no use value but is undertaken in exchange for grades, marks, or stars
- It is mainly performed in isolation rather than in cooperation with others
- It consists of soulless, standardized, and disaggregated tasks

With alienated learning at large, we shouldn't be surprised when disconnected, alienated students respond like alienated workers. We shouldn't be shocked when they cheat, scrawl graffiti on the school premises, create classroom disruption, or simply do the absolute minimum amount of work necessary to get them through the day.

The antidote to alienated learning is learning that has meaning and purpose. It is learning that has use in the real world and not just as a credential or accountability requirement. It connects the learning task to the result through timely and meaningful assessments. It is creative and fulfilling in its production. Last, it occurs in an environment where cooperation among students is frequent and encouraged.

Disassociation

Disengagement can result from disassociation from the basic norms and standards of human communities and their leadership, and from any feeling of association with or belonging to those collectives.

Living in a state of normlessness, or lack of social regulation and belonging in society, is what Emile Durkheim called *anomie*. The online *Encyclopaedia Britannica* describes anomie as "a condition of instability resulting from a breakdown of standards and values or from a lack of purpose or ideals."[316] In his classic study of suicide that documented and explained how suicide rates varied in different cultures at different times, Durkheim linked anomie to conditions of economic depression and despair on the one hand, and, more surprisingly, with the opposite condition of extreme prosperity on the other.[317]

Narcissistic Individualism

At the prosperous end of the scale, anomie is apparent in the kind of mental state that occurred in the Gilded Age of the last quarter of the 19th century, the dot-com boom of the 1990s, and the period immediately preceding the global economic collapse in 2007. It is a state that comes from imagining that anything is possible, that appetites are insatiable, and that everyone is entitled. There is unlimited aspiration, absence of restraint, decline of moral conduct, and a sense that there can never be enough of anything.

Anomie is evident in modern society in financial greed, rampant consumerism, the limitless search for physical and digital perfection, and wanton disregard for the environment. It is visible in obsessions with improbably tall buildings and impossibly high heels. Anomie is addiction to drugs, meaningless sex, binge drinking, and violent video games. It's Madonna as the *Material Girl*[318] and it's the self-absorbed plutocratic elite in Suzanne Collins's *The Hunger Games*.[319] It's also Jeanette Winterson's science fiction novel *The Stone Gods*, in which people can freeze the physical aging process, and where women are then pressured to fix themselves earlier and earlier, as young as age twelve.[320] This dystopian society's greatest punishment for criminals and dissidents is to condemn them to age naturally. To twist the state motto of New Hampshire, anomie is *Live Free and Die.*

An alienated society is one in which work, and therefore life, is meaningless. An anomic society is one in which rules, norms, and boundaries have been abolished or abandoned and life is, literally, limitless. "When there is no other aim but to outstrip constantly the point arrived at," Durkheim argued, "how painful to be thrown back!"[321] Anomic societies are characterized by self-important spectacles, and by corporations engaged in what business guru Jim Collins called "the undisciplined pursuit of more."[322]

What is a life like without horizons, limits, or attachments to some ideal or spiritual being greater than oneself? Individuals in an anomic society are trapped in an endless, frantic search for the next immediate fix of entertainment, excitement, and evanescent satisfaction. "Since imagination is hungry for novelty, and ungoverned, it gropes at random," Durkheim wrote.[323]

The ultimate expression of the more privileged end of the anomie spectrum is *narcissism.* Narcissism comes from the Greek myth of Narcissus, whom the gods punished by making him fall inextricably in love with his own reflection. Narcissism is designated by the American Psychiatric Association as "an all-pervasive pattern of grandiosity, need for admiration or adulation, and lack of empathy."[324]

One of the best known out of many books on narcissism is by Jean Twenge, professor of psychology at San Diego State University, and her colleague W. Keith Campbell. In *The Narcissism Epidemic: Living in the Age of Entitlement*, Twenge and Campbell demonstrate that narcissism is much more than a psychiatric disorder.[325] It doesn't just vary between people. It also varies over time, according to changing conditions in society. It's a sociological phenomenon, then, as well as a psychological one.

Twenge and Campbell looked at comparable data from college students between 1979 and 2006 and how they ranked according to the Narcissistic Personality Inventory. By the end of their data collection in 2006, two-thirds of the sample scored above the earlier average—a 30 percent increase in narcissism in just twenty years.[326] Self-admiration and self-expression began with the self-indulgence and self-absorption of the 1970s, and turned into a shallow and material-istic form of narcissism in the 1980s, which then compounded each other and continued to get worse.

What does narcissism look like? It begins with celebrating and praising an individual child so excessively that the child expects to be in the spotlight at all times and never learns that other individu-als have value and need their own moments in the spotlight, too. It continues with adults giving their children an unwarranted "feeling of royalty" by telling them they deserve the best of everything, even when they've done little or nothing to earn it.[327] Parents who end up raising narcissistic children copy their kids' styles and interests, rather than vice versa, overpraise their children when their first effort is not their best effort, and impart the lesson that winning is all that matters, even if it involves cheating. In schools, narcissism is man-ifested in programs that promote excessive self-esteem, in constant grade inflation, and in assigning credit for just showing up or taking part. Educators frequently experience it when they have to deal with students who demand extra attention and special consideration when their grades are not high enough.

> *Narcissistic students create an exhausting nightmare for teachers, who constantly have to make all learning fun and exciting and stand on their heads and do somersaults to keep everyone happy.*

Instead of aspiring toward meaningful engagement, narcissistic students demand never-ending entertainment. It's an exhaust-ing nightmare for teachers, who constantly have to make all learning fun and exciting, stand on their heads and do somersaults to keep everyone happy, and award endless gra-tuitous praise to prevent these children from tuning out, turning off, and generally look-ing and being disengaged. In a learning world without limits, no wonder teachers often feel they can never really do enough.

There are antidotes to the spread of these narcissistic behaviors in young people. One thing that Twenge and Campbell found is that narcissism declines in times of war, recession, and other kinds of hardship. Perhaps one positive legacy of the coronavirus pandemic may be a reassertion of the importance of having social norms, of making sacrifices for other people, and of putting other people before ourselves. We may relearn the value of saving for the future rather than spending like there's no tomorrow. Obviously, wars, pandemics, and other hardships are not strategies we recommend for dealing with narcissism, but there is a lot we can learn from how these events make people less self-centered.

There are more realistic responses than these to overcoming excessive individualism and anomic collapses of norms and standards in schools. Teachers and their colleagues can and should step in to stop undesirable behavior. They can return students' work that is unsatisfactory (although always with meaningful feedback). They can encourage their students to cultivate self-discipline and perseverance.

Children need to experience the reality of limits and obstacles sometimes, rather than always having them swept out of their way, like Danish and Dutch "curling parents" are inclined to do. When adults show young people how to work as a team, to endure hardship, and to surmount challenging obstacles together, those youngsters can reap the reward of genuine, earned achievement. When they experience deferred, and not just immediate, gratification, they are on the road to emotional maturity and the development of willpower. So, we should allocate and expect children to have responsibilities in school and at home. We should certainly give praise, but not gratuitously, and only where it's due.

None of these things are easy, but they do cultivate enduring engagement. This is engagement with realistic rather than fabricated achievement; commitment to true friends, not just Facebook ones; and making sacrifices for the needs of others, rather than indulging only in oneself.

Durkheim, a former schoolteacher turned social theorist, called these sorts of things *moral education*. The idea was so important to

This is engagement with realistic rather than fabricated achievement; commitment to true friends, not just Facebook ones; and making sacrifices for the needs of others, rather than indulging only in oneself.

him that he dedicated a whole book to it.[328] Moral education is an antidote to anomie. It requires developing a spirit of self-discipline, responsible and autonomous judgment, and willingness to serve the collective interest by developing social solidarity and the sense of belonging to groups. "Morality begins . . . only insofar as we belong to a human group," Durkheim argued. "Morality is complete only to the extent that we feel identified with those different groups in which we are involved—family, union, business, club, political party, humanity," he continued.[329]

The task of the school, perhaps uniquely, was to "breathe life into *the spirit of association*," as Durkheim called it.[330] This could be achieved by forming intentional kinds of human groups and by developing feelings of belonging among their members.

Association and belonging are two of the strongest antidotes to anomie. Belonging to a group of some kind is a way that people engage with each other and with a purpose or cause beyond themselves. "Man cannot become attached to higher aims and submit to a rule if he sees nothing above him to which he belongs," Durkheim wrote.[331]

Not just any kind of belonging is right or appropriate, though. Elite in-groups can actually exaggerate narcissism by enhancing senses of superiority and exclusion. Schools that build their sense of spirit or association in traditional terms through teams, clubs, trophies, uniforms, and the like can unintentionally make young people from ordinary families and non-elite backgrounds feel like they don't belong and can't succeed. Some U.S. college fraternities and sororities perpetuate the very worst of this exclusion.

We have more to say about building senses of belonging in our book *Well-Being and Socio-Emotional Learning: How to Build Everyone Back Better.*[332] The point to establish here is that many disengaged students feel no sense of belonging to their class, their school, or anything else other than perhaps their peer group or street gang. So, building feelings of belonging among young people is essential to engaging them with their learning and to developing their well-being. It's an integral part of practicing cooperative learning in classes, using adventure education as a way to build group solidarity, encouraging students to take up social causes together, and making the school into a space where students with diverse backgrounds and identities feel proud to belong.

Social and Community Breakdown

At the other end of the economic spectrum, anomie manifests quite differently. Here one finds problems of what look like breakdowns of culture and cohesion in poor, working-class communities. One of the biggest challenges of the 21st century is the decline of what social scientists have called *social capital* or the economic value of human relationships.[333] In the West especially, traditional manufacturing has largely disappeared, the low-wage service sector has grown, and workers have had to push themselves ever harder to meet their survival needs.[334] The cost to their families in terms of lost time for human relationships has been immense. Some societies with strong unions and welfare states have been able to protect their social fabric by making sure that everyone has enough restorative time for their families and friends. Others, like the United States and the United Kingdom, have not. Overwork undermines the social cohesion that makes life worth living. According to former U.S. Secretary of Labor Robert Reich, Americans now work:

> 70 hours a year more than the Japanese, 266 hours (six and a half workweeks) more than British workers, 266 hours (six and a half workweeks) more than French workers, and 424 hours (ten and a half workweeks) more than German workers.[335]

The overworked American isn't a figment of everyone's imagination, and the answer to many problems like this isn't more grit. It's restructuring the society so that it's a good place to live and work for everyone.

The opposite problem of overwork is no work at all. Our Boston College colleague David Blustein's 2019 book *The Importance of Work in an Age of Uncertainty* describes how even the most mundane and repetitive work can still provide people with a baseline of fulfillment that comes from making a social contribution. Taking away people's ability to work does a lot more than deprive them of an income. It also strips away their access to supportive social networks, their ability to organize their lives around purposeful routines, and "the importance of a future orientation" that promotes "the capacity to plan ahead" for better times.[336] For writers like Reich and Blustein, the collapse of social cohesion is mainly caused not by unethical individuals, but by social and economic policies. Ultimately, they advocate for political solutions to create more just and caring societies.

Others blame the breakdown of social cohesion not on the *structures of society* but on deeply ingrained *cultures of poverty.* Consider the views of Sir Keith Joseph, the Spokesman on Home Affairs for U.K. Prime Minister Margaret Thatcher. A believer in free markets and small government, Joseph was also concerned about the effects of poverty on society. He controversially argued that the poor were trapped in cycles of deprivation that passed on dysfunctions and social disorganization from one generation to the next. The problem, he claimed, could be attributed to "mothers least fitted to bring children into the world." These mothers, he argued, are "of low intelligence, most of low educational attainment." He concluded, "They are unlikely to be able to give children the stable emotional background, the consistent combination of love and firmness," that they need.[337]

This deficit perspective on poverty that claims disorganization results from cultural breakdown has experienced a revival. One of its leading contemporary exponents is Charles Murray, the W. H. Brady Scholar at the American Enterprise Institute, a conservative think tank. Murray was also the coauthor, in the 1990s, of a controversial book, *The Bell Curve,* on the nature and impact of intelligence distributions in society. There, he and his colleague Richard Herrnstein claim that U.S. policy and welfare benefits effectively subsidize poor women who are "at the low end of the intelligence distribution."[338]

In his 2012 book *Coming Apart: The State of White America, 1960–2010*, Murray takes on very real problems of working-class poverty, and social breakdowns in working-class culture, including an epidemic of opioid addiction.[339] However, he doesn't attribute the cause of the problems to economic inequality and reduced supports from social policy. He attributes the problems to poor people themselves. More children in poor communities, in a "new lower class," are born out of wedlock, Murray claims. Men are less likely to hold jobs. Families don't stay together. Traditional religion is in decline. Drug addiction has spread like wildfire. Consequently, things are "coming apart," not because of the economy or government policy, but because of the bad habits and lack of industriousness among poor people, who are "more politically and socially disengaged."[340]

J. D. Vance, in his *New York Times* best-selling autobiography *Hillbilly Elegy*, about growing up in Appalachia and Middletown, Ohio, is no less harsh in his judgment of the poor communities he left behind.[341] While some of his grandmother's generation still offered some kind of dignity and stability, he reflected, his parents' generation didn't. "We spend our way to the poorhouse," Vance writes, by splurging on "giant TVs and iPads," "expensive clothes," and "homes we don't need."[342] His bitter conclusion is that, in the Appalachian culture that raised him, "Thrift is inimical to our being."[343] Economic policies help, but in the end, Vance says, people like this need to pull themselves together, just like he did.

This is the conservative interpretation of community breakdown as an explanation for increased poverty. Its solutions are cultural, not structural. They are about changing the habits and mindsets of the disadvantaged and their children, rather than restructuring the society that has placed them there and that keeps them in poverty. Grit isn't just a personal character trait, from this viewpoint. Now it's something you can stick on a report card and evaluate just like you do with reading, mathematics, or anything else. Engagement becomes the stoic endurance of a few rare individuals who overcome and rise above their dysfunctional families and friends. Children are encouraged and supported to beat the odds, instead of adults endeavoring to change those odds so that they are fairer for everyone.

Engagement here is about resilience, bouncing back, toughing it out. Schools are places of order and character development. It's the job of educators to inculcate moral virtues in the young, to make up for the morality that their parents' communities are believed to have abandoned.

Anomie (disassociation) and alienation (disconnection) are not necessarily competing explanations for disengagement. Marx, the radical, and Durkheim, the conservative, both have a point. You can and often do have social dislocation *and* economic inequality. Likewise, if you can reduce inequality, you can also reduce people's sense of disassociation. This helps explain why Nordic countries with strong welfare states and commitments to equity rank so highly on measures of well-being.[344]

But even when there is a solid strategy to reduce inequality, disassociation from a community and its values remains an issue. Wearing masks and keeping physical distancing from one another during a pandemic to comply with social norms and meet our obligations to others is about protecting and building an orderly, moral community. The job of the school is to develop the senses of association and belonging that turn behaviors like mask-wearing from a top-down requirement of a bureaucracy into a shared commitment of a community.

Nordic societies combat anomie by having outdoor breaks for play and conversation among children and adults every hour or so. They emphasize free play rather than structured literacy and mathematics programs in early childhood.

Nordic societies combat anomie not just by minimizing economic inequality, but also by having outdoor breaks for play and conversation among children and adults every hour or so. They emphasize free play rather than structured literacy and mathematics programs in early childhood. Children sing songs that emphasize peace and togetherness, and teachers' time is protected so that they can engage in informal discussions over coffee rather than just in official meetings throughout the school day, and so on.[345] From the angle of *alienation*, the curriculum has to be inclusive and responsive. But, if we learn the lessons of *anomie*, we also need to make our schools places where all young people feel they belong and are part of something important, too.

Disempowerment

Disengagement is sometimes a political matter—not just a behavioral, cognitive, or emotional issue. Disengagement may actually mean disempowerment. Students' feelings of powerlessness and lack of voice can result from ingrained cultures of teaching in which teachers feel they have to be individually in charge and in control in their classes all the time.

Sometimes when people use the term *disengagement*, it is a euphemism for disobedience or resistance to teachers. This type of disengagement can be a symptom of an environment with behavior programs that border on cruelty. Students rebel when they are in schools that seem uncaring. They check out inwardly when faced with structures that are unfair.

In his 1932 classic *The Sociology of Teaching*, however, Willard Waller argues that authority relations are the natural state of affairs in teaching. Waller's writing speaks to uncomfortable truths that persist in many schools today. The school, he says, is "a despotism in a perilous state of equilibrium,"[346] and the teacher-pupil relationship is unavoidably "a form of institutionalized dominance and subordination" in which teachers and pupils have a "conflict of desires."[347] Adults and children are pitted against one another: "The teacher represents the adult group, ever the enemy of the spontaneous lives of children . . . Pupils are much more interested in life in their own world than in the desiccated bits of life teachers have to offer," he observes.[348] In this perilous state, "authority is on the side of the teacher. The teacher always wins. In fact, he must win or he cannot remain a teacher."

How do students respond to this? "Whatever rules that the teacher lays down," Waller notes, "the tendency of the pupils is to empty them of meaning." They do this "by mechanization of conformity, by 'laughing off' the teacher . . . by taking refuge in self-initiated activities, that are always just beyond the teacher's reach." While "the power to pass rules is not limited," however, "the teacher's power to enforce those rules is."

When we were in secondary school, we were masters of this. We read superhero comics under the desk, played card games in the back corner of the class, and inflicted practical jokes on the more hapless teachers. In all these ways that superficially appear as mere disengagement, "students attempt to neutralize teacher control."[349] Waller seemed resigned to this situation. Adversarial classroom management came with the territory, in his view. No schools could be free of it. Ultimately, they were autocracies. The only choice was simply how benign or harsh their methods were in dealing with classroom discipline.

Much later, well into the 1960s, John Holt, a future leader of the homeschooling movement, was less pragmatic. In 1964's *How Children Fail* and the 1967 follow-up *How Children Learn*, he records observations of classroom practices familiar to all teachers, but which seem to him strange and unacceptable.[350] Why did teachers keep asking questions to which they already had the answer? Why did students fail to check their work properly? Why did they half-raise their hands in response to questions they didn't really understand? Why did they mumble their answers instead of speaking out clearly? Why did very young children form their letters vaguely in ways that could be interpreted one way or another?

The reason, Holt says, is quite simply *fear*—fear of getting the wrong answer, of finding out how awful your work would be if you checked back over it, of being called on to answer if you raised your hand too obviously or just kept it down, or of just being wrong. So, students developed subterfuges that looked like disengagement, to avoid being found out and getting things wrong. Holt's students felt powerless, and he believed that we should and could put this right.

It's not the teachers that are to blame for this, Holt points out. It's a system that judges teachers and schools on the work they can get their students to produce; on what we would now call outcomes, or test scores. It's a system that is deeply embedded in Tyack and Tobin's traditional grammar of schooling that schools and school leaders have found so hard to change.[351]

The matter of how much power students should have can be polarizing. On the one hand, concentrating power in the hands of teachers can seem oppressive and unfair, so critics advocate for young people to have more agency and voice. On the other hand, many teachers and parents hold steadfast to Waller's view that adult power over students is either necessary or inevitable. In reality, power in schools is more complicated than this. Classical sociological theories of power in organizations and society help us to understand why.

In the 1950s, Robert Dahl, a professor of political science at Yale University, defined power in terms of the ability to participate in decision making. He studied this through "careful examination of a series of concrete decisions" that people made about where to shop, how to vote, and where to work.[352] Whoever ended up making the decisions were the ones who had power, he contended.

Two political scientists at Bryn Mawr College in Pennsylvania, Peter Bachrach and Morton Baratz, later criticized Dahl's model. It "takes no account of the fact that power may be, and often is, exercised by confining the scope of decision-making to relatively 'safe' issues," they claim.[353] Bachrach and Baratz posit that power is not just about whose will prevails. It is also about who decides what appears (or doesn't appear) on the decision-making agenda in the first place.

These two *faces of power*, as Bachrach and Baratz call them, occur all the time in interactions between teachers and students. The first face, for example, is evident when high school teachers (along with many parents) feel they are in a constant battle of wills with teenagers.

It may seem like the teacher usually wins in terms of gaining compliance, but if, by the end of the lesson, a student writes only a couple of sentences rather than the several paragraphs required by the teacher, who has really exercised more power? The first face of power highlights whether students get to choose what they want to learn, and how they want to learn it.

The second face of power—who sets the agenda—alerts us to which decisions teachers allow students to make. This perspective draws attention to how some of the most routine aspects of school are loaded with power implications. For example, teachers get to tell students to raise their hands or turn off their phones, but students aren't permitted to tell teachers to raise *their* hands or turn off *their* phones. Perhaps students can choose the format of certain assignments, but the teacher sets the curriculum topics—potentially precluding controversial topics that students care deeply about but the teacher feels uncomfortable with. It's not on the agenda. Developments like student self-advocacy, or students simply being able to say they may not be comfortable with something their teacher asks them to do, are ways of engaging with this second face of power.

In 1974, British social theorist Steven Lukes published *Power: A Radical View*.[354] His book revolutionized research and thinking about power. The exercise of power is not always observable, Lukes says, in contests of wills, or even in who decides what is on the agenda or not. There is a third face of power that is pervasive, yet invisible. In line with a range of 1970s European writers and ensuing feminist theories, Lukes points out that those with the greatest power are able to shape the very way people think about things by determining language and discourse that serves the interests of the powerful and eliminates vocabularies of opposition among the powerless.[355] "The bias of the system is not sustained simply by a series of individually chosen acts," he argues, "but more importantly by the socially structured and culturally patterned behaviour of groups, and practices of institutions."[356]

This third face of power operates by "influencing, shaping or determining" people's "very wants" by "controlling their thoughts and desires."[357] "Is it not the supreme and most insidious exercise of power," Lukes asks, "to prevent people . . . from having grievances by shaping their perceptions, cognitions and preferences in such a way that they accept their role in the existing order of things?"[358]

When hunger and starvation are relabeled *food insecurity*, the third face of power turns a social problem of inequality into a psychological issue of personal vulnerability. When we call children in poverty *vulnerable* rather than *marginalized* or *oppressed*; when we designate learning as *personalized* even though it is actually digitally *customized*; and when we convert the challenge of transforming a school's *culture* for the better into a simple task of *behavior management*, we are colluding with language that mobilizes bias in favor of the powerful. Terms like these keep opposition out of students' and others' heads, so they are unable to imagine a better future. We are, at these moments, all entrapped in Lukes's third face of power.

In 2005, in a revised and expanded edition of his book, Lukes is self-critical of his earlier views. He now acknowledges how "power over others," in some aspects, "can be productive, transformative, authoritative and compatible with dignity."[359] Sometimes, when adults exert power over children, it's not because they are tyrants, but because, as adult human beings, they often do know best. Any parent who has ever had to deal with serious misbehavior by grounding their children or teenagers, imposing time-outs, or taking away their computers knows exactly what Lukes means. Indeed, Lukes identifies parents, teachers, orchestra conductors, and sports coaches as people who have "command-obedience relationships that are indispensable to valued co-operative activities."[360]

These different perspectives on power can enrich our understanding of an increasingly popular approach to student engagement known as *student voice*. In 2001, University of Sussex professor Michael Fielding—one of the first academics to write about student voice—argued that students should be empowered to address their needs and advance their interests in their schools. Student voice, he says, should be "emancipatory in both process and outcome." He urges teachers to provide students with opportunities to address parts of their identities and aspirations that do not fit neatly into typical schools.[361]

If this call to empower students seems somewhat abstract, our work in Ontario revealed numerous examples of student voice in action. For example, provincial policy was reviewed annually by a diverse group of Ontario students who provided feedback on the impact of the government's new goals. Student mental health committees in schools addressed students' own issues like anxiety or depression.[362] It was also students across the province, not adults, who took the initiative to set up Gay-Straight Alliances in schools to support their LGBTQ communities.

Meanwhile, in the U.S. Pacific Northwest, after a group of English language arts teachers had collaborated with their colleagues across vast distances to develop new units on writing, they then empowered their students to share their writing and give feedback to their peers in other schools in the network. As we will describe further in chapter 6 (page 183), these students also learned to write op-eds and letters to elected officials to express their concerns about issues in their communities.

Uncannily, on the very day we were writing these paragraphs, Andy witnessed the power of student voice at work with his own grandchildren. As May turned into June, and the novelty of learning at home during the coronavirus was wearing off, Andy's wife, Pauline, a former school administrator, suggested that their seven-year-old grandson prepare a lesson to teach to his five-year-old twin sisters. From a point where he was starting to tune out, he perked up instantly. With careful preparation, he presented a lesson on the dinosaur *Spinosaurus* to his sisters, who were enrapt. His presentation came complete with properly labeled pictures, a short video, clear oral delivery, and two paragraphs read out from one of his books. As the twins drew and wrote about what they were learning, he also gave them feedback on how to improve.

Empowerment should not just be a reward for older or well-behaved students. It is something to be experienced and learned from the very moment a child begins school. Can we help children to experience a sense of empowerment by learning to resolve conflicts amicably in open-ended morning meetings in the kindergarten classroom? Can we provide middle school students with opportunities to pursue their own interests in school, and to knit these together with other parts of the curriculum? Can we work with our students in our high schools to devise formative assessments that will help them to grow in confidence and competence as they progress through a challenging curriculum? Can we allow students with learning challenges to express self-advocacy for the things that will help them learn when the need arises, and not just after a formal diagnosis of their disability has been completed? Can we include students with mental health issues on the mental health committee, or involve some of the worst-behaved students on the behavior committee? Student voices should be heard everywhere. Educators must be constantly alert to the possibilities and necessities for their inclusion.

At the same time, when adults must exercise power over students in the best interests of the community and students themselves—in dealing with bullying, for example—they can provide clear and calm explanations of why consequences are being imposed. "Because I said so" disempowers students rather than helping them understand and do better next time. Students need to know what kinds of restorative practices will involve the bullies and the victims. They have to recognize that both the perpetrators and the targets of bullying must be fully heard, rather than summarily dismissed.

Schools are good places for young people to learn to take responsibility for their choices and to find their voices. Like any other aspect of human development, empowerment cannot simply be given to students. It has to be deliberately structured so it can be experienced and learned. It's a matter of trust, say Pasi Sahlberg and Tim Walker, in their book *In Teachers We Trust*. They quote the remarks of one of the Finnish teachers they worked with on why "children often fool around."[363] It's because, many times, "too much responsibility is offered to a student who has very poor self-regulation skills."[364]

The answer is not to take away these children's responsibilities, though. Citing the work of another Finnish primary school teacher, Sahlberg and Walker point to three ascending levels of trust and responsibility she provides for her students when they are working in pairs or groups. Students on the first level work inside the classroom. At the second level, they can work in the hallway, where the teacher can still keep an eye on them. At the third level, they are trusted to work anywhere on the floor, even out of her sight.[365] Sahlberg and Walker explain that these kinds of approaches are typical in Finnish schools. Like trust, responsibility, or self-assessment, empowerment is not a thing that teachers give or take away in an instant. It is something that students themselves are responsible for building over time.

If students are going to grow in confidence and maturity, they need to be able to participate in decision making and not have their ideas and concerns excluded at the outset. Of course, sometimes, empowerment efforts backfire. Children will act irresponsibly. They will disappoint their teachers. We need to have a growth mindset toward empowerment. It has to be *learned*, not just *earned*. Children do not always master a new mathematics concept the first time around and they don't honor the trust that is given to them every time, either. We can't give up on our students whenever they disappoint us or let us down.

> *Empowerment has to be* learned, *not just* earned.

These are the kinds of issues that teachers and other educators need to reflect on and resolve when it comes to empowerment. We must avoid falling into two traps: defending teachers' right to make decisions for students under any circumstances, or romantically assuming that unlimited empowerment will turn every student into a change-making Greta Thunberg. Instead, teachers must ask how they can deliberately develop empowerment and responsibility among their students, even in difficult conditions, for without genuine empowerment, true responsibility will never be learned at all.

Distraction

Distraction occurs when the mind initially sets out to focus on one object of attention but is turned away from it by something more compelling. Pleasant distractions redirect the mind away from what is boring or irrelevant. Unhelpful distractions prevent us from achieving goals that are essential to our fulfillment and well-being.

Paul Atchley, a neuroscientist and university professor, gave a popular TED Talk called "Distraction Is Literally Killing Us." In his talk, Atchley explains that when the mind is caught up in *continuous partial attention*, the cognitive overload becomes too much for a person to handle.[366] Yet the attractions of new technologies are so powerful that, in the United States, two-thirds of adults now check their phones over 160 times a day—often when they are in the middle of doing something else. Three-quarters of adults "consider themselves addicted."[367] Eventually, the most compelling stimulus is what grabs our attention and draws us to it.

Neither of us is immune to the distractions of surreptitiously peeking at messages during long meetings, or scrolling through Twitter accounts when we ought to be planning classes or writing papers. In a coronavirus world of endless Zoom meetings, how many of us have furtively worked on two screens and tasks at the same time? Some of this just helps break up the day. Perhaps it's no different from how people drifted off in their own heads or wrote shopping lists when meetings got tedious in the past. If there's too much distraction, however, people miss out on important knowledge and information—and this is exactly what's happening to students.

In his studies of how educational leaders deal with digital distraction, our Boston College colleague Vincent Cho described how teachers in one school complained that their students were "playing video games constantly" and found that it was impossible to "pull students out" of such distractions when they had become "sucked in."[368] Even when students pulled an all-nighter preparing for a "huge chemistry test," their inability to turn off their "buzzing phone" would take "away from their ability to focus on the test."[369] Cho found that even though "digital distraction did not wreck all instruction" in this school, "it did seem to gnaw at its effectiveness."[370]

The issues of digital attraction and distraction surfaced in one of our ten Ontario school districts that were part of the NPDL network. Over 1,300 schools in eight countries participate in this network.[371] Teachers in the NPDL network are encouraged to take on new roles as activators of student learning. They view themselves as collaborators who are "intentional about fostering . . . new relationships" and partnerships with "students, teachers, families, and communities."[372] This seems like the epitome of engagement.

Many of the Ontario district's educators couldn't say enough positive things about NPDL. One sixth-grade teacher described it as "thrilling," not only because "it suited my personality," but more deeply because "I was able to become more of an educational tour guide facilitating students' experiences rather than me trying to share my experiences with them."[373] A kindergarten teacher stated that "It's perfect for play-based and inquiry learning to have the children discover their interest in learning." A fifth-grade teacher said that "It really engaged my students" and has "also made me look at the curriculum in a totally different way, going into the skills that we want our students to learn as life-long learners." One kindergarten teacher liked how it "just blends so well with the curriculum."

Teachers followed the exhortations of their administrators to make the most of new pedagogies. They taught their students how to create websites, post blogs, and make videos. Two upper-elementary teachers created:

> a "virtual symposium" because we were trying to "leverage digital" to students (regarding) how they could use it to communicate. The final projects had to be in digital format. We had websites. We had Google classrooms. We had blogs. We had slideshows. We had videos. Then, we created a Google classroom and invited all of our other classes in the school to participate and to give feedback.

For these teachers, access to the internet provided a learning opportunity for everyone. Digital skills, they felt, would help students represent what they had learned in ways that were playful and creative. They then could "teach their parents and the other students in the school things that they learned in the process, that other people didn't know."

School administrators also expressed enthusiasm about new pedagogies. When asked if they had any problems with the push for ubiquitous use of digital tools, one principal's response was that:

> How we were using technology wasn't as deep as it could have been. We looked at our Smart boards, and we realized that we were only using them for their intended purpose 30% of the time. Most of the time we were using them as overhead projectors. As we were discovering this, and telling ourselves that technology is important, we realized that the kinds of technological tools we chose to use were as important as us moving in technology. By that definition, there's been growth in deeper learning, because teachers are learning how we use technologies in integrated ways to deepen kids' learning.

For this principal, professional development of the staff in how to use new technologies was equated with *deeper learning*, rather than in terms of learning how to solve complex problems or moral dilemmas, for example. Deeper learning here meant skill in using new technologies.

Ironically, at the same time that districts like this one and networks like NPDL are pushing for digital use *ubiquitously*, major technology companies have moved in the opposite direction. Sherry Turkle is the Abby Rockefeller Mauzé Professor of the Social Studies of Science and Technology at the Massachusetts Institute of Technology. In her book *Reclaiming Conversation*, she reports that increasing numbers of corporations "devise strategies for workplace teams built on face-to-face meetings" in which "there are no phones" or other distractions.[374] "Others begin the day with technology-free 'stand-up meetings,'" she says.[375] Still others "ask employees to take a break" from technology and encourage them "not to check their email after business hours."[376]

What is going on when major technology companies are alert to the dangers of digital distraction, and school innovation networks are not? It was only in a focus group of the district's mental health consultants (typically called school counselors in the United States) that we heard a sense of alarm about the negative impacts of technology on students. One consultant stated that she had observed "astronomical increases in explosive behaviors in the classroom, kids just not sitting down and not coping well. We're living in a time right now, there has been so much transformation as a result of technology." Another consultant said that new technologies were having "huge impacts that we're seeing on mental health and well-being." A third noted that "It is one of those hidden stressors that we talk about, on a very physiological level, that when we're staring at screens so much and at certain times, how it's changing the way that our biology is working." For this reason, a fourth consultant argued that there needed to be stricter "parameters around use."

For this district's mental health consultants, the downsides of the distraction caused by excessive use of new technologies were obvious. But "then we run smack into New Pedagogy's endorsement of new technologies," one complained. The consultants regretted that many educators in their system were so smitten with technology that they failed to see how it may also be creating a whole generation that finds it hard to focus on just one thing for any length of time. They were exasperated that the leadership of the school district continuously communicated that "We need more! The kids love it."

The mental health consultants were then left to address the symptoms with students who suffered from sleep deprivation, cyberbullying, and addictive checking of their phones for new messages more than eighty times a day by some accounts. The sheer volume of digital distraction led one consultant to comment, "I'm not anti-technology, but I also recognize the huge impacts we're seeing on mental health and well-being." As we saw in chapter 1 (page 13), despite everyone's efforts to make the best of an almost impossible situation, the coronavirus pandemic has, in many ways, only exacerbated the problems of distraction from deeper engagement that digital technology poses in home learning environments.

Is there a way to reconcile the drive that is led by movements like NPDL to use new digital tools ubiquitously, while ensuring that students do not fall prey to endemic digital disturbances? To be honest, children and teenagers are already a bundle of biological distractions! Additional and unnecessary distractions can therefore pose serious problems to the deeper learning that should be at the heart of schools. They can undermine students' capacity to read long texts and not just short ones. It takes more time to embrace extended works of imaginative fiction than to do a quick cut-and-paste of online information. Students should be able to exercise good judgment in order to do both under the proper circumstances. Likewise, we should want our students to play physically in rough-and-tumble sports that develop strength and agility, as well as virtually in sophisticated gaming environments that many workplaces also use to simulate real-life challenges in firefighting or hospital operating rooms, for example.

There are practical ways to address these matters. As in the CHENINE Charter we presented in chapter 3 (page 102), they begin with candid acknowledgment of the risks that accompany the introduction of new technologies in schools, as well as an appreciation of their benefits.

In France, which, according to OECD data from fifty countries, already has one of the two lowest rates of technology use in schools,[377] smartphones have been banned in schools.[378] But such draconian regimes that amount to digital prohibition or total abstinence may be counterproductive. There's no point removing digital distractions if regular classes continue to be filled with disengaging worksheets or didactic presentations by teachers. Kids will just go back to the other old-fashioned distractions like paper planes, doodling, or daydreaming.

Rather, digital distraction can be taken as a prime opportunity for learning why easily distracted students have become disengaged in the first place. Do they find the curriculum alienating? Is it devoid of any mystery or magic? Do they understand what they are asked to learn, and why? What might motivate them to such an extent that they wouldn't even want to look at their phones anymore? If we can engage students as well as teachers with motivating content and classroom practices, we can recapture their attention. Together, we can learn how to stay off the slippery slope of digital distraction in favor of more paradisiacal pathways of full engagement.

Defeating Disengagement

The enemies of engagement we've been discussing are outside us and also within us—*all* of us. They are outside us in outdated examination pressures that sacrifice intrinsic engagement to anxious memorization. They are in curricula cluttered with uninteresting content and cleansed of controversy. They are in cultures of market competition that set students and schools against each other instead of building senses of community and belonging among them. They are in overly strict behavior management systems that secure short-term compliance at the expense of empowering students to develop their capacities for self-determination. And they are in over-exuberant rather than evidence-informed adoptions of digital technologies.

Systems of policy and leadership have a lot to answer for as enemies of student engagement. But teachers and other educators can't just sit back and blame everything on "the system," tempting as that is. As we said previously, teachers are part of the big picture of engagement and disengagement. When we look for the enemy, the most important realization is that, in important respects, the enemy is not just out there. The enemy is also within.

What do we mean by this? Well, our schools and universities don't only fail to engage students. They often actively disengage those students, too. Unless we fight off these enemies ourselves, then we all, in a way, become responsible. The good news, though, is that if we *are* the enemy—in teaching, leadership, educational policy, or universities—because we spend too much time trudging through the curriculum, teaching to the test, or enforcing unreasonable behavior policies—we can also switch sides. We can join with our students to create a more engaging experience of education together.

So what clues has this sociologically informed chapter given us about how we might flip schools from producing disengagement to doing the opposite?

If disengagement results from *disenchantment* with a system that has become obsessed with win-lose examinations on quickly forgotten content, the remedy will require nothing less than wholesale assessment reform. Using the best of modern technology, this can combine shared digital feedback and more flexible systems of certification with collective professional judgment about student learning and performance. This transformational alliance of digital sophistication and collaborative professionalism will protect certification of standards while sustaining the joy of learning. These changes will enable *creativity and magic* to be injected back into schools to ignite all students' intrinsic motivation for learning.

If disengagement is the consequence of alienated and *disconnected* teaching that makes students feel estranged from their schoolwork and its relationship to their own lives, then systemic, sustained efforts must be made to connect the curriculum and students' work assignments more closely to their interests, identities, and cultures. Above all, students need to find some deep personal sense of *meaning and purpose* in what they are learning and why.

If disengagement is a consequence of *disassociation* from communities that have weakened because of narcissistic individualism or social disorganization, then schools and school systems must recreate senses of *attachment and belonging* among all their students, whatever their circumstances, in their learning, their classrooms, their schools, and their communities.

If disengagement is really student *disempowerment* as a result of teachers' clinging too tightly to autonomous control over their own classes, or to behavior management systems that enforce top-down compliance, then we must expand the rights of students while also developing their capabilities and responsibility to express their *voice and involvement* in the classroom, the school, and the system's policy-making processes.

Finally, if destructive digital *distraction* becomes endemic because commercial interests in technology profits and political interests in quick fixes combine to drive educational reform, then we need to develop strategies for more ethical and targeted uses of digital technologies on educational grounds instead. These will strengthen students' *concentration and focus* on their learning and, with patience and relentless persistence, they will also build students' capacities for true *mastery* of knowledge, expertise, and themselves.

Disengagement comes in many forms and occurs for a number of reasons. In this chapter, we have looked at five formidable enemies of engagement that usually masquerade as less controversial manifestations of disengagement. Once we acknowledge these enemies of engagement for what they are, we can then defeat them with strategies that reverse their effects, as shown in table 4.1.

TABLE 4.1: Types of Disengagement and Their Antidotes

Disenchantment	Creativity and Magic	
Disconnection	Meaning and Purpose	
Disassociation	Attachment and Belonging	
Disempowerment	Voice and Involvement	
Distraction	Focus and Mastery	

Disengagement is often treated as a *wall* that students erect to barricade themselves off from their teachers and the learning. Instead, we should think of disengagement as a *window* into how young people are actually feeling about their learning and their lives.

Think back to when you started reading this chapter and you were asked to reflect about a student who was disengaged and about your own experiences of disengagement. Now that you've considered the five enemies of engagement, has your view shifted about what's been causing disengagement for you and for your students? Do you have some new ideas that suggest some different, better approaches than ones you have tried so far?

If we confront the five enemies of engagement and take our lead from understanding the deeper forces that are at work behind student disengagement, and then respond accordingly, we will make considerable progress. Imagine how much more engaging our classes and schools could be if we infused more learning with creativity, magic, and a sense of meaning and purpose. Imagine how much more engaged children and teenagers could be if they had a voice in their learning and their schools and all of them felt like they truly belonged there. Imagine if we used digital technology more thoughtfully and critically so that it *enhanced* great teaching and learning, instead of being adopted overzealously and distracting everyone from the quality of their educational experience. How much more engaging our schools would become for all our students then! As Freddie Mercury once sang, it would, indeed, be "a kind of magic."[379]

> *Disengagement is often treated as a* **wall** *that students erect to barricade themselves off from their teachers and the learning. Instead, we should think of disengagement as a* **window** *into how young people are actually feeling about their learning and their lives.*

CHAPTER 5

Standardized Testing: The Archenemy of Engagement

There's scarcely anything more disengaging for students than high-stakes standardized testing. Of course, like any stressful event, a test or examination can actually provoke intense engagement —for a while. Preparation, revision, practice exams, sample questions, asking friends to test you—all these things can definitely grab young people's attention in the short term. Fear is engaging. Intense worry is also engaging. Knowing that your entire future may rest on a single test result or that a school's reputation might depend on how many students reach and exceed proficiency—this succeed-or-fail, life-and-death mentality is certainly engaging, in a way. So, too, is the national fervor that is whipped up among students in many East and Southeast Asian nations when they take the international PISA tests on which their countries' subsequent rankings and reputations will depend. But in any deep and lasting sense, high-stakes tests for accountability or systemic comparison purposes are the antithesis of engaging learning. As soon as the tests are over, most people will never have to recall or use most of the knowledge they have been tested on ever again.

High-stakes testing—especially when it doesn't involve the kind of certification that might benefit the student—is disengaging for almost everyone associated with it. It is an

> *High-stakes testing is an archenemy of engagement—a Darth Vader or Lord Voldemort of education that must be confronted and defeated.*

archenemy of engagement that embodies all the five forms of disengagement in a single phenomenon—a Darth Vader or Lord Voldemort of education that must be confronted and defeated.

- With their emphases on basic skills, formulaic answers, and factual recall, high-stakes tests drain learning of its creativity and magic and *disenchant* students with their education.

- High-stakes tests *disconnect* or alienate students from any sense of meaning or purpose as their only value is to exchange what is learned in order to hit a target, get a grade, or pass a course—and often, the tests don't even provide that.

- High-stakes tests pit students against students and schools against each other in a winner-takes-all process of competitive achievement that creates *disassociation* and lack of belonging among diverse students and across schools and systems. This undermines collaboration, teamwork, and common good.

- High-stakes tests *disempower* almost everyone. They destroy the dignity of many students with disabilities and students who are second language learners. These students cannot express what they know and have no voice in their own learning and its assessment.

- High-stress and time-consuming tests *distract* students from other kinds of engaging learning, and they produce outcomes of no real value for students and their teachers who normally don't receive the results until months after the tests have been taken.

It's little wonder that, in the throes of COVID-19, although teachers, students, and families wanted to look forward to returning to teaching, learning, and caring for students in physical schools, hardcore advocates in politics and government bureaucracies pressed for the reintroduction of the standardized tests that had been suspended during the pandemic. Battle lines are being drawn between diehard defenders of standardized tests and a groundswell of public opinion and professional opposition that is pressing for their permanent abolition and promoting more constructive alternatives in their place.

The Impact of Testing

Daniel Koretz is the Henry Lee Shattuck Professor of Education at the Harvard Graduate School of Education and a friend and neighbor of Dennis's. Over the years, the two of them have run into each other at their local grocery store, and have swapped stories about their latest experiences with educational change. While the exchanges have always been amicable, they aren't always upbeat. That's because Koretz's research, as summarized in his book *The Testing Charade: Pretending to Make Schools Better*, provides a bracing depiction of educational reforms that have gone awry for decades.[380]

Koretz has studied the impact of high-stakes testing on students' reading and mathematics achievement since 1990. First, "in the case of reading," he writes, "the trend data show that students' learning hasn't improved much, despite decades of unrelenting pressure to raise the test scores in reading."[381] Second, while fourth graders' mathematics scores have improved, by the time students reach high school, there is a strong "fade-out" in the results, such that "since its first implementation in 2003, PISA has shown no consistent improvement of our students in math."[382] Koretz concludes that, "On balance, then, the reforms have been a failure."[383]

High-stakes testing has been the embodiment, the epitome, and the apogee of the Age of Achievement and Effort. It has been denounced by the statistical societies of both the United States and United Kingdom, discredited by respected academics on both sides of the Atlantic, abandoned outright by Wales and Scotland, and targeted by mounting opposition during the pandemic. High-stakes testing may finally be on the run. Its unconvincing results and its widely acknowledged negative side effects on students' and teachers' engagement have it on the ropes.[384] Defenders of testing are not going down without

a fight, though. Arguments in favor of retaining testing for accountability, equity, and intervention purposes after COVID-19 continue
to materialize.[385]

However, not all large-scale assessments need be high stakes.
Among the attempts to address the interests of accountability and
measurable, systemwide improvement while avoiding the negative side
effects, one response has been to keep the large-scale tests but lower
the stakes a bit to reduce incentives to game the system. In this spirit,
Ontario tried to learn from the mistakes made by high-stakes systems
in the United States, the United Kingdom, and elsewhere. These mistakes include imposing punitive measures on schools that failed to
reach their test score targets, like closure, takeover, or termination of
leaders and other staff.

The Ontario government has used full-cohort testing of all students
in grades 3, 6, 9, and 10 to meet accountability targets and guide
interventions. But it has also sought to avoid the "perverse incentives" of what had come to be known as *Campbell's Law*. Named after
Dartmouth College professor Donald T. Campbell in 1976, this law
states that "the more any quantitative social indicator is used for social
decision-making, the more subject it will be to corruption pressures
and the more apt it will be to distort and corrupt the social processes
it is intended to monitor."[386] In other words, people will do practically
anything in a high-stakes environment to meet the targets and avoid
performing badly on the test.

From the early 2000s, Ontario therefore repurposed its test, known
as the EQAO (short for Education Quality and Accountability
Office), for monitoring and intervention purposes as well as traditional accountability ones. It also lowered the stakes. Schools were
not ranked publicly, principals were not fired, and schools were not
shut down if they struggled. However, results were still known to the
government, and provincial targets for 75 percent proficiency (what
teachers called *the drive to 75*) by the next election were based on
them. Schools still had to undertake data-driven performance reviews
through repeated six-week teaching-learning cycles.[387]

All of this put a lot of pressure on school districts, the schools, and many of their teachers, particularly at the elementary school level. The tests were not high-stakes, but they were not low-stakes or no-stakes either. In this respect, they are best understood as being what Jaekyung Lee and Chungseo Kang call *mid-stakes* in nature.[388]

As we explained in previous chapters, in 2014, we led a Boston College research team to study and work with ten school districts that had joined an innovative Consortium sponsored by the Council of Ontario Directors of Education (CODE). Our purpose was to investigate how the districts were responding to the government's new reform agenda of *Achieving Excellence*, with its focus on broad excellence, equity understood as inclusion, well-being, and maintaining public confidence.[389] In the course of interviewing 222 teachers, school leaders, district leaders, and policymakers, we learned about many positive aspects of how the new policy was being implemented, which we describe later. In the course of our work, we also learned about the impact of the mid-stakes EQAO tests, including whether they had managed to overcome or offset the "corruption pressures" that Campbell's Law describes.[390]

Some senior administrators still felt that EQAO "helped with accountability" and "helped drive standards," in one director's words. A superintendent added that it had a "place in terms of accountability." Some principals were proud when students with learning disabilities showed gains on EQAO literacy scores and said that the test helped them to know their students.[391] EQAO "drives the conversations," one principal remarked. Another commented, "You can certainly see those students and where they're struggling. Sometimes you didn't even know they were struggling until you had that data."

Once again, though, no one justified mid-stakes testing on the grounds that it made learning engaging for students themselves. The silence was deafening. However, now that Ontario's learning goals had broadened beyond literacy and mathematics, other administrators were becoming more ambivalent about the testing. One system administrator wrestled aloud with the test's pros and cons:

> Is it the perfect way to measure that? No, but can a stan-
> dard like that drive the way that I might teach better and
> help kids be clear around expressing their thoughts? I
> don't know. I don't think it's a bad thing. The fact that
> our kids with learning disabilities are challenged by that
> bothers me immensely. But I don't know a better way.[392]

Here, mid-stakes testing no longer seemed like a desirable strategy as it had in the first decade of the 21st century. Having secured some achievement gains and narrowed some achievement gaps in previous years, the law of diminishing returns appeared to be setting in. The test was now just the least-bad option, which had to be employed in the absence of anything better. As a result of being in daily, direct contact with students in the emerging Age of Engagement, Well-Being, and Identity, teachers were even more critical of Ontario's mid-stakes test than before. They pointed to five negative side effects it exerted on students' learning and engagement.

1. Cultural bias

2. Exclusion of the most vulnerable

3. Eclipse of learning

4. Inhibition of innovation

5. Spinning cycles of improvement

Cultural Bias

Teachers provided examples of test questions that were culturally biased. Items about Canada's nationally famous ice hockey star Wayne Gretzky would have been unknown to most newcomers from the Global South. Other items that referred to winter vacations in warm places probably made little sense to children from low-income families. A question about choosing appetizers from a menu was simply insulting to children in poverty for whom fancy restaurants were an unknown quantity. Even efforts to represent greater cultural diversity, like including an item on tae kwon do, had little meaning for the Indigenous students we saw responding to them. It's hard to feel engaged if the curriculum or assessment system is biased against your culture.[393]

Exclusion of the Most Vulnerable

It's also hard to feel engaged if the testing and evaluation procedures are not inclusive. Educators were concerned about students who had no chance of succeeding on the test, yet whose scores would be counted in the school's final profile. A coordinator explained:

> They don't report on the participating students. They report on *all* students. The kids with developmental disabilities who do not write are still in the denominator. Students who don't write the test and who are exempt are then given a zero.

One teacher summed up what the test meant for these vulnerable students themselves:

> I have students that are non-verbal and autistic, that there's no way, shape, or form, can write that test. It's ridiculous that they would even get on the list. It doesn't take into consideration the poverty in my school. It doesn't take into consideration the (child services) involvement, the families that are living in motels. All those things that set my families back are not even considered. It's hugely detrimental to my kids when we get into those scenarios. It's very stressful for them. It's very stressful for the teachers. And, quite frankly, it seems to be unfair.[394]

Mid-stakes testing was not inclusive. It was exclusionary. It was unable to engage many kinds of students with their learning or with demonstrating and expressing what they knew and could do, especially those who had learning disabilities, spoke a different language, or had just arrived from a country at war.

Eclipse of Learning

The standardized tests drove teachers to devote excess instructional time to test preparation rather than new learning.[395] As early as kindergarten and first grade, teachers introduced vocabulary included in the test and asked the children to practice shading in test bubbles.

Even though one district director publicly stated that he didn't "give a rat's ass" about the test, because the most important thing was learning rather than test scores, his schools still moved the desks into rows so students could get accustomed to the testing environment. In one school where test practice had been part of the school's weekly routine from the start of the school year, we observed students reluctantly redoing a practice test on reading comprehension because many of them had performed poorly on it the day before.[396] The principal frankly admitted that the purpose was to familiarize students with testing.

Some educators were quite content to focus on test preparation. In the words of one district leader:

> EQAO really sets the bar. I find when you put grade 3 questions on the table in front of a group of primary teachers, K to 3 . . . "Let's talk about, as a community here, how can we support the grade 3 teachers in the building? This isn't about one year captured on a test. This is an accumulation of the years." We started to talk about what are the things that you can do in grade 4 to support your grade 6 teacher? We talked about doing daily, if not weekly, multiple-choice experiences in your room so that the children learn the strategies to conquer those types of questions with ease.[397]

A second-grade teacher also focused on preparing her students for the test in grade 3:

> I did give them a question from the EQAO because I have a couple of the grade 2s, just to see how they did. Then I sat with them and looked at what were the barriers. Was it the language? Was it the vocab? Was it that it was written? Was it that they had to communicate it? That they had to write it in that box? That helped me understand maybe what I need to do next year to be able to have them be successful.[398]

Whether they agreed with test preparation, or not, though, these teachers' and leaders' focus, goals, and priorities were still directed toward helping students to be successful on the test, rather than to become more engaged with their learning.

Inhibition of Innovation

In previous chapters, we mentioned that one of our ten districts participated in the New Pedagogies for Deep Learning (NPDL) network.[399] In some grades, NPDL's promotion of innovation and self-directed learning seemed at odds with the demands and constraints of the EQAO. "I feel like EQAO is preparing students for a very antiquated version of education," one grade 3 teacher said. A grade 5 teacher agreed. "The standardized testing is so far removed from what we're doing. There's nothing standard about what we're doing. We're taking each child where they come from," they said. "All the things that we establish in our classrooms, the accommodations, all the tools that we give our students cannot be used on EQAO," another grade 5 teacher observed. "I do have EQAO pending as a grade 3 teacher," another teacher in the same focus group added. "I do have content that I'm expected to teach and assess. Hopefully, some of the critical thinking skills would come through, when the students are presented with a pencil-paper test for three days in a row. There's a complete disconnect."

Teachers outside the grades where EQAO was administered did not experience its pressures and constraints to the same degree. Among early years teachers, EQAO was not raised as an issue. And when teachers moved out of tested grades, they could suddenly feel liberated from the strictures of EQAO. "Last year, I was in grade 6 when I did my *New Pedagogy* project and I was like, 'Come on, I've got to get it done. EQAO is coming," one teacher remarked. But "this year," in a different grade, "it was like, 'Let's fly with this!' It's a big difference. If we didn't do math today, it doesn't matter. We'll catch up with it. The kids are engaged."

Spinning Cycles of Improvement

Drawing on Peter Hill and Carmel Crévola's research and development work in Australia, Ontario had developed a six-week teaching-learning cycle across its elementary schools.[400] Progress for each individual student was monitored and shared on a six-week basis—initially, on publicly displayed data walls—and students were tagged as being green (meeting or exceeding proficiency), yellow (at risk of not meeting proficiency), or red (falling short of proficiency). A range of data including proxies for EQAO assessments were used to make these determinations. After collaborative discussions about each student measuring below proficiency, teachers designed and implemented interventions, and then reviewed progress once more at the end of the next cycle.

These teaching-learning cycles were originally part of Ontario's effort to raise achievement results and narrow achievement gaps quickly in literacy and mathematics during the Age of Achievement and Effort. They were designed to catch students early, in real time, before they fell through the cracks. However, after 2014, when the province's reforms began to encompass wider aspects of students' learning and development, these six-week cycles of data-driven intervention came under pressure. In one district, a teacher expressed uncertainty about managing the reams of data:

> Everybody's gathering data, which is good, but what do we do with it, and what is the best data to gather? Now you see the teachers are taking pictures, they're observing, they have checklists, they're gathering it too, but what to do with it?[401]

Teachers in this district felt that six weeks was not sufficient to collect masses of data, identify issues, set objectives, and meet periodically to assess progress—while still attempting to manage classrooms full of diverse learners.[402] The teaching-learning cycle seemed to be turning into a rapidly accelerating spinning cycle like one in a washing machine or a gym. "The classroom's a busy place. There are always problems that need to be addressed immediately, so it's just a question of time," one teacher remarked. Another commented:

> Within the space of three weeks, we need to determine what our goal is, have built that up with our students and clearly established what the criteria are with our students, collect the data, and be working on it before that mid-point meeting. Then, we have another three weeks to keep going with that, to continue collecting data, to hopefully bring them to a successful conclusion of that

> project, to then have our data for the final meeting. I
> think my colleagues and I are all in agreement that 6
> weeks is too short of a time.[403]

A principal added that:

> The time between the meetings is sometimes too short
> because we establish learning outcomes, let's say at the
> first PLC meeting, then three weeks later we have the
> mid PLC, and sometimes, with all of the school activi-
> ties and other workshops, teachers find it very hard to
> establish the strategies to reach the learning outcomes
> that we've set.[404]

The broader goals of the Age of Engagement, Well-Being, and Identity incorporate deeper explorations into the nature and source of students' learning problems and strengths.[405] They therefore require wider spans of data than just measures of literacy and mathematics to inform professional judgments. This has meant that the original, fast-paced, data-team design no longer fits the deeper and broader learning agenda of *Achieving Excellence*. The EQAO and the six-week teaching-learning cycle are outdated remnants from a previous change strategy that have hindered the pursuit of more ambitious goals.

The Battle Over Mid-Stakes Testing

Like a number of other systems, Ontario was striving to embrace the innovative and inclusive goals of the Age of Engagement, Well-Being, and Identity while continuing to operate in a standardized testing environment inherited from the Age of Achievement and Effort. Our research into how the ten Consortium districts were try-ing to implement the province's more expansive and inclusive policy agenda brought the clash between these new goals and the old testing system into the spotlight. The many side effects of mid-stakes testing included five that had direct consequences for student engagement.

1. How can Indigenous students, speakers of minority
    languages, and recent newcomers to the country
    experience learning and success when not only the

content but also the linguistic structures of items are alien to their own cultures?

2. How can vulnerable students become engaged in their learning if the tests and all the time it takes to prepare for them do not acknowledge and include their gifts and talents?

3. What are we really doing when we teach kindergarten students how to fill in test bubbles when we could be helping them to start learning in depth instead?

4. What sense is there in promoting engaging forms of innovation in some grades, only to abandon or reverse those processes in other grades that deliver standardized learning for upcoming tests instead?

5. What is the point of repetitive six-week cycles of inquiry and intervention that must feel like a frenetic spinning class at the gym, when we should be giving teachers time to reflect together about their students' and their own deeper learning processes?

Mid-stakes testing does not eradicate unwanted side effects simply by lowering the stakes.

It's good to get beyond high-stakes testing, but mid-stakes testing does not eradicate unwanted side effects simply by lowering the stakes. It's time to rethink our assessment practices altogether.

The original purpose of EQAO was educational accountability. With the drive to 75, the test also became a tool for tracking, monitoring, and intervention.[406] It tried to maintain what was felt to be the best way to ensure accountability and provide systemwide evidence of progress. It tried to lower the stakes and consequences from high-stakes to mid-stakes, so that there would be no direct, punitive consequences.

Although many district leaders, principals, and staff saw value in this large-scale assessment, and despite the fact that, for a time, it definitely narrowed some achievement gaps, teachers became increasingly critical of it, not least in terms of its negative consequences for students' engagement.

In the face of Ontario's 21st century goals for deeper learning, the province's disenchanting, disempowering, and distracting testing strategy created a test-centric, culturally biased, uninventive, over-hasty culture of teaching that short-circuited teachers' opportunities to develop more engaging learning for their students. A 21st century movement toward deeper, more engaging learning was being constantly pulled back and weighed down by Ontario's 20th century system of large-scale, mid-stakes assessment. Whether it's mid-stakes or high-stakes, large-scale standardized testing of entire cohorts of students is now a major battleground on which the future of all students' engagement and success will be fought.

In 2017, prompted by the findings of our research, Ontario's premier announced that the province's six advisors (including Andy) would conduct an independent review of assessment and reporting practices, including EQAO. The review concluded that "using large scale provincial assessments for student diagnostic purposes, to infer evaluation of educators, and for ranking schools and school boards" was "inappropriate."[407] It recommended phasing out and ending EQAO tests before grade 6; paying "vigilant attention to ensuring curriculum and assessment materials provide linguistically, culturally and geographically relevant items and materials";[408] and ending the use of tests to rank schools or drive interventions in particular schools and districts.

The premier accepted all the recommendations in principle. One month later, however, in May 2018, the newly elected Progressive Conservative government disbanded the team of advisors and removed the report from its Ministry website. In the midst of the coronavirus pandemic in September 2020, it went one step further and called for bids to create a way to move EQAO testing online.

A battle over educational testing and its consequences for student engagement has also been raging in Australia. In 2008, the Australian government introduced a federal test known as NAPLAN (National

Assessment Program: Literacy and Numeracy). With close similarity to Ontario's mid-stakes EQAO, NAPLAN's tests in literacy and mathematics were administered in years 3, 5, 7 and 10. Three leading researchers published a review of the tests in 2020 and proposed only minor alterations. The review recommended changing the time of year for administering the test, revising the content of writing assessments, extending the number of subjects to be tested, and giving NAPLAN a new name, for example.[409] The minister for education swiftly responded that even these minor changes were unnecessary.[410]

Commenting on the review and on the test itself, Canadian change expert Michael Fullan—who was once a strong supporter of Ontario's mid-stakes tests, but who has been persuaded otherwise by the mounting evidence of their side effects—acknowledged that Australia's schools had "shown little or no improvement" for the duration of NAPLAN's existence. The review's mere "tinkering with the system," he said, will continue to "narrow the curriculum, without addressing the motivation of students or those that teach them."[411]

There are a lot of vested political and economic interests in perpetuating large-scale testing. Political leaders can deploy test results to demonstrate numerical improvements in education within their terms of office. Schools can use high scores as a Pied Piper's flute to lure elite parents and their children from other schools. System leaders can use poor results as a pretext for closing schools down and keeping principals in line. And let's not forget that for technology and testing companies, testing and data are billion-dollar businesses. These interests have little to do with students' learning and success.

As evidence mounts about the negative impacts of testing, more and more people are turning against the excessive systems of top-down accountability and intervention that have been put in place in the past decades. Recovery from the coronavirus pandemic will surely accelerate these trends. The 2020s are going to see a monumental global battle over the future of standardized testing between educational interests in students' learning, engagement, and well-being on the one hand and political and business interests in top-down accountability on the other. The result of this battle will be a decisive factor in determining whether the Age of Engagement, Well-Being, and Identity will or will not truly transform children's futures.

As our contribution to this struggle, we make ten policy recommendations for large-scale assessment reform. These reconcile two legitimate concerns. One is the need for at least some accountability, along with administrators' need for systemwide data that can guide improvement efforts. The other is to eliminate or at least mitigate the negative side effects that undermine students' engagement and success.

> *The 2020s are going to see a monumental global battle over the future of standardized testing between educational interests in students' learning, engagement, and well-being, on the one hand, and political and business interests in top-down accountability on the other.*

1. *Apply the European Union's Purpose Limitation Principle* that data collected for one purpose should not be used for another. Large-scale assessment can perform valuable accountability and monitoring purposes.[412] It should not also be used to drive micro-interventions as if it were a formative or diagnostic assessment with individual students, teachers, and schools.

2. *Prevent the use of large-scale assessment data for explicit or implicit ranking* of schools or systems by inhibiting or prohibiting publication of school scores.

3. *Create a professional culture of large-scale assessment* in which school and system leaders take collective responsibility for putting an end to unethical testing practices like narrowing the curriculum, teaching to the test, using test scores to entice students from competing schools, and concentrating undue attention on "bubble kids," who score just below the measured point of

proficiency, to artificially elevate their schools' scores. This culture can be enshrined in an ethical leadership assessment charter and in professional standards frameworks for educational leaders.

4. *Detach testing from imposed, time-bound targets* for numerical school and system improvement.

5. *Abandon spinning cycles* of short-term, intensive, data-driven improvement based on large-scale assessment instruments or proxies for them.

6. *Use large-scale assessments to inform teachers' collective professional judgments* as a basis for improvement at the school level, while still monitoring overall performance at the system level, as is done in Scotland.[413]

7. *Do no harm.* Suspend all large-scale standardized testing before grade 6 to avoid substantial negative effects on young children's learning, engagement, and well-being.

8. *Establish an independent watchdog* to undertake triennial reviews of the positive and negative consequences of large-scale government tests on cultural bias, innovation, student engagement and well-being, and distraction from core purposes. Make the findings of the reviews public and publish action plans to respond to problems the reviews identify.

9. *Where possible, use samples to measure and monitor system performance*, as in Finland,[414] or the U.S. National Assessment of Educational Progress, rather than whole-cohort assessments that are more prone to perverse incentives.

10. *Explore the power of technology to transform student assessment*, not by moving high-stakes testing online, but by developing, expanding, and sharing continuous assessments and self-assessments. Transformational assessment processes of this kind will increase all parents'

knowledge of their children's learning and understanding, and of teachers' responses to that learning. This may obviate the current last-resort dependency on high-stakes testing scores in the absence of other information.

We're often afraid to let go of something we've known and used for a long time, even when it's not perfect. We fear that the alternative will be worse or that we won't know what to do with it. Change entails loss.[415] We fear letting go of control. That's why people stay in bad relationships, hang on to falling investments, resist new technologies, and keep on with familiar ways of teaching even when they no longer seem to work. For years, administrators have been trying to get teachers to let go of familiar habits and change their practices. It's now time to turn the tables. Administrative and political leaders must let go of ineffective old assessment policies and embrace better ones instead.

In our own childhoods, teachers regarded the ballpoint pen as an instrument of the devil that would destroy the beauty of cursive writing. There was outrage in 1972 when a new women's magazine legitimized the title of *Ms.* over *Mrs.* or *Miss.* As recently as 1986, physical punishment was still practiced in U.K. schools because teachers and school leaders feared that chaos would ensue if this deterrent was abolished. In the third decade of the 21st century, some people break into an uproar when the topic of gender-neutral bathrooms appears on school meeting agendas.

Change entails loss. We fear letting go of control. That's why people stay in bad relationships, hang on to falling investments, resist new technologies, and keep on with familiar ways of teaching even when they no longer seem to work.

But cursive writing survived the advent of the ballpoint pen. The progression of ballpoint and then fiber tip technology preserved and even enhanced the flow of traditional, pen-and-ink writing while eliminating its blots and smudges. *Ms.* has become the accepted title for millions of women. The abolition of physical punishment forced schools to develop more humane discipline strategies and more motivating learning environments for their students.

And gender-neutral bathrooms have been an unremarkable feature of passenger airplanes ever since they started to fly.

We predict that by the year 2030 we will all look back at the battles over large-scale standardized assessments and wonder what all the fuss was about. Stodgy, traditionalist leaders will have been forced to take their analog obsessions with bureaucratic control out of governments and school systems. Rising generations of teachers and leaders will use digital technologies to effortlessly share information and ideas about students' work and give more voice to their students in the process. Following on from the pandemic, when virtual schools opened up classrooms to parents all over the world, the guarded entrances of schools and awkward parent-teacher meetings will give way to continuous flows of news and updates about what students are learning and doing in real time.

We can and should make large-scale transformations in testing and examinations in our systems. Meanwhile, there is a lot that all of us, teachers and professors alike, can already be doing in our own classes to make assessment a more engaging experience for everyone.

Assessment for Engagement

If high-stakes and mid-stakes tests are abolished or their roles reduced, people always ask, what are the other practical options? Not all testing and assessment is villainous. Assessment *can* be one of our tools of engagement too.

This is where small-scale and psychology-informed strategies come into their own. As most teachers and other educators know, standardized test scores and grades on completed assignments represent *summative assessment*, which happens after the learning is over. One widely used alternative is *formative assessment*, which provides feedback on the learning as it is in process. This practice can enhance and advance the quality of learning and is a major contributor to what is known as *assessment for learning*. There is a host of books on assessment for learning—using formative assessment strategies like peer assessment, self-assessment, and real-time feedback that actually enhance students' learning. Far fewer books address how assessment can improve student engagement. There are more and more instruments for assessing levels *of* student engagement, but there is far less information on how to assess *for* student engagement. There are important exceptions, though.

One of the gurus of assessment for learning is University College London professor Dylan Wiliam. He argues that formative assessment can increase student achievement via *pedagogies of engagement*, an idea first introduced by Stanford University professor Lee Shulman, though in a different context from Wiliam's.[416] Promoting pedagogies of engagement through formative assessments is not just an inspiring philosophy or theory; it includes quite simple and practical strategies. In his books and videos, Wiliam sets out a number of these, many of which we have used, including the following.[417]

- Call on any students at any time, and use simple devices to do so. In our workshops in large ballrooms or gymnasiums, we sometimes allocate numbers and letters to rows and columns of tables and then randomly call on people from tables G5, F2, and A7 for answers, for example.

- Use mini whiteboards or blackboards so students can display their responses to their lessons. Andy first saw these in a Hong Kong secondary school as part of its approach to developing self-regulated learning. Students exchanged and edited each other's mini blackboards as part of their collaborative learning. They have, of course, also become a vital tool of at-home learning during the pandemic, to enable children to write or draw their ideas or answers and send them by screenshot to their teachers.[418]

- Employ red, yellow, and green signals that students display to demonstrate their levels of understanding—giving the teacher a quick indicator of whether the degree of understanding is strong, whether students need more help, or whether green students can be paired with red and yellow ones for a bit of peer tutoring, perhaps. In our work in the U.S. Pacific Northwest, we used red, orange, and green paddles with groups of network leaders in meetings to determine not just understanding, but also agreement or disagreement with items like whether the network should be expanded, or how the project could be made sustainable.

- Provide tools, not just encouragement, for self-assessment. One example used by Wiliam is the use of heart monitors in physical education classes for students to check their heart rates before, during, and after class.[419]

- Eliminate fear of making mistakes by employing the language and strategy of growth mindsets. These point out that something has not been learned *yet*. Andy taught his own young grandson that for all of us, there is a moment just before we can do something, when we can't do it. He later discovered that his grandson went on to say the very same thing to one of his friends.

- Use technology to share classroom learning. Technology, and its capacity to provide feedback in real time, is bringing us to a point where we can totally transform how we understand and display student assessment. In one of our Ontario districts, teachers photographed or made short film clips with tablets or smartphones of students working with mathematics manipulatives, making words and sentences on magnetic boards, or building with blocks. These pictures and clips were shared with colleagues and parents on Google docs and became items for discussion with students themselves. These assessments were referred to throughout the year to compare present with past performance. One principal noted that they now "had stuff that they could share with parents, that they could share with the children, and that the children could share with each other."

Another educator who offers insight into how assessment can increase student engagement is Ross Morrison McGill, a nationally acclaimed expert on teaching, teacher development, and assessment in the United Kingdom. His *TeacherToolkit* Twitter account has almost a quarter of a million followers, the most of any U.K. educator's.[420] As a deputy head teacher (that is, vice principal) turned consultant, he is cherished by legions of teachers for being a thorn in the side of England's national inspection service, Ofsted, which he calls *the grim reaper*. McGill is familiar with the leading research on and major advances in student assessment, but like all good professionals, he also uses his own practical experience and knowledge as a source of positive strategies that can help engage students too.

McGill is a truly inspiring educator and yet his best-selling book, *Mark. Plan. Teach.*, begins with probably the least-inspiring aspect of teaching and learning of all: marking, or grading.[421] Grading is usually the last thing teachers think about. The actual teaching is what teachers live for—being in the moment, holding the class spellbound, dealing with the unexpected, seeing the light bulbs turn on. Grading comes last. Like death and taxes, that big pile of papers or books at the end of the week or the semester is something awful that just can't be avoided.

McGill turns this all on its head—making marking one of the *first* things to think about, and transforming it into a source of increased engagement for kids and for teachers, rather than the opposite. Here are five of his strategies for using more engaging marking as a form of assessment.

1. Provide written feedback or "live marking" during the lesson. Draw a box around one part of the work on a student's paper to comment on a single aspect of learning in a pinpointed way. This should create an opportunity for dialogue with the student and leave time, within the lesson, for the student to respond in the assignment itself.

2. Develop assessment rubrics with students by providing various ungraded exemplars of work for them to consider as they do so.

3. Present oral feedback in real time, especially if it is precise and offers just the right amount of challenge. Not all assessments have to be written down.

4. Use self-assessment for students to find and fix specific things that can be improved relatively swiftly, making remaining needed improvements seem less overwhelming.

5. Adopt self-assessment and peer-assessment routines as foundations for learning, not as add-ons to other assessments, or breaks from them. This can help ensure that the process of continuous learning through formative assessment drives the learning in the class, instead of getting hung up on right answers for summative assessments.

You can thrive in a learning environment where you have made assessment, and even marking or grading, an engaging and uplifting experience for everyone. And you can fight off the grim reaper of bureaucracy and testing in the wider system, too. You can be part of the big picture and the little picture together. That is the secret of confronting the archenemy of engagement out in the world and inside your own classroom by developing positive assessment practices as well as combatting bad ones.

Dispatching the Archenemy

Wiliam and McGill are just two of the many assessment experts who remind us of the power of formative assessments and assessment for learning, as opposed to relying too much on summative assessments or high-stakes tests as ways to measure achievement or drive improvement. But as much as work like theirs is widely admired by educators, school systems and political leaders typically treat their strategies as being supplements to, not replacements for, large-scale assessments and standardized testing. To change this situation, we must take the dual approach of making assessment more engaging—not just by supporting and promoting alternative assessments that are more formative in nature, but also by deliberately making large-scale assessments and standardized testing less disengaging, too. That is what we have tried to do in this chapter.

As we learned from our work in Ontario, if we persist with even moderate versions of existing approaches to testing entire student cohorts as ways to drive improvement, this will undermine the efforts to bring about the changes in learning and innovation that many now want. Revving each other up or jollying each other along the pathways of engagement is an admirable thing to do for our students. But if the dragon of disengagement remains firmly astride our route, we cannot avoid dealing with it. Whether the archenemy of engagement assumes the form of Ross McGill's grim reaper, Diane Ravitch's biblical Goliath,[422] or J. K. Rowling's fictional Voldemort, we will never reach our goal of learning for everyone until it is vanquished, once and for all.

Revving each other up or jollying each other along the pathways of engagement is an admirable thing to do for our students. But if the dragon of disengagement remains firmly astride our route, we cannot avoid dealing with it.

CHAPTER 6

The Five Paths of
Student Engagement:
In Theory and Practice

The quest to forge and follow different paths of student engagement in order to achieve success and fulfillment for all students is by no means easy or straightforward. We need a clear sense of where we are going and why. We're after more engagement not for its own sake, but for when and only when it helps our students thrive and succeed. Engagement is sometimes nothing more than mere entertainment, and our students deserve more than that.

We've been careful to pack the right gear and provisions to sustain us along our journey. These have taken the form of knowledge, theories, and evidence provided by experts who have passed this way before. Theories of self-actualization, intrinsic motivation, mastery, and flow, to mention just a few, can all equip us in our quest for learning and success for everyone.

When we heard the siren calls of relevance, technology, and fun, we let ourselves enjoy some of the attractions of each of them, without getting pulled into their whirlpools of excess.

And then we had to confront five formidable enemies of engagement, and slay each one of these political, bureaucratic, and commercial dragons—including the greatest archenemy of them all: large-scale standardized testing.

Now, at last, the paths to student engagement are opening up. Our way is becoming clearer. It's time to push on. In that spirit, this chapter lets us take a breather at first, to recap the psychological and sociological theories and understandings that brought us to where we are now. The chapter then describes our five paths of student engagement in action in the classrooms of the teachers with whom we collaborated in our work with rural schools in the U.S. Pacific Northwest.

A New Theoretical Framework for Student Engagement

How should teachers go about engaging their students? We can now appreciate that students must be engaged psychologically in terms of their emotions, cognition, and behavior. Engagement may involve transcendence in committing to something greater than oneself. It can and should harness the motivational power of flow. Intrinsic interest can maximize student engagement, but so can the struggle and suffering that must sometimes be required if students truly want to achieve excellence and mastery. Engagement is intense, can be serious, and is not always enjoyable in the short term. It's now clear that simplistic and singular approaches like relevance, technology, and fun are insufficient to get students fully engaged in their learning.

Engagement, we have argued, has sociological as well as psychological dimensions. For this reason, researchers should not only pick it apart in a laboratory or isolate it in the neurons of people's brains. Of course, we should improve engagement wherever we can by changing our classroom practices. However, student engagement is also shaped by what surrounds those practices—like assessment and testing policies, curriculum content, school culture, and technology. If all our efforts to improve engagement are simply tacked onto conventional teaching and learning practices, we will miss the opportunity to transform levels and patterns of engagement on a substantial scale that can reap benefits for everyone.

In chapter 2 (page 43), alongside the psychological theories that have dominated the field of student engagement, we proposed a sociological approach that was relevant not just to the interactions in individual classrooms, but also to the nature and direction of the whole curriculum and the culture of the school. In chapter 4 (page 117), this approach examined engagement in the context of teacher-student power dynamics, the nature of schools as communities and bureaucracies, the cultural relevance (or not) of curriculum content, and the impact of digital technology. Drawing on sociological theories and insights, we identified five enemies of engagement that we expressed as forms of *disengagement*, with opposites that also suggested the best ways to defeat them.

Despite some points of similarity, these two frameworks—from psychology and sociology—have rarely been brought together. When we combine and integrate psychological and sociological theories of engagement, we can start to see our way forward through engagement toward learning and success for all young people. The integration of the two perspectives both broadens and sharpens our vision. It reveals five distinct paths forward. Together, these define a new way to think about student engagement theoretically, and to make it come alive practically.

1. *Intrinsic value* is closely related to the enchantment, creativity, and magic of a puzzle or activity. It runs counter to the disenchantment that is common in standardized curricula and bureaucratic testing procedures.

2. *Importance* or attainment value has affinity with the social and personal meaning and purpose of activities. It is the opposite of the alienated or disconnected learning described in chapter 4 (page 117).

3. *Association* is about learning cooperatively with others in a group, network, or team that confers senses of attachment, belonging, and solidarity. It cultivates mutual obligations in a shared community.

4. *Empowerment* concerns developing students' confidence and capacity to acquire the skills and dispositions to

shape their own futures and participate in the broader society. Students' autonomy over their own choices and decisions is an integral part of empowerment.

5. *Mastery* involves pursuing excellence and high performance to a degree that involves intense focus, concentration, discipline, persistence, stretching, struggle, and sometimes even suffering to become supremely competent in a new area of knowledge or skill. It is the obverse of transient distraction, and part of the quest to dedicate oneself to producing work or performances of the highest quality.

These five paths of student engagement that result from the integration of psychological and sociological perspectives are represented in figure 6.1.

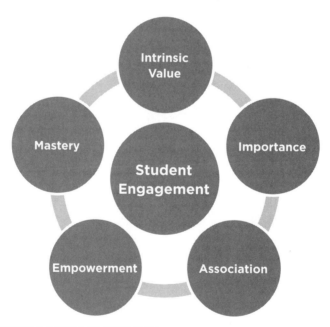

FIGURE 6.1: The five paths of student engagement.

There is no order of priority among these five paths. They are often intertwined, but not always. For instance, it's possible to find art, poetry, and music intrinsically rewarding for their own sake, and perhaps even sources of lifelong pleasure and mastery, even when they are not especially related to important political and social issues of the day. Alternatively, students might get fully engaged in a task because they think it is important for their future, even though the task itself is not all that interesting intrinsically.

Focus on just one of the five paths to engage your students, and you will have a chance of succeeding with some of them, some of the time. Address each one of the paths at some point or other, on the other hand, and it is likely that all your students will get engaged.

The five paths of engagement do not always align or converge, then. Focus on just one of the five paths to engage your students, and you will have a chance of succeeding with some of them, some of the time. Address each one of the paths at some point or other, on the other hand, and it is likely that all your students will get engaged. They will come to excel in their studies and experience enhanced well-being, too!

Five Paths of Engagement in Practice

Our framework of five paths of student engagement is derived from the literature we have reviewed in different disciplines and from our first-hand research and development work with school districts. This section describes our work with the Northwest Rural Innovation and Student Engagement (NW RISE) network that led us into the field of student engagement in the first place, where the five paths of engagement emerged out of educators' own practice.

In 2012, Danette Parsley of the Northwest Comprehensive Center in Portland, Oregon, invited us to serve as technical consultants to create a network of remote rural schools in the U.S. Pacific Northwest. We knew it would be a daunting undertaking. The schools were scattered over a vast region. Many of the region's rural communities had suffered economic devastation. We looked into the research on rural schools and communities and came across books with titles like *Hollowing Out the Middle: The Rural Brain Drain and What It Means for America* and *Survival of Rural America: Small Victories and Bitter Harvests.*[423] Rural American education had suffered from years of neglect. Although many schools and communities had fallen on hard times, we also came across pockets of rural communities and schools that were flourishing.

With educators from the participating states, we connected teachers to each other, face-to-face and online, and helped them build *professional capital* together.[424] We were insistent that the participants set their own direction. Indeed, we urged them to come up with a name for their network themselves. With more than a little irony, we warned them that if they couldn't find a name within a reasonable time period, they would have to accept our default option—*Understanding Rural Improvement Networks in Education*, or URINE for short. "If you don't find your own name and direction," we warned, "you will have to tell other people you're working in URINE!"

In the end, after we had shown them examples of other networks, they decided to focus their own network on building teams of teachers in similar jobs in the same grade or subject to plan curriculum collaboratively. The focus of the network, they decided, should be on student engagement. On June 18, 2013, when the network was just starting, we recorded the following:

> There was significant agreement that student engagement is an important goal of the network. The team discussed the links between increasing student engagement and achievement and that there are tools and instruments to measure student engagement. Team members agreed that building the professional capital of adults is connected to student engagement.

Our design team agreed to call the new network the *Northwest Rural Innovation and Student Engagement* (NW RISE) network. We wanted not just to improve academic achievement, but also to empower students and increase their sense of attachment or belonging to their own communities, and to communities like theirs, even if economic necessity might drive them to leave their hometowns in search of better opportunities after high school graduation.

To achieve these goals, we would have to come to grips with student engagement. We conducted school surveys and found that students reported levels of engagement and disengagement similar to broader trends in the United States. We then asked educators to join what we called "job-alike" groups that would bring them together by discipline, grade level, or type of job (for example, principal or counselor). These groups were linked through online communities of support on a platform called *Schoology*. The job-alike groups became the heart and soul of biannual NW RISE conferences, where educators could share their challenges, find kindred spirits who would brainstorm possible strategies for engaging their students, and enable them to return renewed and inspired to their schools.

We also studied the communities in which NW RISE schools were located to understand their demographics, their cultures, and the aspirations of their students. To do so, we worked with our colleagues at the Northwest Comprehensive Center to undertake a review of the school districts by creating summary profiles for each of them. As an example, the profile for Cusick, Washington, appears in figure 6.2 (page 190).

Cusick is similar to many of its companion NW RISE schools. Like most of the schools in the network, it serves a small population: just 239 students in this case. Almost two-thirds of the students receive free or reduced-price lunches, reflecting the far higher rates of poverty in rural America than in the cities or suburbs.[425] Cusick also has distinctive demographics. Almost one-third of its students are members of the Kalispel Native American tribe and receive instruction in their Indigenous Salish language.

Every rural school district is unique, of course. Some of the NW RISE schools were White working class in composition. In others, almost half the population was Hispanic, serving the children of migrant farm laborers and their families. If a school was close to a national park, some of the students might also come from affluent

CUSICK SCHOOL DISTRICT

Cusick School District is a rural district located approximately 53 miles north of Spokane.

Cusick School District has one school, Cusick, serving students in Kindergarden through twelfth grade (K-12). Cusick draws students from the nearby Kalispel Indian Reservation and the communities of Cusick and Usk. In addition to core academic classes, curriculum features Salish–the native language of the Kalispel tribe, American Sign Language, Robotics, Digital Photography, Small Engines, and Design & Commerical Arts.

WA

| **239** Students | **18** Teachers | **13** Student-Teacher Ratio |

| **59%** ELA Proficiency | **56%** Math Proficiency | **100%** Graduation Rate | **76%** Attendance Rate |

Occupation of the Adults Living in the District

Male

- Education, Legal, Arts, Media — 1% / 0%
- Health Practitioners — 27%
- Natural Resources, Construction, Maintenance
- Service — 14%
- Management, Business, Financial — 21%
- Science, Computer, Engineering — 8%
- Sales — 5%
- Other Occupations — 25%

Female

- Education, Legal, Arts, Media — 13%
- Health Practitioners — 4% / 0%
- Service — 40%
- Management, Business, Financial — 13%
- Science, Computer, Engineering — 0%
- Sales — 22%
- Other Occupations — 7%

Student Demographics

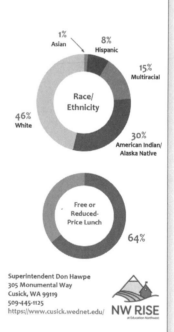

Race/Ethnicity
- 1% Asian
- 8% Hispanic
- 15% Multiracial
- 30% American Indian/ Alaska Native
- 46% White

Free or Reduced-Price Lunch — 64%

Superintendent Don Hawpe
305 Monumental Way
Cusick, WA 99119
509-445-1125
https://www.cusick.wednet.edu/

NW RISE
at Education Northwest

This document was created as part of the Northwest Rural Innovation and Student Engagement Network (NW RISE), a project of the Northwest Comprehensive Center and Education Northwest. © 2018 Education Northwest.

Source: © 2018 by Education Northwest. Used with permission.

FIGURE 6.2: NW RISE profile of Cusick, Washington.

professional families who worked in the tourism industry or as park rangers. Just like in cities and suburbs, there is plenty of diversity in rural America.

The five paths of engagement we describe in this chapter come directly from the research we carried out with educators in these districts, and then from consulting the relevant literature on engagement and motivation. The following sections illustrate how each path of engagement manifested itself among students, teachers, and leaders themselves in the NW RISE districts.

Intrinsic Value

Chris Spriggs and her husband, Rob, first drove to Glenns Ferry, Idaho, in 2001. "My husband complained immediately that he didn't even see a McDonald's, and the town obviously didn't have a lot to offer," Chris writes. She and Rob both accepted jobs at the high school, almost on a whim. They didn't anticipate they would stay for long.

To their surprise, however, they quickly adapted to their new home. They loved the natural beauty of the region, perched between majestic Bennett Mountain and the Snake River. The area has a rich history. It stands on the ancestral homelands of the Shoshone and Bannock Native American peoples. In the early 19th century, the Lewis and Clark expedition—the first recorded transit of the entire United States by White explorers—crossed the Snake River at what is now Glenns Ferry, named after the ferry that was established in 1869 to carry travelers on the Oregon Trail to California.

Although it was the history and natural beauty of the region that was a magnet for this young couple, in the end, it was the people of Glenns Ferry, and the students in their school, that kept Chris and Rob there for almost twenty years. A turning point, Chris recalls, was when Rob "was diagnosed with brain cancer in 2012":

> The town rallied behind us, holding fundraisers, making shirts that everyone in town bought, wore, and photographed themselves in, and posted on Facebook, so my family could view them while we were sitting in the

hospital. People mowed our lawn, brought us food, and ultimately, made us feel supported and loved. One of the most touching moments for us was when the varsity football team that my husband coached ran to our house (literally) during practice and brought Rob a football that they had all signed.[426]

It's not always obvious at what point something shifts from having an extrinsic value to an intrinsic one for a person. Chris and Rob went to Glenns Ferry to teach for a year or two at most. Yet as time passed, they found so much more than they ever expected. "It is a combination of the community's support, the sense of safety provided, the laid-back comfort, the connection to nature, and the desire of the town to hold on to traditional values and beliefs that have kept us here," Chris writes.

As time passed and Chris came to know everyone in Glenns Ferry so well, she also saw the hardships some of her students went through. Sixty-four percent of Glenns Ferry students were on free or reduced-price lunch. Chris tells the story of one of her former students who grew up with a mother in prison and a father who was unemployed. He could easily have become angry with "a place that disenfranchised him," as she puts it, but Chris could see that he had a fighting spirit for building a better life for himself that she wanted to support.

Chris gave her students an opportunity to do a "community study" project, which prompted students to make a time-lapse video of their lives, supplemented with writing assignments and a presentation to their classmates. For a student like the one Chris describes, who was being raised by his grandparents and given the task of "taking care of his own cousins who were basically abandoned by their own parents," the project was just the lifeline that he needed. For "this kid who had very little to call his own in life," the chance to make a film of his everyday comings and goings, while also capturing the "beautiful scenery and nature" of his native Idaho, was intrinsically rewarding. It also inspired his "peers, who loved his video" and were so pleased that he "had found the beauty in his life" and shared it with them.

Students experience *intrinsic value* in their schools when they have opportunities to engage in activities that are inherently interesting, playful, or beautiful. This is especially important for students coming from difficult family backgrounds with few visible means of support. School doesn't have to be a long, dreary march through the Common Core State Standards or any other government mandate. Nor do teachers just have to rely on their state curricular frameworks alone. Finding a way to appeal to students' *intrinsic* interests and to give them academic expression is a surefire strategy to engage many students like the ones in Glenns Ferry.

To the west, on a rain-soaked day in February, we visited the combined elementary and secondary public school in Wishram, Washington, on the banks of the Columbia River. To begin with, students were dissecting salmon for their science class. Animal dissection is a clinical laboratory routine in many biology classes. But teachers and a local park ranger made the subject highly engaging for their students with intrinsically interesting instruction. The animated and enthusiastic park ranger led the dissection activity. She taught the students the parts of the salmon and asked them to carefully observe the gills, fins, and scales, and to understand what purposes the different parts of the salmon serve. She taught them that the mucus that covers the salmon protects them against diseases and also aids in their ability to slide through the water easily. The students were totally captivated. And just in case they weren't, to add a touch of levity to the class, whenever she wanted to capture her students' attention, or if the class had simply become a bit noisy, she told them she would clap her hands three times and shout, "Fish!" at which point they were all to raise their hands in the air and shout, "Slime!"

Two hundred seventy miles east of Wishram is the small community of Genesee, Idaho, with only 955 people. More than a six-hour drive north of the state capital of Boise, Genesee's students are used to a much slower pace of life than city dwellers. Most families grow wheat and chickpeas in the vast Palouse plains that cover thousands of miles in northern Idaho, eastern Washington, and northeast Oregon.

When we asked the high school students what it was like to live in Genesee, compared to other places they knew, they didn't mention other countries or even states, but began by complaining about "how fast everyone drives in *southern* Idaho," and how unfriendly and even "snotty" they are there.

As in other parts of the NW RISE network, we witnessed a lot of student engagement at the Genesee School. In one memorable lesson, the school's charismatic music teacher had all the students playing in a marimba orchestra! She had taught them how to play their instruments with disciplined syncopation (a nod here to the importance of mastery) and joyful execution. These students were experiencing the intrinsic rewards of artistic expression, and they loved it.

To our surprise and delight, the students invited us to join them. They gave us mallets to strike away on the xylophones and offered us constant encouragement. As a certain indicator that this performance wasn't just for our benefit, in between songs they shouted out to their teacher, "We love you, miss!" and "You're our second mother!" Surely, you might think, it can't be all that hard to develop intrinsic engagement in elementary school music. The subject matter almost demands it. But what about teachers of bread-and-butter material like mathematics? How can they make learning joyful and playful, too?

We asked Genesee's music teacher where she got her inspiration and ideas from. When she had been a student, she explained, she originally wanted to become a mathematics teacher because her own mathematics teacher had been so inspiring. She only ended up teaching music by accident. It just so happened that this inspiring mathematics teacher was still teaching in the same school, just down the hallway. So that's where we headed next. What could he possibly be doing that was so engaging?

Jay Derting was teaching square roots. This must be the ultimate challenge for any teacher who believes that anything can be made engaging. But Jay had his students drawing and calculating how to work out the angles of a roof they planned to put on a shed in the schoolyard. Square roots were connected to geometry, and geometry was connected to real life. This certainly ticked the *importance* box for student engagement.

But there was more to it than this. As an old-fashioned Socratic teacher, Jay was, unknowingly, an accomplished exponent of what Dutch professor Gert Biesta calls the "beautiful risk" of teaching that engages us cognitively, emotionally, and spiritually.[427] The fashionable push to think about *facilitating* learning as the only important priority, and to disparage the personal and even charismatic dimension of teaching, Biesta argues, amounts to *learnification*.[428] This destroys the beautiful risk that is the promise of all inspiring teaching and replaces it with indirect facilitation that can become strangely soulless in nature. Biesta's work reminds us that we shouldn't write off the best kinds of traditionally engaging teaching just yet. If millions of adult viewers are motivated to tune into online TED Talks delivered by inspiring experts, don't children deserve to have their own version of this experience some of the time in their classes too?

The way Jay talked about mathematics captivated his students. He knew how to conduct rapid-fire question-and-answer dialogue in ways that gripped their attention. Jay accepted estimates rather than seeking correct responses, translated mathematical concepts into ordinary language, and made sure to call on a wide range of students rather than just one or two. He gave constant, accurate, and positively intoned feedback as he did so. The students didn't take their eyes off him for one second.

School subjects aren't just bodies of knowledge; they are also cultures and communities of teachers who have different ways of being.[429] Mathematics teachers often do not engage their students or engage with each other in the same ways that social studies, or English, or music teachers do. When teachers in the NW RISE project met with each other twice a year to engage in collaborative curriculum planning, the English teachers got straight to it. The mathematics teachers tended to choose their words more sparingly and were less likely to plunge headfirst into new relationships. In addition, the NW RISE mathematics teachers found out that they had vast differences among them with regard to their confidence in the subject. While Jay had been a finalist for Idaho's Teacher of the Year, another mathematics colleague confessed that he had never liked mathematics at all. He went into teaching because he loved coaching and wanted to be a physical education instructor. But in a rural environment short on specialists, he had been assigned to teach mathematics as part of his multidisciplinary course load.

At some point, though, one member of the mathematics job-alike group came up with the idea of designing "escape boxes" with chains and combination locks that could be opened by solving a series of mathematical puzzles. The group got incredibly excited about this, brought actual boxes to their next planning sessions, and designed activities that, they reported, were as engaging for their students as they had been for them. There was no obvious relevance to or importance for this activity. There was no digital technology, no gadgets or gizmos either—just the tactile apparatus of combinations and locks. But the activity was certainly creative, imaginative, sufficiently challenging, and completely fun—just like the full-size escape rooms that draw in groups of adult consumers around the world.

A couple of years later, the entire mathematics group stood up in front of more than a hundred colleagues at a NW RISE meeting and made a moving testimony. They described how their energizing collaboration had brought new pleasures and rewards to teaching mathematics, even for those who originally lacked confidence in the material. They showed film clips of their students engaging with measurement problems that were drawn from the popular young adult novel *Holes* by Louis Sachar. They also took delight in challenging their NW RISE colleagues to struggle with and tease out some of the students' mathematical problem-solving strategies.[430] Mathematics, we saw, could and can have just as many intrinsic delights as fish dissection in science class or playing the marimba in music.

We can't design intrinsically rewarding tasks all of the time in our schools, but we can do it a lot more than we do right now. As Jay Derting shows, it can even be done with learning about square roots in mathematics classes! Jay himself is beguiled by the beauty of mathematics, and conveys that infectious enthusiasm to students. Factor in the inherent interest in puzzle solving that not only was engaging for Harry Harlow's monkeys but also applies to all primates, including humans, and key elements of intrinsic motivation are there. When we can reach this level of engagement across all grade levels and the entire curriculum, we will get closer to the joy of playing that Sahlberg and Doyle rightly say we should bring into all our schools.

Importance

Students experience attainment value when what they are learning is so *important* to them that it begins to influence their identities, their goals, and their desire to make a difference in the world. It's the difference between *learning to play the piano* and *becoming a pianist*. When you *want* to play the piano and it has become an essential way of expressing who you are and what you value, you've reached what our Boston College colleague Stanton Wortham calls *social identification* with an art form or a discipline.[431]

What does importance look like in remote rural classrooms? Let's start with some examples from NW RISE social studies teachers.[432]

In 2016, when antigovernment militias protested the enormous expanse of federal lands in the West at Oregon's Malheur National Wildlife Refuge, NW RISE social studies teachers regarded this as a fantastic "teachable moment." They created and shared lesson plans about the U.S. Constitution, the history of the national parks, and contemporary debates between environmentalists and business groups. Rural America is far from homogenous, and it's not uncommon for small communities to consist of a blend of park rangers in favor of conservation and loggers

> *Students experience attainment value when what they are learning is so important to them that it begins to influence their identities, their goals, and their desire to make a difference in the world. It's the difference between learning to play the piano and becoming a pianist.*

and miners who resent restrictions on private enterprise and threats to local jobs. Curriculum units organized around the protests and the response of the federal government gave students ways to understand their own communities, the grievances of some groups, and the concerns of others.

The social studies teachers shared their classroom experiences on the NW RISE Schoology online platform. They then helped each other to develop their lesson plans so they would be engaging for all their students, including ones who hadn't initially been interested in the topic. These lessons didn't just consolidate the idea of a rich and shared rural American identity; they also taught students that they, too, could appreciate the importance of participating in spirited democratic debate and compromise.

Rob Coulson, a social studies teacher in the isolated forest community of Powers, Oregon, was frustrated with some of his students' failure to engage sufficiently with their academics. In this high school, which served a student population of just sixty, Rob decided to offer two electives he thought would grab his students' attention: 20th century U.S. history, as seen through the lens of sports on the one hand, and music on the other. "It's the spoonful-of-sugar approach," he said, in which students were exposed to sports and music "as the entryway" to deeper historical study and analysis.

He organized lengthy playlists with film and music clips, articles, and interpretations of critical incidents for the students. The playlists exposed students to material that took them into the heart of U.S. history. He organized the class thematically around critical incidents, such as the Great Depression, World War II, and the War in Vietnam. Spirituals, the blues, ragtime, big band, the Beatles, and David Bowie, along with hip-hop artists like Public Enemy and Coolio, were all integrated into his curriculum. He was combining importance with intrinsic interest.

Rob was especially keen to introduce students to genres and artists with which they were unfamiliar. He was eager to introduce students to new interests as well as follow any interests they already had. He wanted them to come to appreciate music that was angry, funny, and socially critical, all at the same time. For example, few of them had heard of legendary guitarist Josh White, the first African American man whose music sold over one million records. White's classic, "One Meatball," told the plaintive story of a hungry man with only fifteen cents. When the only item he could afford on the menu was a single meatball, the song's lyrics rang out, "The waiter hollered down the hall, / 'You gets no bread with one meatball!'"[433]

While many students had expected a light-hearted course, through songs like this, they found, "All of a sudden we'd be talking about pretty heavy stuff: massive poverty, racism, drug use, all of those things." They learned that White's civil rights activism led him to be blacklisted by the U.S. entertainment industry and that he had to relocate to London in the 1950s to keep his career afloat. In their analysis of songs like "One Meatball," students learned to treat a catchy song as a historical primary source, just as musicologists do every day, and to develop more critical perspectives on the United States' past than they might otherwise have had.

Not all of the music that students studied had to do with social or political themes like poverty, war, and racism. In a study of Pink Floyd's iconic *Dark Side of the Moon* album, for example, the students "listened to the album in class, uninterrupted, as the life of one individual from birth to death." The students then "wrote about the meaning of life and philosophy, by analyzing the album as one unit unto itself." Rob described this as "one of the most engaged classes I have ever seen." Students could see themselves as part of a dynamic life cycle shared by all human beings, in every culture, across the millennia. The engagement here was existential. It exemplified transcendence, the highest level of Maslow's hierarchy of needs.

Back in Wishram, the dissection of salmon was not just handled in a way that made it an intrinsically interesting task. The school served the Wishram people, a Native American tribe. Fishing for salmon at the nearby Celilo Falls was a central part of their cultural heritage. The school also catered to a White working-class community in a town that had been cut off from passing tourists by a new highway, and that had been plunged into unemployment when the local rail yards closed down. Many of the town's residents had become financially dependent on welfare benefits, and we heard complaints about some who were involved in the illegal drug trade in crystal meth. Salmon and the salmon-fishing industry were seen as a way to revive the town's tourist trade in the future, while honoring an important part of Indigenous heritage. As a curriculum topic, it had unarguable local importance.

Importance needn't become self-important, though. We can't expect all students of every age to be studying issues of earth-shattering significance all the time. With younger children, for example, importance may be connected to other aspects of life than it might be for older students. We saw this in a class of fifth graders in the small town of Ione in eastern Oregon. The students were reading aloud from a magazine article on malfunctioning dolls that exploded, faulty battery-operated toys that gave small electrical shocks to children, and contaminated stuffed animals that gave unwary youngsters skin rashes that lasted many weeks. The article provoked a lively conversation about manufacturers' responsibilities and consumer safety. Students learned how it was useful to always be alert to health hazards in regard to anything they might bring into their home.

Through small-group, then whole-class activities, students shared stories about their own misadventures with their favorite toys or with products their families had acquired that had malfunctioned. They learned that when consumers have problems with any kind of commodity that they've purchased, they need not be left on their own to grapple with the issue because their government allocates resources to make sure that people are not cheated or harmed by products. The children shared stories of false advertising scams with which they were familiar, and they seemed relieved to learn that there are options for redress when

> *Importance needn't become self-important. We can't expect all students of every age to be studying issues of earth-shattering significance all the time.*

something goes awry. These youngsters were able to engage with a topic that conveyed important information for them and their families. They were so motivated by this topic that they didn't want to leave for lunch!

The impetus to learn about important topics can come from the students or their teachers. Often, students won't even know about the existence of an issue until their teachers introduce it to them. This requires teachers to exercise their professional judgment to anticipate what might arouse students' interests and keep them engaged throughout a curricular unit. This could be something that is deep and interconnected in a social sense, or enchanting and magical in an existential one. Teachers who live in the communities where they teach (as rural teachers often do), rather than commuting in from afar, have an advantage here because they know those communities inside and out. Whether their students were studying antigovernment militias, investigating popular culture as expressed in sports or popular music, or learning about consumer rights through toys that malfunction, NW RISE teachers found ways to identify topics that their students considered important enough to stick with them, because they truly mattered.

Association

There are few greater challenges to young people's well-being and achievement than lack of belonging. Students who feel isolated and are treated like outsiders are more likely to experience mental health problems and suffer from underachievement. Perpetrators of school shootings tend to be the apocryphal loners who have often felt bullied or marginalized by peers.[434] Writing in *The Atlantic* magazine about ironic aspects of learning at home during the coronavirus pandemic, Erika Christakis reports research indicating that emergency psychiatric visits between 2009 and 2012 more than doubled during the months when school was in session, compared with during the summer and vacations, and that youth suicide rates drop during vacations.[435] Just as much as isolation, negative social interactions at school can also have highly detrimental effects.

Proactively building belonging is a key component of engagement with learning, with the local community, and with life. In schools it can happen in the hallways, out in the yard, in team sports, and in extracurricular activities. But the most important place to start fostering young people's positive relationships with each other is in the classroom, in close relations with the teachers, in how and where the curriculum can connect with issues in the local community, and in how cooperative the learning is itself.

Proactively building belonging is a key component of engagement with learning, with the local community, and with life.

Michael O'Connor, a former doctoral student who worked with us on the NW RISE network, wrote his dissertation on the English language arts job-alike group.[436] He found that students in NW RISE schools were mainly positive about their schools. One said that "the teachers all know us" and that they know "when we're not performing to our best, they push us even more to get to that spot." The low student-teacher ratio in their rural schools was seen as a real asset: "There's less kids, so it's easier for teachers to focus on students and to be able to help them specifically instead of having a lot of kids that they would have to deal with," one teacher remarked. At their best, schools felt like an extension of home. One student said:

> We're like a family here. Our class advisor, our home-room [teacher], says she feels like our mom, because she says we act like brothers and sisters around here. We argue, we love each other. I think that's really nice about here, because it's all one big family.

Even when there might be some inevitable sources of tension in a rural area, students found that "when you have different kinds of people socially, they're still accepted by the community because they're somebody's uncle or aunt." More than a few NW RISE teachers described students who had given them trouble when they were in middle school, but who turned out to be of real value years later when help was needed with some landscaping or electrical repairs, for example.

Nonetheless, students also held critical perspectives about growing up in tight-knit communities. "Everybody knows everybody's business, which is where things can go awry," one student observed. If students are in with the popular group of athletes, they're set, but if they are not, it's "hard to fit in" because there just aren't enough young people of other kinds to interact with. "If one person doesn't like you, you're pushed out," one student said. "If you don't get along with the people here, you don't get to meet new groups, because everybody here is pretty much the same general group of people."

Feeling a sense of belonging with other students around you is in many ways easier in rural schools than in urban metropolises. But intense bonding with others locally can sometimes lead to prejudice or mere discomfort in relation to strangers from afar—even to people from the other end of your state who seem "snotty"! When they anticipated interacting with others in the larger world after high school graduation, students' awareness of their insulated rural world, and feelings of insecurity that went along with it, became apparent to their teachers. Teachers were surprised by some of the apprehensions that students revealed when they shared samples of their essays with peers in other network schools. "Miss, I don't want them to think I'm stupid," one teacher's student worried. "The kids from the other school will think we're *gangsta*," another student said. "I don't want them judging me," a third told her. "It nearly made *me* panic," this teacher recalled. "Their fear was palpable in the classroom."

Teachers were taken aback by their students' obvious uneasiness about associating with students in other schools. But they were determined that students should learn that, whenever they wrote, they should always have an audience in mind. Like it or not, they would have to learn sooner rather than later how to feel comfortable associating with others outside their own group as well as within it. Students understood this and sent their writing out for review. Once they overcame their initial disappointment at receiving critical comments from peers in other NW RISE schools, this teacher "began to notice a change." Her students were spending more time making sure their drafts and posts were intelligible and edited to the best of their ability. Students were finding that they shared a sense of belonging with other students in the remote rural communities of the NW RISE network. "They learned how to develop their skills as editors, and they found that once they swallowed their pride, they could learn from others, too," the teacher said. Best of all, "they learned to have more confidence in themselves."

In *Democracy and Education*, John Dewey devotes one section to "The Implications of Human Association." Dewey valued democracy as "a mode of associated living, of conjoint communicated experience."[437] For democracy to work, he asserted, everyone needs to experience "free and equitable intercourse which springs from a variety of shared interests." This kind of intercourse or association does not come naturally to students. It has to be designed and sustained by their teachers.

Empowerment

As we learned in chapter 2 (page 43), Daniel Pink argues that autonomy is one of the essential elements of intrinsic engagement. Autonomy is not about having control over other people, but about having power over one's fate. This is what being *empowered* means: to have control over one's own actions and choices. One of the worst states of human existence is to be deprived of autonomy. Zero autonomy is a state of totalitarianism that robs us of our ability to determine our own futures.

The path to autonomy occurs through empowerment. In the curriculum, empowerment means that the teacher does not always determine what might be best or most relevant for a student. It can also start with helping students figure out what might be most relevant, useful, or important for themselves. Empowerment is about helping students become increasingly self-directed and self-determined learners, so they can prosper during remote learning in a pandemic, and everywhere else besides. It is about pursuing the spirit of Kieran Egan's proposals for learning in depth, so that, over time, on at least some learning topics, students will end up knowing more than their teachers.

This contrast between student autonomy and teachers' benevolent control became strikingly apparent in one of the NW RISE writing projects, where students were invited to inquire into and develop independent opinions about one-to-one technology in schools. Teachers thought that their students would enjoy debating back and forth with one another about the use of digital tools in schools. But the topic failed to ignite their interests. It was too commonplace, students said. While it seemed relevant to the teachers, nothing about it excited their students.

Teachers responded by asking their students what kinds of topics might pique their interest and found out that they were alert to a real transformation underway on farms and ranches in the area: the use of drones in agriculture. In many rural communities, drones are an increasingly popular way to keep track of the health of crops, and to undertake planting and harvesting. But farmers are not always fully informed about the potentially negative aspects of drones for their farms and communities. While drones can eliminate the need for backbreaking agricultural labor, they can also lead to workers being let go. And in small rural communities, the ramifications of these job losses can be substantial.

The technological aspects of drones are also complicated. Who would learn how to assemble them and put them to work? What if they didn't work perfectly from the start and required adjustments? Who would repair them when they broke down? Would proudly independent rural communities now find themselves drawn into dependency on remote technology companies for basic information about planting, care for crops, and harvesting?

None of these questions have easy answers. Even experts in robotics and business confess that they barely understand the kinds of disruptions that will be brought about by developments like drone technology. Some foresee millions of job losses. Others anticipate job creation in areas like customer service and marketing.

Given a truly difficult and challenging subject to study, students responded with gusto. Some of their writing reflected unabashed enthusiasm for drones. "Since Idaho has a large amount of people who farm," one student wrote, "drones could be a great beneficiary device for them. The drones would be able to fly over the field and take high-definition photos of the crops for the farmer to see." When teachers taught their students about some of the new capabilities of drones, such as being able to detect areas of insect infestations in crops, or areas needing additional watering, their students could see the benefits immediately. "Oh, that would be so cool!" they shouted out.

At the same time, students also expressed concerns about the unintended consequences of drone usage. They learned that drones have caused accidents due to malfunctioning equipment, and that, notwithstanding their value in providing farmers with aerial photographs of their crops, privacy advocates worry that drones in agriculture, like drones elsewhere, could also be used to snoop on neighbors. These trade-offs then found their ways into op-eds that students wrote. In addition to writing to their peers in other rural schools in the network, they also composed letters to local political leaders.

Empowerment seems like a viable path for high school students who are moving toward adulthood. What about elementary students, though? Is empowerment a realistic path of engagement for them?

Karen Martin is a rural Alaskan teacher in the Denali Borough School District. Karen's village, Healy, only has "about 1,000 people" and it wasn't until 2017 that it even had its "first full-service grocery store." While Karen is awestruck by the beauty of the Alaskan wilderness, she knows her small town isn't easy for everyone. There is a clear social-class division between those who earn their living as coal miners and those who work as park rangers in nearby Denali National Park or in the tourism industry.

Karen knows all about how to engage with her students' questions about what they are learning. On one occasion, when she was teaching her fourth graders about the history of the women's suffrage movement, she thought they would be inspired by the social justice activism of feminists a century ago. After all, Karen's own mother had to struggle to support her three children on welfare when Karen was growing up. Many of Karen's students who are from working-class coal-mining families have encountered similar hardships of their own. Healy is "a difficult and challenging place to live, especially in the cold and darker times of the year," Karen pointed out. Wouldn't students want to know about how other hard-working women had protested and fought for their rights and for their families in the past? Her own mother let her children know that education was "essential" and was the surest route out of poverty and dependency. She wanted her own working-class students to realize this too. But the history of women's rights wasn't what troubled Matthew, one of the kids in Karen's class. His ideas about what was worth studying were challenging and profound. "Students should be allowed to protest," he declared. "We should protest if we think school doesn't have a purpose." Matthew was expressing his outrage about disempowerment.

Karen was a member of the NW RISE Writers' Group of teachers who wanted to share their reflections and disseminate them to others in the profession. In her journal entry about Matthew, she remembered that she "was automatically defensive inside." Karen asked Matthew to elaborate on his thinking. "Shouldn't we understand the purpose of how we spend our time in school?" he asked. "Why can't we choose our classes or the things that we do and think are worth doing?"

Matthew's comments "hurt, because of course, I took his words personally," Karen recalled. But then she challenged herself to be more empathetic. "For the first time, I understood a little better what school looked like through his eyes," she went on. It was a turning point. "I told my students that day that they should question the purpose of their use of their time. Better yet, we should craft our purpose together and they should indeed have agency with respect to their own life's time."

Even in elementary school, teachers have to be willing to listen to their students' questions and then respond to them with open hearts and minds. No one wants to feel condemned to sit by and watch while others decide their fates, whether in their communities or in their classrooms. The struggle to find the right projects not just *for* students, but also *with* students, especially those who are economically or culturally marginalized, ultimately represents movement toward developing greater student autonomy, engagement, and empowerment.

Mastery

Mastery is about acquiring knowledge, skill, or expertise that involves challenge and difficulty. A sense of mastery brings about fulfillment once dexterity of skill, or wisdom in grasping something conceptually difficult, has been attained. Mastery cannot be bestowed as a gift; it has to be earned. In fact, the easier that something is, the less likely it becomes possible to experience mastery.

In 1984, the late Ted Sizer, founder of the Coalition of Essential Schools, formerly a network of over one hundred innovative schools in the United States, argued that a lot of high schools tacitly encouraged the very opposite of mastery. Teachers laboring under impossible workloads and time pressures learned to give students what they wanted by lowering standards, and students did the same with their teachers by complying with their minimal requests—even when they didn't know why they had been asked to do their assignments in the first place.[438] It was a vicious cycle that needed to be broken by giving students genuine challenges, then providing the supports they needed to meet them.

What was Sizer's solution to this dilemma? His Coalition of Essential Schools developed a set of "common principles" for redesigning schools. One of the most important of these was the concept of "student as worker, teacher as coach." In this model, "a prominent pedagogy will be teaching students how to learn and thus to teach themselves."[439] In this way, the Coalition would help students to achieve another one of the common principles, which was the "demonstration of mastery" through the completion of "real tasks" that possessed personal meaning for students and others as well.

While the Coalition was eventually consigned to oblivion by the relentless juggernaut of the Age of Achievement and Effort, its ideas about the student as worker and the demonstration of mastery continue to live on in the countless schools it inspired—including the rural schools of NW RISE.

Mark Martin, Karen's husband, is a science teacher who was attracted to the Denali region by the prospect of long treks through the magnificent wilderness. At one NW RISE conference, we talked about how our Boston College colleague Mike Barnett had successfully engaged urban youth in science classes with inexpensive aquaponics kits that they assembled. "Why not do something like this in my school?" Mark thought. Like their peers in schools over four thousand miles away in Boston, Mark's students would be able to learn about the difference between hydroponics, in which plants grow without soil in nutrient-enriched water, and aquaponics, in which fish are added to the mix and their excreted waste provides an additional source of organic nutrients for the plants.

Rather than just order the kits, though, Mark encouraged his students to engineer their own aquaponics system from scratch. He was delighted to see how some of his most recalcitrant students took up his challenge. They became so engaged in designing and then assembling the aquaponics system, and monitoring the right balance of water, lighting, polycrystals, and nutrients, that they began staying after school just to care for the fish and the plants and to make sure everything was in order. Students "collected data, including nutrients and growth rates," and were fascinated to see that they could successfully grow lettuce in this environment. In the end, they had a "small class celebration when it got large enough to eat."

The culminating aquaponics activity was a presentation at the school's annual "gallery walk" of student learning. "It's a great, authentic audience where the students had to know the science and understand the data they collected to a high enough level to explain it to the public," Mark explains. "I have seen this activate my students," he writes, and "it has helped to improve understanding, effort, and engagement in my classroom." For these previously reluctant students, science class changed from being an obligatory course requirement to becoming a discipline in which they exhibited great enthusiasm and demonstrated true mastery of something that was important for them and that might also have utility when they graduated.

Once again, this example illustrates how the five pathways of engagement often intersect and sometimes even merge into an expansive highway that leads toward inclusive learning and success. Mastering aquaponics got students engrossed in the *intrinsically* intriguing task of building their own kits. In an ever-threatened economy, it built and modeled local enterprise that was also connected to the environment. It had undeniable *importance*. It *empowered* students to take responsibility for something that was not just an assignment for its own sake but one that could have community impact. They couldn't do any of this on their own, like they could when they took a standardized test, filled in worksheets, or even learned online. The success of their project depended on working together with each other, building *association* not just around learning, but also through the very act of learning itself.

Finding the Way Forward

In theory and in practice, we have now seen, student engagement is a sociological as well as a psychological phenomenon. Student engagement is about so much more than just getting individual teachers to try harder or think differently in order to interest their students in learning. The sociological approach calls for us not just to *up our game* in our own classrooms, but also to *change the game* in our schools and school systems. This chapter has delved deeper into student engagement by drawing on and then expanding the traditional research base in this field to set out five bolder paths of student engagement.

Student engagement that activates the *intrinsic value* of learning connects students with issues that excite them emotionally, intrigue them cognitively, and turn their classrooms into places of magic and wonder. Engaging learning is often important, and even relevant in the conventional sense, but this doesn't mean that all learning must become serious or sanctimonious. The curriculum can be connected to students' personalities and to ways of knowing that are familiar to their cultures, as in the salmon-dissection lesson in Wishram. It

The sociological approach calls for us not just to up *our game* in our own classrooms, but also to *change the* game *in our schools and school systems.*

can also liven everyone up with laughter-filled chants that flood classrooms with feelings of joy and belonging. Students can listen to the lyrics of protest songs and also get lost in the intrinsic pulse and flow of psychedelic music or hip-hop. In a post-pandemic world, this energizing potential of music and the arts must not become the first casualty of austerity that tends to protect the standardized staples of the Age of Achievement and Effort. Areas of learning that are inspiring, intrinsically engaging, personally empowering, and socially important must not be economically expendable. They are actually indispensable if we want to engage *all* our students.

Student engagement that is *important* can't only be justified in relation to distant payoffs in work and higher education. It must also be connected to acquiring real-world skills, expressing students' identities, and addressing compelling problems and issues in the environment and society. These can include topics as disparate as contemporary political problems, the history of sports, and the interpretation of musical lyrics. Learning like this connects students to who they are, where they live, and what matters in the world. To sustain this move, we must also ensure that bureaucratic obsessions with pre-specified standards and high-stakes tests don't disengage students by squeezing out these opportunities for learning that has meaning and purpose for them.

Engagement is also about *association* with or belonging to a group or community that means something has value and strengthens one's own sense of identity and worth. It is the teacher's job to build student engagement by developing strong senses of association and belonging not just among a few students—the star athletes or future valedictorians, for example—but inclusively among all students of many different backgrounds, classes, cultures, and dispositions. This means creating culturally responsive teaching, promoting cooperative learning, refusing to tolerate face-to-face or online bullying, and holding the bureaucratic forces of unresponsive standardization and testing at bay.

Engaging all our students means understanding that a good education entails *empowerment.* All teachers who oppose being micromanaged, distrusted, constantly told what to do, and persistently threatened with sanctions if they digress from bureaucratic expectations must understand that this is how their students feel about these issues, too. Teachers must want for their students what they already want for themselves. The needs for power and autonomy are universal. It is not enough to enhance student engagement by making psychological adjustments within unchanged power relationships—more encouragement, focus, growth mindsets, colored cards, hand signals, or emojis, for example. The goal must also be to figure out how to enable and empower students to have more voice and choice in determining their own futures.

Students also want to develop a sense of *mastery* so that they can experience the thrill of genuine accomplishment. In sociological rather than psychological terms, this means that teachers will not only have to be entertaining and interesting to keep their students amused, but they will also have to present them with daunting challenges from time to time, and know how to give their students enough support to meet the challenge while feeling their accomplishments have been independently earned. Beyond the school itself, as populist leaders, social media platforms, and reality TV formats drag citizens into a pernicious herd mentality of in-group virtue and out-group vice, empowerment also means giving students the critical thinking skills they need to be active, democratic citizens. Teachers should help students to distinguish what is fact from what is fake, as well as how to examine issues from different standpoints. They should want their students to be able to debate different viewpoints with rational arguments and authoritative evidence, and also to empathize with the positions of their opponents. Mastery should not just be the accomplishment of a single goal. It should become a habit—a lifelong thirst for knowledge and competence that builds from one level of attainment to the next.

These five paths of student engagement and their sociological as well as psychological underpinnings draw us deeper and further into thinking about how student engagement must go beyond individual teachers changing a strategy or two here or there. It must also reconfigure the relationships between teachers and students, and society and its schools. Only then will we truly be blazing new trails to learning and success.

> *The five paths of student engagement must reconfigure the relationships between teachers and students, and society and its schools. Only then will we truly be blazing new trails to learning and success.*

The Promise of Engagement and the Battle for Change

Engagement is the new frontier of student achievement. It is the route from the Age of Achievement and Effort to the Age of Engagement, Well-Being, and Identity. Given the calamity of the global pandemic, ongoing struggles over social and racial justice, the continuing threat of climate change, and the worldwide threats to democracy, it has become increasingly untenable to restrict our focus to driving up achievement scores by concentrating on impersonal data and metrics. Nor will endless appeals to grit or exhortations to transform learning through technology cut the mustard, either. Learning in and beyond the third decade of the 21st century needs not just to encourage high levels of academic achievement; it also needs to win young people's hearts and minds, and acknowledge their own aspirations, too.

To advance the transition from one age to the next, we have integrated two perspectives on student engagement. The widely used *psychological* perspective helps identify problems and specify solutions that can be addressed by individuals and school teams to bring about positive change. It promotes strategies that include improving motivation, attention, focus, and interest in conventional classrooms. Our complementary *sociological* perspective moves beyond the established trinity of behavioral, cognitive, and emotional issues. Sociological

> *Engagement is the new frontier of student achievement.*

perspectives raise additional questions of what needs to change in the culture, curriculum, testing regimes, and power dynamics of existing school systems. As U.S. President Joe Biden is fond of saying, we can walk and chew gum at the same time.[440] We can have both things together.

Moreover, as we set about upping the intensity of engagement in our classes with all students, it's important to stay vigilant about the three myths—strategies that seem enticing but can sometimes fall short, or even fall foul of true or complete engagement.

For example, while engagement can and should often be *relevant* and culturally responsive to children's everyday lives, especially when there is injustice at stake, teachers can, do, and must also engage children with new interests and take them on leaps of imagination away from their everyday experience too—into fantasy literature, creative arts, or the mysteries of the universe in mathematics and science, for instance.

Similarly, while digital *technology* opens up important new avenues for learning and engagement, it is not a silicon bullet that can eliminate every problem of disengagement by itself. Digital technologies can provide instantaneous access to worlds that are unavailable in a traditional classroom. They can engage young people in learning by making it feel like a game sometimes. They have also been a virtual lifesaver for vast numbers of students during the coronavirus epidemic. But technology can also be distracting, fuel digital addictions, and displace other valued activities like learning outdoors.

Last, while it's terrific when learning can feel genuinely like *fun*, when the time passes swiftly, and when students just don't want any of it to end, engaging learning can and sometimes must also be difficult and challenging. It can even be frustrating, sometimes, before an ultimate breakthrough is achieved. This might be the mountain peak above the clouds at the end of a rain-swept hike, the new idea that no one had ever quite thought of before, or the virtuoso performance that had to undergo endless rehearsals before it finally felt just right.

The multidimensional and integrative approach we have set out in this book has identified not one, but five paths to greater engagement along with five enemies of engagement that must be confronted and defeated along the way.

First, our approach seeks an end to *disenchanting* top-down bureaucracies of standardization and testing that steal the magic of *intrinsic value* from learning. It argues in favor of schools and school systems that value teachers' collective judgment based on their professional knowledge and on the students they know best. It proposes that, as certified professionals, teachers are allowed and empowered to be the first responders to their students' needs when there is a crisis. And it challenges school systems to quit their dysfunctional dependency on antiquated high-stakes examination and testing systems that destroy teachers' and students' motivation, and replace them with more humanistic and digitally sophisticated forms of feedback instead.

Second, our approach asks for the curriculum and for teachers' pedagogies to be less alienating and *disconnected* from students' everyday experience, more responsive to young people's cultures and identities, and more connected to topics that cultivate a sense of *importance* in students' lives. It strives for schools where students are able to see the point of what they are studying beyond getting a good grade, passing a test, or pleasing their teachers. This raises the stakes for students and teachers alike. Instead of sitting back and waiting to be entertained, or refusing to comply with teachers' demands, students should, from their very first years in school, be able to explain what they are learning and why they are learning it. They should be given and also take responsibility to become self-determined learners. The stakes for teachers are also raised when it becomes *their* responsibility to establish a sense of meaning and purpose for everything on the curriculum, from Isaac Newton's laws of motion to the value of mathematical square roots.

Third, our integrated perspective advocates for students to have stronger senses of *association* with their schools, with each other in their learning communities, and with a sense of moral order, purpose, and direction in society. This requires more than joyful songs and developing a stronger sense of school spirit. It also means changing how and what teachers teach. School life has to be designed so that it brings young people together rather than sets them apart. Streaming and tracking students by attainment separates students of different social classes and ethnocultural groups from each other in school and then in life. So, as challenging as it can sometimes be for teachers, we must work harder to change pedagogies and school organization so that mixed-ability classes can be both inclusive and effective. We must commit to programs that prevent bullying in schools and head off hate in society. And we must put principles like peace and dignity not just on the periphery in social studies programs, but at the very heart of everything our schools do.

School life has to be designed so that it brings young people together rather than sets them apart.

Fourth, our perspective promotes the *empowerment* of student voice, so students can have more influence over their own learning and become knowledgeable, well-informed, and actively engaged citizens within their societies.[441] This means putting an end to *disempowering* structures, cruel and unusual behavior programs, and the entire philosophies of some schools and systems that demand militaristic-style compliance from students at all times. It also means involving students in all aspects of their learning. This includes developing their own realistic assessments about their work rather than waiting to accept or reject the assessments that adults make of them. It means actively participating in setting the rules for group work, for their classroom, and for their entire school—then taking responsibility for ensuring they and their peers stick to those rules. It also entails developing more self-advocacy among all students, not just those who have identified disabilities. And it means policymakers designing clear strategies for soliciting student input and feedback on government policies and their implementation.

Last, our distinctive approach issues warnings about *distractions*, such as excessive screen time and evanescent entertainment, that draw young people away from the focus and persistence that are necessary if they are to achieve true *mastery* in their learning and well-being. This kind of mastery is vital for building the platforms that underpin fulfilling careers as well as engrossing and enriching life interests once young people's school days are over. Alongside (not just instead of) learning that feels like fun or seems completely relevant, therefore, schools need teachers who can set and help students meet high expectations that at first might seem beyond them. Teachers must nurture and nudge students to stay focused on their goals, make sacrifices, persist through adversity, face their fears, and avoid giving up when the going gets tough. It means embracing the Buddhist mentality that suffering is an important part of learning and life sometimes. Isn't it more important to master a hard mathematics concept than to give up and play a video game sometimes? These are the examples we must set out for our children, and the dispositions we must help them develop, not as the opposite of engagement, but as part of its very essence.

Transforming student engagement certainly does mean promoting positive changes in individual schools and classrooms wherever possible through strategies like interdisciplinary projects or innovative uses of technology, for example. But if many students, not just a few, are going to benefit from increased engagement, then a transformational agenda for all students' engagement should also mean the following.

- Undertaking profound changes in curriculum and assessment, and transferring more power over learning from the teacher to the student

- Subjecting the opportunities and threats of digital technology to the thoughtful scrutiny and professional judgment of educators who know their students, communities, and curricula better than computer algorithms ever could

- Building schools as communities that develop senses of belonging among the diverse students and families that make up our world today

- Ultimately, transforming the very nature of public education itself so that learning, well-being, and quality of life for all students become the drivers of educational improvement—not data, testing, technology, and accountability[442]

These changes represent the promise of engagement that we have set out in this book, a promise that can be fulfilled by taking different paths that ultimately yield fulfillment and success for all students. Improving the achievement of hard-pressed and easily distracted students depends far less on buildings, spreadsheets, algorithms, market branding, and performance numbers than on the quality of the interactions between teachers and students that support and stimulate engagement with learning.

We have emphasized how the idea of engagement has two main origins. One meaning is about a promise—a pledge of lifelong love and commitment. The other is about a battle—a confrontation with dangerous enemies. Although these two meanings of engagement seem contradictory, when it comes down to engagement with learning, they are not.

Student engagement is a promise *and* a battle. It is a battle for involved and empowered learning in the face of unnecessary restrictions and endless distractions. Student engagement is also a promise. Engagement to be married is a promise to live together, for better or worse, as long as you both are able. Engagement in education is a promise as well—to expect and enable students to undertake something hard, to the best of their ability, in ways that are psychologically and socially meaningful, and to experience fulfillment along the way.

It's easy to make promises. It's essential to keep them. If we are to follow the paths of student engagement to learning and well-being, we must draw on all the tools and resources we have at our disposal and apply them with relentless commitment and determination. We must not treat engagement as an optional extra, as something that's nice if you can get it. It shouldn't just be a treat offered to some children, some of the time, on a field trip, or a Friday afternoon, or once tests have been taken, when there's time to do something more interesting instead. Engagement, rather, is a battle for the hearts and minds of all our students, especially the most vulnerable and marginalized, every minute of the day. And it's a battle against the enemies that constantly impede our efforts—against the excesses of standardized testing, against ever-present digital distractions, against narcissistic senses of entitlement among some privileged families and their children, and against snake-oil salespersons who claim there is just one program, one answer, their answer, that will get all students engaged forever.

Engagement is a battle for the hearts and minds of all our students, especially the most vulnerable and marginalized, every minute of the day.

It's every teacher's responsibility to fight their *inner battles* that can fulfill the promise of engagement for all their students. It's also their professional duty to fight the *outer battles* beyond their own classrooms and schools that constantly frustrate their efforts. This is the engagement agenda for all educators everywhere.

Our world needs a profound transformation, environmentally, socially, and politically. It needs to be put back on its axis. Everyone's engagement is called for if we are to be able to promise a better tomorrow and if we are prepared to battle hard to fulfill that promise. The best and most important place to begin is with how we engage our students today.

References

1   Hargreaves, A., Shirley, D., Wangia, S., Bacon, C., & D'Angelo, M. (2018). *Leading from the middle: Spreading learning, well-being, and identity across Ontario*. Toronto, Canada: Council of Ontario Directors of Education. Accessed at http://ccsli.ca/downloads/2018-Leading_From_the _Middle_Final-EN.pdf on February 12, 2021.

2   Hargreaves, A. (2021). The day after: Education and equity after the global pandemic. In M. Soskil (Ed.), *Flip the system U.S.: How teachers can transform education and save democracy* (pp. 64–73). New York: Routledge; Hargreaves, A. (2020). Austerity and inequality; or prosperity for all? Educational policy directions beyond the pandemic. *Educational Research for Policy and Practice*; Hargreaves, A. (2020, March 10). #WorldTeachersDay: Lessons from the pandemic: "A world without teachers." Accessed at www.ei-ie.org/en/woe_homepage/woe_detail/16957 /worldteachersday-lessons-from-the-pandemic-"a-world-without-teachers" -by-andy-hargreaves on December 3, 2020; Hargreaves, A., & Fullan, M. (2020). Professional capital after the pandemic: Revisiting and revising classic understandings of teachers' work. *Journal of Professional Capital and Community*, 5(3/4), 327–336. Accessed at https://doi.org/10.1108 /JPCC-06-2020-0039 on December 3, 2020; Hargreaves, A. (2020). Large-scale assessments and their effects: The case of mid-stakes tests in Ontario. *Journal of Educational Change*, 21, 393–420. Accessed at https:// doi.org/10.1007/s10833-020-09380-5 on December 3, 2020; Hargreaves, A. (2020, April 16). What's next for schools after coronavirus? Here are 5 big issues and opportunities. *The Conversation*. Accessed at https:// theconversation.com/whats-next-for-schools-after-coronavirus-here -are-5-big-issues-and-opportunities-135004 on December 3, 2020; Hargreaves, A. (2020, August 6). The education technology students will need—and won't—after coronavirus. *Washington Post*. Accessed at www .washingtonpost.com/education/2020/08/06/education-technology-students -will-need-wont-after-covid-19/ on December 3, 2020; Hargreaves, A. (2020, April 7). A complete list of what to do—and not do—for everyone teaching kids at home during the coronavirus crisis. *Washington Post*. Accessed at www.washingtonpost.com/education/2020/04/07/complete-list- what-do-not-do-everyone-teaching-kids-home-during-coronavirus-crisis on December 3, 2020; Hargreaves, A., & Shirley, D. L. (2020). Leading from the middle: Its nature, origins and importance. *Journal of Professional Capital and Community*, 5(1), 92–114; Hargreaves, A., Washington, S., & O'Connor, M. T. (2019). Flipping their lids: Teachers' wellbeing in crisis. In D. M. Netolicky, J. Andrews, & C. Paterson (Eds.), *Flip the system Australia: What matters in education* (pp. 93–104). New York: Routledge; Shirley, D. (2021). An American education system with integrity. In M. Soskil (Ed.), *Flip the system U.S.: How teachers can transform education and save democracy* (pp. 9–21). New York: Routledge; Johnston, C., Kim, M. J., Martin, K., Martin, M., Shirley, D., & Spriggs, C. (2018). Rural teachers forging new bonds—and new solutions. *Educational Leadership*, 76(3),

56–62; Hargreaves, A. (2021). Digital technology after COVID-19 and the CHENINE Charter for Change. In R. Turok-Squire (Ed.), *Rainbows in our windows: Childhood in the time of corona* (pp. 3–19). Coventry, England: University of Warwick Department of English and Comparative Literary Studies. This essay originally appeared in *Issues in English*, volume 15, a publication of the English Association (www.englishassociation.ac.uk).

3   Organisation for Economic Co-operation and Development. (2018). *Country Notes: Canada*. Paris: Author. Accessed at www.oecd.org/pisa /publications/PISA2018_CN_CAN.pdf on March 24, 2021.

4   For examples, see Barber, M. (2007). *Instruction to deliver: Fighting to transform Britain's public services*. London: Methuen; Gamoran, A. (Ed.). (2007). *Standards-based reform and the poverty gap: Lessons for No Child Left Behind*. Washington, DC: Brookings Institution; Tucker, M. S. (Ed.). (2011). *Surpassing Shanghai: An agenda for American education built on the world's leading systems*. Cambridge, MA: Harvard Education Press.

5   Hodges, T. (2018, October 25). School engagement is more than just talk. *Gallup Education*. Accessed at www.gallup.com/education/244022/school -engagement-talk.aspx on December 3, 2020.

6   Association for Supervision and Curriculum Development. (2016). *The engagement gap: Making each school and every classroom an all-engaging learning environment*. Alexandria, VA: Author.

7   Hodges, T. (2018, October 25). School engagement is more than just talk. *Gallup Education*. Accessed at www.gallup.com/education/244022/school -engagement-talk.aspx on December 3, 2020.

8   Organisation for Economic Co-operation and Development. (2000). *Student engagement at school: A sense of belonging and participation*. Paris: Author, p. 4.

9   Organisation for Economic Co-operation and Development. (2000). *Student engagement at school: A sense of belonging and participation*. Paris: Author, p. 4.

10   Sato, M. (2011). Imagining neo-liberalism and the hidden realities of the politics of reform: Teachers and students in a globalized Japan. In D. B. Willis & J. Rappleye (Eds.), *Reimagining Japanese education: Borders, transfers, circulations, and the comparative* (pp. 225–246). Oxford, England: Symposium Books, p. 226.

11   Sato, M. (2011). Imagining neo-liberalism and the hidden realities of the politics of reform: Teachers and students in a globalized Japan. In D. B. Willis & J. Rappleye (Eds.), *Reimagining Japanese education: Borders, transfers, circulations, and the comparative* (pp. 225–246). Oxford, England: Symposium Books, pp. 226–228.

12   Organisation for Economic Co-operation and Development. (2000). *Student engagement at school: A sense of belonging and participation*. Paris: Author, p. 9.

13   Organisation for Economic Co-operation and Development. (2020). *PISA 2018 results (Volume III): What school life means for students' lives*. Paris: Author, p. 130.

14   Organisation for Economic Co-operation and Development. (2020). *PISA 2018 results (Volume III): What school life means for students' lives*. Paris: Author, p. 132.

15   Organisation for Economic Co-operation and Development. (2020). *PISA 2018 results (Volume III): What school life means for students' lives.* Paris: Author, p. 132.

16   Organisation for Economic Co-operation and Development. (2020). *PISA 2018 results (Volume III): What school life means for students' lives.* Paris: Author, p. 98.

17   Schleicher, A. (2019). *PISA 2018: Insights and interpretations.* Paris: Organisation for Economic Co-operation and Development, p. 48.

18   Booth, R. (2019, February 4). Anxiety on rise among the young in social media age. *The Guardian.* Accessed at www.theguardian.com/society/2019/feb/05/youth-unhappiness-uk-doubles-in-past-10-years on December 3, 2020.

19   Damon, W. (2008). *The path to purpose: How young people find their calling in life.* New York: Free Press, p. 8.

20   Damon, W. (2008). *The path to purpose: How young people find their calling in life.* New York: Free Press, p. 8.

21   Damon, W. (2008). *The path to purpose: How young people find their calling in life.* New York: Free Press, p. 8; Shirley, D. (2020). Beyond well-being: The quest for wholeness and purpose in education. *ECNU Review of Education, 3*(3), 542–555.

22   In our earlier book, *The Fourth Way*, we described this period as the *second way* of educational change—a way of markets, testing, and standardization that had followed a 1960s and 1970s *first way* of innovation and inconsistency. See Hargreaves, A., & Shirley, D. (2009). *The fourth way: The inspiring future for educational change.* Thousand Oaks, CA: Corwin.

23   National Commission on Excellence in Education. (1983). *A nation at risk: The imperative for educational reform.* Washington, DC: Government Printing Office.

24   Baker, M., & Foote, M. (2006). Changing spaces: Urban school interrelationships and the impact of standards-based reform. *Educational Administration Quarterly, 42*(1), 90–123; Hargreaves, A. (2003). *Teaching in the knowledge society: Education in the age of insecurity.* New York: Teachers College Press.

25   Hargreaves, A. (2020). Large-scale assessments and their effects: The case of mid-stakes tests in Ontario. *Journal of Educational Change, 21,* 393–420. Accessed at https://doi.org/10.1007/s10833-020-09380-5 on February 12, 2021, p. 401.

26   No Child Left Behind (NCLB) Act of 2001, Pub. L. No. 107-110, § 101, Stat. 1425 (2002). Accessed at www2.ed.gov/policy/elsec/leg/esea02/index.html on December 3, 2020.

27   Shirley, D. (2006). The Massachusetts Coalition for Teacher Quality and Student Achievement: An introduction. *Equity and Excellence in Education, 39*(1), 4–14.

28   GovTrack. (n.d.). *H.R. 1532 (112th): Race to the Top Act of 2011.* Accessed at www.govtrack.us/congress/bills/112/hr1532 on December 3, 2020.

29   Barber, M. (2009). From system effectiveness to system improvement: Reform paradigms and relationships. In A. Hargreaves & M. Fullan (Eds.), *Change wars* (pp. 71–94). Bloomington, IN: Solution Tree Press.

30   Hargreaves, A. (2014, September 26). Why we can't reform literacy and math all at once. *Washington Post.* Accessed at www.washingtonpost.com /news/answer-sheet/wp/2014/09/26/why-we-cant-reform-literacy-and-math -all-at-once on February 15, 2021.

31   Bird, S. M., Cox, D., Farewell, V. T., Goldstein, H., Holt, T., & Smith, P. C. (2005). Performance indicators: Good, bad, and ugly. *Journal of the Royal Statistical Society: Series A, 168*(1), 1–27.

32   Tymms, P., & Merrell, C. (2007). *Standards and quality in English primary schools over time: The national evidence.* Cambridge, England: University of Cambridge, p. 14.

33   Tymms, P., & Merrell, C. (2007). *Standards and quality in English primary schools over time: The national evidence.* Cambridge, England: University of Cambridge, p. 19.

34   Tymms, P., & Merrell, C. (2007). *Standards and quality in English primary schools over time: The national evidence.* Cambridge, England: University of Cambridge, p. 26.

35   See Shirley, D. (2017). *The new imperatives of educational change: Achievement with integrity.* New York: Routledge.

36   See, for example, Tucker, M. (2019). *Leading high-performance school systems: Lessons from the world's best.* Alexandria, VA: Association for Supervision and Curriculum Development.

37   Organisation for Economic Co-operation and Development. (2015). *OECD country note: Results from PISA 2015—Massachusetts.* Paris: Author.

38   Baroutsis, A., & Lingard, B. (2017). Counting and comparing school performance: An analysis of media coverage of PISA in Australia, 2000– 2014. *Journal of Education Policy, 32*(4), 432–449.

39   Organisation for Economic Co-operation and Development. (2014). *Improving schools in Wales: An OECD perspective.* Paris: Author.

40   Bray, M. (2006). Private supplementary tutoring: Comparative perspectives on patterns and implications. *Compare: A Journal of Comparative and International Education, 36*(4), 515–530.

41   Organisation for Economic Co-operation and Development. (2017). *PISA 2015 results (Volume III): Students' well-being.* Paris: Author. Accessed at http://dx.doi.org/10.1787/9789264273856-en on December 3, 2020.

42   Carr, J. (2020, March 6). Government behaviour tsar calls out "contradictory" Ofsted report. *Schools Week.* Accessed at https://schoolsweek .co.uk/government-behaviour-tsar-calls-out-contradictory-ofsted-report/ on December 3, 2020; Golann, J. W., & Torres, A. C. (2020). Do no-excuses disciplinary practices promote success? *Journal of Urban Affairs, 42*(4), 617–633.

43   Elk, M. (2018, April 2). Wave of teachers' wildcat strikes spreads to Oklahoma and Kentucky. *The Guardian.* Accessed at www.theguardian .com/us-news/2018/apr/02/teachers-wildcat-strikes-oklahoma-kentucky -west-virginia on March 24, 2021.

44   Ravitch, D. (2020). *Slaying Goliath: The passionate resistance to privatization and the fight to save America's public schools.* New York: Knopf.

45 Coughlan, S. (2016, May 3). Parents keep children off school in test protest. *BBC News.* Accessed at www.bbc.com/news/education-36188634 on December 3, 2020.

46 Landau, C. (2020, August 6). We already had a mental health epidemic among young people: Then came the coronavirus. *Psychology Today.* Accessed at www.psychologytoday.com/ca/blog/mood-prep-101/202008 /we-already-had-mental-health-epidemic-among-young-people on December 3, 2020.

47 Twenge, J. M. (2017). *iGen: Why today's super-connected kids are growing up less rebellious, more tolerant, less happy—and completely unprepared for adulthood.* New York: Atria.

48 Human Rights Watch. (2017). *World report 2017: Events of 2016.* Accessed at www.hrw.org/sites/default/files/world_report_download/wr2017-web .pdf on December 3, 2020; Hooper, K., Zong, J., Capps, R., & Fix, M. (Eds.). (2016). *Young children of refugees in the United States: Integration successes and challenges.* Washington, DC: Migration Policy Institute.

49 Beckman, P. J., & Gallo, J. (2015). Rural education in a global context. *Global Education Review, 2*(4), 1–4. Accessed at http://ger.mercy.edu/index .php/ger/article/view/238/151 on February 18, 2018; Strange, M., Johnson, J., Showalter, D., & Klein, R. (2012). *Why rural matters 2011–12: The condition of rural education in the 50 states.* Arlington, VA: Rural School and Community Trust. Accessed at www.ruraledu.org/articles.php?id=2820 on December 3, 2020.

50 Siegel, B., & Waxman, A. (2001). *Third-tier cities: Adjusting to the new economy.* Somerville, MA: Mt. Auburn Associates.

51 Yeats, W. B. (1933). *The collected poems of W. B. Yeats.* New York: Macmillan.

52 Fullan, M., & Rincón-Gallardo, S. (2016). Developing high quality public education in Canada: The case of Ontario. In F. Adamson, B. Astrand, & L. Darling-Hammond (Eds.), *Global education reform: How privatization and public investment influence education outcomes* (pp. 69–93). New York: Routledge.

53 Norwegian Directorate of Education and Training. (2020). *See new curricula: The knowledge promotion 2020.* Accessed at www.udir.no/laring -og-trivsel/lareplanverket/fagfornyelsen/nye-lareplaner/ on December 3, 2020.

54 Organisation for Economic Co-operation and Development. (2015). *Improving schools in Scotland: An OECD perspective.* Paris: Author.

55 Donaldson, G. (2015). *Successful futures: Independent review of curriculum and assessment arrangements in Wales.* Cardiff, Wales: Welsh Government. Accessed at https://gov.wales/sites/default/files/publications/2018-03 /successful-futures.pdf on December 3, 2020.

56 GovTrack. (n.d.). *S. 1177 (114th): Every Student Succeeds Act.* Accessed at www.govtrack.us/congress/bills/114/s1177 on December 3, 2020.

57 Min, K.-S., Jung, H., & Kim, C. M. (2017). Examining a causal effect of Gyeonggi innovation schools in Korea. *Korean Educational Development Journal, 14*(2), 3–20.

58 Ng, P. T. (2020). The paradoxes of student well-being in Singapore. *ECNU Review of Education, 3*(3), 437–451. Accessed at https://doi.org/10.1177 /2096531120935127 on December 3, 2020.

59   Singapore Ministry of Education. (2016). *Developing rugged and resilient youths through outdoor education.* Accessed at www.moe.gov.sg/news/press-releases/developing-rugged-and-resilient-youths-through-outdoor-education on December 3, 2020.

60   Association for Supervision and Curriculum Development. (2019). *The learning compact renewed: Whole child for the whole world.* Alexandria, VA: Author. Accessed at http://files.ascd.org/pdfs/programs/WholeChild Network/2020-whole-child-network-learning-compact-renewed.pdf on December 3, 2020.

61   Organisation for Economic Co-operation and Development. (2019). *OECD future of education and skills 2030: OECD learning compass 2030.* Paris: Author. Accessed at www.oecd.org/education/2030-project/contact /OECD_Learning_Compass_2030_Concept_Note_Series.pdf on December 3, 2020.

62   Hargreaves, A. (2020). Large-scale assessments and their effects: The case of mid-stakes tests in Ontario. *Journal of Educational Change, 21,* 393–420. Accessed at https://doi.org/10.1007/s10833-020-09380-5 on December 3, 2020.

63   Ontario Ministry of Education. (2014). *Achieving excellence: A renewed vision for education in Ontario.* Toronto, Canada: Queen's Printer for Ontario. Accessed at www.msdsb.net/images/ADMIN/correspondence/2014/MEDU %20Renewed%20Vision%20for%20Education.pdf on December 3, 2020.

64   Hargreaves, A. (2020). Large-scale assessments and their effects: The case of mid-stakes tests in Ontario. *Journal of Educational Change, 21,* 393–420. Accessed at https://doi.org/10.1007/s10833-020-09380-5 on February 12, 2021.

65   See Hargreaves, A., & Shirley, D. (in press). *Well-being and socio-emotional learning: How to build everyone back better.* Alexandria, VA: Association for Supervision and Curriculum Development.

66   Gray, P. (2013). *Free to learn.* New York: Basic Books.

67   UNESCO. (n.d.). *COVID-19 impact on education.* Accessed at https:// en.unesco.org/covid19/educationresponse on December 3, 2020.

68   See, for example, Brill, S. (2011). *Class warfare: Inside the fight to fix America's schools.* New York: Simon & Schuster; Page, R. (2006). *The war against hope.* Nashville, TN: Thomas Nelson.

69   Trilling, D., & Fadel, C. (2009). *21st century skills: Learning for life in our times.* San Francisco: Jossey-Bass.

70   Moe, T. M., & Chubb, J. E. (2009). *Liberating learning: Technology, politics, and the future of American education.* San Francisco: Jossey-Bass.

71   Abrams, S. E. (2016). *Education and the commercial mindset.* Cambridge, MA: Harvard University Press; Verger, A., Fontdevila, C., & Zancajo, A. (2016). *The privatization of education: A political economy of global education reform.* New York: Teachers College Press.

72   Ravitch, D. (2020). *Slaying Goliath: The passionate resistance to privatization and the fight to save America's public schools.* New York: Knopf.

73   Illich, I. (1972). *Deschooling society.* New York: HarperCollins; Freire, P. (1970). *Pedagogy of the oppressed.* New York: Continuum.

74   Strauss, V. (2020, May 6). Cuomo questions why school buildings
     still exist—and says New York will work with Bill Gates to 'reimagine
     education.' *Washington Post.* Accessed at www.washingtonpost.com
     /education/2020/05/06/cuomo-questions-why-school-buildings-still-exist
     -says-new-york-will-work-with-bill-gates-reimagine-education/ on December
     3, 2020.

75   Hargreaves, A., & Fullan, M. (2020). Professional capital after the
     pandemic: Revisiting and revising classic understandings of teachers' work.
     Journal of Professional Capital and Community, 5(3/4), 327–336. Accessed at
     www.emerald.com/insight/content/doi/10.1108/JPCC-06-2020-0039/full
     /html on February 12, 2021.

76   Mitchell, C. (2020, July 29). Schools seek cover from special education
     lawsuits, but advocates see another motive. *Education Week.* Accessed at
     https://blogs.edweek.org/edweek/speced/2020/07/schools_seeks_cover_from
     _special_education_lawsuits.html on December 3, 2020.

77   Fishburn, D. (2020, May 29). *Contribution to webinar 9, An International
     Perspective: What's Happening in Other Countries?* of the Teaching Council
     of Ireland, Kildare.

78   Hargreaves, A., & Fullan, M. (2020). Professional capital after the
     pandemic: Revisiting and revising classic understandings of teachers' work.
     Journal of Professional Capital and Community, 5(3/4), 327–336. Accessed at
     www.emerald.com/insight/content/doi/10.1108/JPCC-06-2020-0039/full
     /html on February 12, 2021.

79   Association for Supervision and Curriculum Development. (2020). *Ed
     advantage: Low tech–No tech.* Accessed at www.dropbox.com/s/rzwzn7
     qm2z9f5bn/Matheson%20Redmond%20Collaborating%20to%20Ensure
     %20Access%20for%20ALL%20Students%20During%20a%20Global%20
     Pandemic%204.22.mp4?dl=0 on December 3, 2020.

80   Ali, T. T., Chandra, S., Cherukumilli, S., Fazlullah, A., Hill, H.,
     McAlpine, N., et al. (2021). *Looking back, looking forward: What it will
     take to permanently close the K–12 digital divide.* San Francisco: Common
     Sense Media.

81   University of Helsinki, Centre for Educational Assessment. (2020, August
     7). *Corona spring strained guardians and teachers, students' experiences of
     distance learning varied.* Accessed at www.helsinki.fi/en/news/education
     -news/corona-spring-strained-guardians-and-teachers-students-experiences
     -of-distance-learning-varied on December 3, 2020.

82   Berry, B., Dickenson, T., Harrist, J., Pomey, K., Zheng, J., Irvin, M., et
     al. (2020). *Teachers and teaching in the midst of a pandemic: Implications
     for South Carolina's policy leaders.* Columbia: South Carolina Teacher
     Education.

83   McGinn, D. (2020, July 20). Parents struggle to wean children off 'perfect
     storm' of screen time during pandemic. *The Globe and Mail.* Accessed at
     www.theglobeandmail.com/canada/article-parents-struggle-to-wean
     -children-off-perfect-storm-of-screen-time/ on December 3, 2020.

84   Nitcher, E. (2020, May 4). OPS will buy about 54,000 iPads—one for every
     student—for $27.6 million. *The World-Herald.* Accessed at https://omaha
     .com/news/education/ops-will-buy-about-54-400-ipads-one-for-every
     -student-for-27-6-million/article_f5314757-de00-5ce0-a9b0-a63688f1cee3
     .html on March 15, 2021.

85   Samba, M. (2020, October 19). Nearly 2,000 TDSB students still waiting to receive laptops, tablets for virtual learning. *CBC News*. Accessed at www .cbc.ca/news/canada/toronto/tdsb-students-devices-for-remote-learning -1.5766694 on March 15, 2021.

86   Dvorak, P. (2020, August 27). When 'back to school' means a parking lot and the hunt for a WiFi signal. *Washington Post*. Accessed at www .washingtonpost.com/local/when-back-to-school-means-a-parking-lot -and-the-hunt-for-a-wifi-signal/2020/08/27/0f785d5a-e873-11ea-970a -64c73a1c2392_story.html on December 3, 2020; Hargreaves, A., & Fullan, M. (2020). Professional capital after the pandemic: Revisiting and revising classic understandings of teachers' work. *Journal of Professional Capital and Community, 5*(3/4), 327–336. Accessed at www.emerald.com /insight/content/doi/10.1108/JPCC-06-2020-0039/full/html on February 12, 2021.

87   Gouëdard, P., Pont, B., & Viennet, R. (2020). Education responses to COVID-19: Implementing a way forward. *OECD Education Working Papers*, 224. Accessed at https://doi.org/10.1787/8e95f977-en on December 3, 2020.

88   Hargreaves, A. (2020, April 7). A complete list of what to do—and not do—for everyone teaching kids at home during the coronavirus crisis. *Washington Post*. Accessed at www.washingtonpost.com/education /2020/04/07/complete-list-what-do-not-do-everyone-teaching-kids-home -during-coronavirus-crisis on February 12, 2021.

89   Association for Supervision and Curriculum Development. (2020). *Ed advantage: Low tech–No tech*. Accessed at www.dropbox.com/s/rzwzn7qm 2z9f5bn/Matheson%20Redmond%20Collaborating%20to%20Ensure%20 Access%20for%20ALL%20Students%20During%20a%20Global%20 Pandemic%204.22.mp4?dl=0 on December 3, 2020.

90   Balingit, M. (2021, February 25). Unprecedented numbers of students have disappeared during the pandemic. Schools are working harder than ever to find them. *Washington Post*. Accessed at www.washingtonpost.com/education /pandemic-schools-students-missing/2021/02/25/f0b27262-5ce8-11eb-a976 -bad6431e03e2_story.html on March 24, 2021.

91   UNESCO, UNICEF, & World Bank. (2020). *What have we learnt? Overview of findings from a survey of ministries of education on national responses to COVID-19*. Paris, New York, Washington, DC: Authors.

92   Korman, H. T. M., O'Keefe, B., & Repka, M. (2020, October 21). *Missing in the margins: Estimating the scale of the COVID-19 attendance crisis*. Sudbury, MA: Bellwether Education Partners. Accessed at https:// bellwethereducation.org/publication/missing-margins-estimating-scale -covid-19-attendance-crisis on March 24, 2021.

93   Levi, S. K. (2020, March). *If coronavirus doesn't kill us, distance learning will* [Video file]. Accessed at www.youtube.com/watch?v=8U6zU4MXmnA on December 3, 2020.

94   Lenz, L. (2020, June 1). My third-grader was remote learning in a pandemic. I wasn't going to worry about a C- in PE. *Washington Post*. Accessed at www.washingtonpost.com/lifestyle/2020/06/01/my-third -grader-was-remote-learning-pandemic-im-wasnt-going-worry-about-c-pe on December 3, 2020.

95 Sullivan, E. J. (2020, April 7). Kids won't stop fighting? A bouncer, a therapist and a referee have advice. *New York Times.* Accessed at www.nytimes.com /2020/04/07/parenting/break-up-kids-fight.html on December 3, 2020.

96 Hargreaves, A., & Fullan, M. (2020). Professional capital after the pandemic: Revisiting and revising classic understandings of teachers' work. *Journal of Professional Capital and Community, 5*(3/4), 327–336. Accessed at www.emerald.com/insight/content/doi/10.1108/JPCC-06-2020-0039/full /html on February 12, 2021.

97 Herold, B., & Kurtz, H. Y. (2020, May 11). Teachers work two hours less per day during COVID-19: 8 key EdWeek survey findings. *Education Week.* Accessed at www.edweek.org/ew/articles/2020/05/11/teachers-work-an-hour-less-per-day.html on December 3, 2020; Hargreaves, A., & Fullan, M. (2020). Professional capital after the pandemic: Revisiting and revising classic understandings of teachers' work. *Journal of Professional Capital and Community, 5*(3/4), 327–336. Accessed at www.emerald.com/insight /content/doi/10.1108/JPCC-06-2020-0039/full/html on February 12, 2021.

98 Hargreaves, A., & Fullan, M. (2020). Professional capital after the pandemic: Revisiting and revising classic understandings of teachers' work. *Journal of Professional Capital and Community, 5*(3/4), 327–336. Accessed at www.emerald.com/insight/content/doi/10.1108/JPCC-06-2020-0039/full /html on February 12, 2021.

99 Mintz, V. (2020, May 5). Why I'm learning more with distance learning than I do in school. *New York Times.* Accessed at www.nytimes.com/2020 /05/05/opinion/coronavirus-pandemic-distance-learning.html?search ResultPosition=1 on December 3, 2020; Hargreaves, A., & Fullan, M. (2020). Professional capital after the pandemic: Revisiting and revising classic understandings of teachers' work. *Journal of Professional Capital and Community, 5*(3/4), 327–336. Accessed at www.emerald.com/insight /content/doi/10.1108/JPCC-06-2020-0039/full/html on February 12, 2021.

100 Whitley, J. (2020, June 1). Coronavirus: Distance learning poses challenges for some families of children with disabilities. *The Conversation.* Accessed at https://theconversation.com/coronavirus-distance-learning-poses-challenges-for-some-families-of-children-with-disabilities-136696 on December 3, 2020.

101 Doyle, W., & Sahlberg, P. (2020, April 8). A proposal for what post-coronavirus schools should do (instead of what they used to do). *Washington Post.* Accessed at www.washingtonpost.com/education/2020/04/08 /proposal-what-post-coronavirus-schools-should-do-instead-what-they -used-do on December 3, 2020; Hargreaves, A., & Fullan, M. (2020). Professional capital after the pandemic: Revisiting and revising classic understandings of teachers' work. *Journal of Professional Capital and Community, 5*(3/4), 327–336. Accessed at www.emerald.com/insight /content/doi/10.1108/JPCC-06-2020-0039/full/html on February 12, 2021.

102 Hargreaves, A., & Fullan, M. (2020). Professional capital after the pandemic: Revisiting and revising classic understandings of teachers' work. *Journal of Professional Capital and Community, 5*(3/4), 327–336. Accessed at www.emerald.com/insight/content/doi/10.1108/JPCC-06-2020-0039/full /html on February 12, 2021.

103 Rothstein, R. (2020, April 17). Why COVID-19 will "explode" existing academic achievement gaps. *Washington Post*. Accessed at www.washington post.com/education/2020/04/17/why-covid-19-will-explode-existing-academic -achievement-gaps/ on December 3, 2020.

104 Giles, C. (2016, June 9). Middle-class children increasingly hothoused to stay ahead. *Financial Times*. Accessed at www.ft.com/content/34d85918 -2e52-11e6-a18d-a96ab29e3c95 on December 3, 2020.

105 Bielski, Z. (2020, April 10). Social media awash with bragging about pandemic productivity. *The Globe and Mail*. Accessed at www.theglobe andmail.com/canada/article-social-media-awash-with-pandemic-productivity -bragging/ on December 3, 2020.

106 Braff, D. (2020, September 28). The new helicopter parents are on Zoom. *New York Times*. Accessed at www.nytimes.com/2020/09/28/parenting /helicopter-parent-remote-learning.html?referringSource=articleShare on December 3, 2020.

107 Khazad, O., & Harris, A. (2020, September 3). What are parents supposed to do with their kids? *The Atlantic*. Accessed at www.theatlantic.com/politics /archive/2020/09/limited-child-care-options-essential-workers/615931/ on March 24, 2021.

108 Long, H. (2020, December 16). Nearly 8 million Americans have fallen into poverty since the summer. *Washington Post*. Accessed at www .washingtonpost.com/business/2020/12/16/poverty-rising/ on March 24, 2021.

109 Haider, A. (2021, January 12). *The basic facts about children in poverty*. Center for American Progress. Accessed at www.americanprogress.org /issues/poverty/reports/2021/01/12/494506/basic-facts-children-poverty on February 28, 2021.

110 Butler, P. (2020, November 30). Almost 700,000 driven into poverty by Covid crisis in UK, study finds. *The Guardian*. Accessed at www .theguardian.com/society/2020/nov/30/almost-700000-driven-poverty -covid-crisis-uk-study on March 24, 2021.

111 von der Brelie, H. (2020, December 14). COVID-19 has created a new poverty class in Europe. *European News*. Accessed at www.euronews .com/2020/12/11/new-poverty-hits-europe on March 24, 2021.

112 Boghani, P. (2020, December 8). How COVID has impacted poverty in America. *PBS Frontline*. Accessed at www.pbs.org/wgbh/frontline/article /covid-poverty-america/ on March 24, 2021.

113 Boghani, P. (2020, December 8). How COVID has impacted poverty in America. *PBS Frontline*. Accessed at www.pbs.org/wgbh/frontline/article /covid-poverty-america/ on March 24, 2021.

114 Mattinson, D. (2020). *Beyond the red wall: Why Labour lost, how the Conservatives won and what will happen next*. London: Biteback Publishing; Davis, N. K. S. (2020, October 16). Higher Covid deaths among BAME people 'not driven by health issues'. *The Guardian*. Accessed at www.the guardian.com/world/2020/oct/16/bame-people-more-likely-to-die-from -covid-than-white-people-study on March 24, 2021.

115 Downey, D. B. (2020). *How schools really matter: Why our assumption about schools and inequality is mostly wrong*. Chicago: University of Chicago Press.

116 Downey, D. B. (2020). *How schools really matter: Why our assumption about schools and inequality is mostly wrong.* Chicago: University of Chicago Press.

117 Boushey, H. (2019). *Unbound: How inequality constricts our economy and what we can do about it.* Cambridge, MA: Harvard University Press; Sasson, I. (2016). Trends in life expectancy and lifespan variation by educational attainment in the United States, 1990–2010. *Demography, 53,* 269–293.

118 Reston, M. (2020, July 25). Donald Trump's mind-bending logic on school re-openings. *CNN.* Accessed at www.cnn.com/2020/07/25/politics/donald -trump-schools-reopening-coronavirus/index.html on December 3, 2020.

119 Turner, C. (2020, June 29). Parents who fail to send their children to school in September will be fined, education secretary says. *The Telegraph.* Accessed at www.telegraph.co.uk/news/2020/06/29/parents-fail-send-children-school -september-will-fined-education/ on December 3, 2020.

120 Alphonso, C. (2020, May 5). Quebec school boards provide a glimpse of the new normal in classrooms. *The Globe and Mail.* Accessed at www .theglobeandmail.com/canada/article-quebec-school-boards-provide-a -glimpse-of-the-new-normal-in-classrooms/ on December 3, 2020.

121 Hargreaves, A. [@hargreavesbc]. (2020, May 5). Quebec sends children back to the 1950s. No phys ed, arts, group work, or play as schools are turned into warehouses just so parents can be put back to work https:// theglobeandmail.com/canada/article-quebec-school-boards-provide-a -glimpse-of-the-new-normal-in-classrooms/ @calphonso @pasi_sahlberg @GHCDon @arceducation1 @CarolCampbell4 @BrookingsInst @ GLoganEd [Tweet]. Accessed at https://twitter.com/HargreavesBC /status/1257635637483704320 on March 24, 2021; McCloy, B. [@bruce _mccloy]. (2020, May 5). There has to be a better way of educating and looking after children right now that is not a devastating for them. All the great educational minds and after months this is the best we can do? [Tweet]. Accessed at https://twitter.com/bruce_mccloy /status/1257664355899850752 on March 24, 2021; Gauthier, A. [@ angela_gauthie]. (2020, May 5). Shameful! Disrespect for staff's safety & reinforcement of education as a babysitting service! [Tweet]. Accessed at https://twitter.com/angela_gauthie/status/1257702494764924933 on March 24, 2021.

122 Noack, R. (2020, September 16). In Denmark, the forest is the new classroom. *Washington Post.* Accessed at www.washingtonpost.com/world/2020/09/16 /outdoor-school-coronavirus-denmark-europe-forest/ on December 3, 2020.

123 For a one-minute demonstration of this among boys in the Urban Prep Charter Academy for Young Men, see Edutopia. (2020). *60-second strategy: Snowball toss* [Video file]. Accessed at www.youtube.com/ watch?v=Iuu8 _Ga63J8&feature=emb_imp_woyt on March 24, 2021.

124 Hargreaves, A. (2020, April 7). A complete list of what to do—and not do—for everyone teaching kids at home during the coronavirus crisis. *Washington Post.* Accessed at www.washingtonpost.com/education /2020/04/07/complete-list-what-do-not-do-everyone-teaching-kids-home -during-coronavirus-crisis on December 3, 2020.

125 Fine Dictionary. (n.d.). *Engagement definitions.* Accessed at www.fine dictionary.com/engagement.html on December 7, 2020.

126 Online Etymology Dictionary. (n.d.). *Engagement*. Accessed at www
     .etymonline.com/word/engagement on December 7, 2020.

127 Online Etymology Dictionary. (n.d.). *Engagement*. Accessed at www
     .etymonline.com/word/engagement on December 7, 2020.

128 Noguera, P. (2018, March 1). *Deeper learning: An essential component of
     equity*. Accessed at https://learningpolicyinstitute.org/blog/deeper-learning
     -essential-component-equity on December 3, 2020.

129 Noguera, P. (2018, March 1). *Deeper learning: An essential component of
     equity*. Accessed at https://learningpolicyinstitute.org/blog/deeper-learning
     -essential-component-equity on December 3, 2020.

130 Christenson, S. L., Reschly, A. L., & Wylie, C. (Eds.). (2012). *Handbook of
     research on student engagement*. Dordrecht, Netherlands: Springer.

131 Fredricks, J. A., & McColskey, W. (2012). The measurement of student
     engagement: A comparative analysis of various methods and student self-
     report instruments. In S. L. Christenson, A. L. Reschly, & C. Wylie (Eds.),
     Handbook of research on student engagement (pp. 763–782). Dordrecht,
     Netherlands: Springer.

132 Maslow, A. H. (1954). *Motivation and personality*. New York: Harper.

133 Maslow, A. H. (1969). *The psychology of science: A reconnaissance*. Chicago:
     Gateway, pp. 52–53.

134 Maslow, A. H. (1971). *The farther reaches of human nature*. New York: Viking.

135 Liu, P. (2017). A framework for understanding Chinese leadership: A
     cultural approach. *International Journal of Leadership in Education, 20*(6),
     749–761.

136 Blum, D. (2002). *Love at Goon Park: Harry Harlow and the science of affection*
     (1st ed.). Cambridge, MA: Perseus.

137 Harlow, H. F. (1949). The formation of learning sets. *Psychological Review,
     56,* 51–65. Accessed at https://doi.org/10.1037/h0062474 on December
     8, 2020.

138 Harlow, H. F. (1950). Learning and satiation of response in intrinsically
     motivated complex puzzle performance by monkeys. *Journal of Comparative
     and Physiological Psychology, 43*(4), 289–294. Accessed at https://doi.org
     /10.1037/h0058114 on December 3, 2020.

139 Deci, E. L., & Ryan, R. M. (1985). *Intrinsic motivation and self-
     determination in human behavior*. New York: Plenum.

140 Ryan, R. M., & Deci, E. L. (2000). Self-determination theory and the
     facilitation of intrinsic motivation, social development, and well-being.
     American Psychologist, 55(1), 68–78.

141 Pink, D. H. (2009) *Drive: The surprising truth about what motivates us*. New
     York: Riverhead.

142 Pink, D. H. (2009). *Drive: The surprising truth about what motivates us*. New
     York: Riverhead, pp. 24–25.

143 Pink, D. H. (2009). *Drive: The surprising truth about what motivates us*. New
     York: Riverhead, p. 46.

144 Csikszentmihalyi, M. (1975). *Beyond boredom and anxiety.* San Francisco: Jossey-Bass; Csikszentmihalyi, M. (1987). The flow experience. In M. Eliade (Ed.), *The encyclopedia of religion* (Vol. 5, pp. 361–363). New York: Macmillan; Csikszentmihalyi, M. (1990) *Flow: The psychology of optimal experience.* New York: Harper & Row.

145 Csikszentmihalyi, M. (2004). *Flow: The secret to happiness* [Video file]. Accessed at www.ted.com/talks/mihaly_csikszentmihalyi_flow_the_secret_to_happiness?language=en on December 3, 2020.

146 Peifer, C., & Engeser, S. (Eds.). (2021). *Advances in flow research* (2nd ed.). Dordrecht, Netherlands: Springer.

147 Robinson, K., & Aronica, L. (2016). *Creative schools: The grassroots revolution that's transforming education.* New York: Penguin.

148 Loehr, J., & Schwartz, T. (2003). *The power of full engagement: Managing energy, not time, is the key to high performance and personal renewal.* New York: Free Press, p. 5.

149 Lewis, B. (2018). *Keep calm and carry on: The truth behind the poster.* London: Imperial War Museum.

150 Cummings, D. (2020, January 2). *"Two hands are a lot"—We're hiring data scientists, project managers, policy experts, assorted weirdos . . .* [Blog post]. Accessed at https://dominiccummings.com/2020/01/02/two-hands-are-a-lot-were-hiring-data-scientists-project-managers-policy-experts-assorted-weirdos/ on December 3, 2020.

151 Cummings, D. (2020, January 2). *"Two hands are a lot"—We're hiring data scientists, project managers, policy experts, assorted weirdos . . .* [Blog post]. Accessed at https://dominiccummings.com/2020/01/02/two-hands-are-a-lot-were-hiring-data-scientists-project-managers-policy-experts-assorted-weirdos/ on December 3, 2020.

152 Walker, T. D. (2017) *Teach like Finland: 33 simple strategies for joyful classrooms.* New York: Norton; Sahlberg, P., & Walker, T. D. (2021). *In teachers we trust: The Finnish way to world-class schools.* New York: Norton.

153 Magister. (n.d.). In *Merriam-Webster's online dictionary.* Accessed at www.merriam-webster.com/dictionary/magister on December 8, 2020.

154 Masterpiece. (n.d.). In *Merriam-Webster's online dictionary.* Accessed at www.merriam-webster.com/dictionary/masterpiece on December 8, 2020.

155 Mastery orientation. (n.d.). In *American Psychological Association's dictionary of psychology.* Accessed at https://dictionary.apa.org/mastery-orientation on December 8, 2020.

156 Bloom, B. S. (1968). Learning for mastery. *UCLA Evaluation Comment, 1*(2), 1–12.

157 Bloom, B. S. (1986). Ralph Tyler's impact on evaluation theory and practice. *Journal of Thought, 21*(1), 36–46, p. 37.

158 Bloom, B. S. (1986). Ralph Tyler's impact on evaluation theory and practice. *Journal of Thought, 21*(1), 36–46, p. 37.

159 Bloom, B. S. (1986). Ralph Tyler's impact on evaluation theory and practice. *Journal of Thought, 21*(1), 36–46, p. 37.

160 Bloom, B. S. (1968). Learning for mastery. *UCLA Evaluation Comment*, *1*(2), 1–12, p. 1.

161 Bloom, B. S. (1968). Learning for mastery. *UCLA Evaluation Comment*, *1*(2), 1–12, p. 1.

162 Bloom, B. S. (1984). The search for methods of group instruction as effective as one-to-one tutoring. *Educational Leadership*, *41*(8), 4–17. Accessed at www.ascd.org/ASCD/pdf/journals/ed_lead/el_198405_bloom .pdf on December 8, 2020.

163 Guskey, T. R. (2009). Mastery learning. In T. L. Good (Ed.), *21st century education: A reference handbook* (Vol. 1, pp. 194–202). Thousand Oaks, CA: SAGE.

164 Mastery Transcript Consortium. (2020). Accessed at www.mastery.org on December 8, 2020.

165 Cox, R. H. (2002). *Sport psychology: Concepts and applications* (5th ed.). New York: McGraw-Hill.

166 Gustafsson, H., & Lundqvist, C. (2016). Working with perfectionism in elite sport: A cognitive behavioral therapy perspective. In A. P. Hill (Ed.), *The psychology of perfectionism in sport, dance and exercise* (pp. 203–221). New York: Routledge.

167 Ntoumanis, N., & Biddle, S. J. H. (1999). A review of motivational climate in physical activity. *Journal of Sports Sciences*, *17*, 643–665. doi:10.1080/026404199365678

168 Ames, C. (1984). Competitive, cooperative and individualistic goal structures: A motivational analysis. In R. Ames & C. Ames (Eds.), *Research on motivation in education: Student motivation* (Vol. 1, pp. 177–207). New York: Academic Press; Ames, C. (1990). Motivation: What teachers need to know. *Teachers College Record*, *91*, 409–421; Ames, C. (1992a). Achievement goals and the classroom motivational climate. In D. H. Schunk & J. L. Meece (Eds.), *Student perception in the classroom* (pp. 327–348). Hillsdale, NJ: Erlbaum; Ames, C. (1992b). Classrooms: Goals, structures, and student motivation. *Journal of Educational Psychology*, *84*(3), 261–271. Accessed at http://groups.jyu.fi/sporticus/lahteet/LAHDE_17.pdf on December 8, 2020.

169 Epstein, J. (1984). Family structures and student motivation: A developmental perspective. In C. Ames & R. Ames (Eds.), *Research on motivation in education* (pp. 259–295). New York: Academic Press.

170 Ames, C. (1992). Achievement goals, motivational climate, and motivational processes. In G. C. Roberts (Ed.), *Motivation in sport and exercise* (pp. 161–176). Champaign, IL: Human Kinetics.

171 Maslow, A. H. (1943). A theory of human motivation. *Psychological Review*, *50*(4), 370–396. Accessed at https://doi.org/10.1037/h0054346 on March 24, 2021; Pink, D. H. (2009). *Drive: The surprising truth about what motivates us.* New York: Riverhead.

172 Cecchini, J. A., Fernandez-Rio, J., Mendez-Gimenez, A., Cecchini, C., & Martins, L. (2014). Epstein's TARGET framework and motivational climate in sport: Effects of a field-based, long-term intervention program. *International Journal of Sports Science & Coaching*, *9*(6), 1325–1340. Accessed at https://doi.org/10.1260/1747-9541.9.6.1325 on December 3, 2020.

173 Bowler, M. (2009, September 2–5). *The influence of the TARGET motivational climate structures on pupil physical activity levels during year 9 athletics lessons.* Paper presented at the annual conference of the British Educational Research Association, Manchester, United Kingdom.

174 Braithwaite, R., Spray, C. M., & Warburton, V. E. (2011). Motivational climate interventions in physical education: A meta-analysis. *Psychology of Sport Exercise, 12*(6), 628–638. doi:10.1016/j.psychsport.2011.06.005

175 Senge, P. (1990). *The fifth discipline: The art and practice of the learning organization* (1st ed.). New York: Doubleday.

176 Senge, P. (1990). *The fifth discipline: The art and practice of the learning organization* (1st ed.). New York: Doubleday, p. 3.

177 Senge, P. (1990). *The fifth discipline: The art and practice of the learning organization* (1st ed.). New York: Doubleday, p. 147.

178 Senge, P. (1990). *The fifth discipline: The art and practice of the learning organization* (1st ed.). New York: Doubleday, p. 7.

179 Senge, P. (1990). *The fifth discipline: The art and practice of the learning organization* (1st ed.). New York: Doubleday, p. 141.

180 Senge, P. (1990). *The fifth discipline: The art and practice of the learning organization* (1st ed.). New York: Doubleday, p. 142.

181 Eccles, J. (2005). Subjective task value and the Eccles et al. model of achievement-related choices. In C. J. Elliot & C. S. Dweck (Eds.), *Handbook of competence and motivation* (pp. 105–121). New York: Guilford Press.

182 McClelland, D. C. (1987). *Human motivation.* Boston, MA: Cambridge University Press.

183 Atkinson, J. W. (1957). Motivational determinants of risk-taking behavior. *Psychological Review, 64*(6), 359–372, p. 359.

184 Atkinson, J. W. (1964). *An introduction to motivation.* Princeton, NJ: Van Nostrand.

185 Eccles, J., & Wang, M. T. (2018). So what is student engagement anyway? In S. L. Christenson, A. L. Reschly, & C. Wylie (Eds.), *Handbook of research on student engagement* (pp. 133–145). Dordrecht, Netherlands: Springer, p. 142.

186 Eccles, J. (2005). Subjective task value and the Eccles et al. model of achievement-related choices. In C. J. Elliot & C. S. Dweck (Eds.), *Handbook of competence and motivation* (pp. 105–121). New York: Guilford Press.

187 Wigfield, A., & Eccles, J. (1992). The development of achievement task values: A theoretical analysis. *Developmental Review, 12*(3), 265–310, p. 280.

188 Wigfield, A., & Eccles, J. (1992). The development of achievement task values: A theoretical analysis. *Developmental Review, 12*(3), 265–310, p. 280.

189 Lawson, M. A., & Lawson, H. A. (2013). New conceptual frameworks for student engagement research, policy, and practice. *Review of Educational Research, 83*(3), 432–479.

190 Lawson, M. A., & Lawson, H. A. (2013). New conceptual frameworks for student engagement research, policy, and practice. *Review of Educational Research, 83*(3), 432–479, p. 437.

191 Christenson, S. L., Reschly, A. L., & Wylie, C. (Eds.). (2012). *Handbook of research on student engagement.* Dordrecht, Netherlands: Springer.

192 Lawson, M. A., & Lawson, H. A. (2013). New conceptual frameworks for student engagement research, policy, and practice. *Review of Educational Research, 83*(3), 432–479, p. 443.

193 Lawson, M. A., & Lawson, H. A. (2013). New conceptual frameworks for student engagement research, policy, and practice. *Review of Educational Research, 83*(3), 432–479, p. 434.

194 Anderson, S. E. (2009). Moving change: Evolutionary perspectives on educational change. In A. Hargreaves, A. Lieberman, M. Fullan, & D. Hopkins (Eds.), *Second international handbook of educational change* (pp. 65–84). Dordrecht, Netherlands: Springer.

195 Mehta, J., & Fine, S. (2019). *In search of deeper learning: The quest to remake the American high school.* Cambridge, MA: Harvard University Press.

196 Central Advisory Council for Education. (1967). *Children and their primary schools* (*The Plowden report,* Vol. 1). London: HMSO, p. 187.

197 Hargreaves, A. (2020). *Moving: A memoir of education and social mobility.* Bloomington, IN: Solution Tree Press, p. 45.

198 Ontario Ministry of Education. (2014). *Achieving excellence: A renewed vision for education in Ontario.* Toronto, Canada: Queen's Printer for Ontario. Accessed at www.msdsb.net/images/ADMIN /correspondence/2014/MEDU%20Renewed%20Vision%20for%20 Education.pdf on December 3, 2020, p. 13.

199 Ontario Ministry of Education. (2014). *Achieving excellence: A renewed vision for education in Ontario.* Toronto, Canada: Queen's Printer for Ontario. Accessed at www.msdsb.net/images /ADMIN/correspondence/2014/MEDU%20Renewed%20Vision%20 for%20Education.pdf on December 3, 2020, p. 4.

200 Ontario Ministry of Education. (2014). *Achieving excellence: A renewed vision for education in Ontario.* Toronto, Canada: Queen's Printer for Ontario. Accessed at www.msdsb.net/images/ADMIN/correspondence /2014/MEDU%20Renewed%20Vision%20for%20Education.pdf on December 3, 2020, pp. 13–14.

201 Hargreaves, A., Shirley, D., Wangia, S., Bacon, C., & D'Angelo, M. (2018). *Leading from the middle: Spreading learning, well-being, and identity across Ontario.* Toronto, Canada: Council of Ontario Directors of Education. Accessed at http://ccsli.ca/downloads/2018-Leading_From_the_Middle _Final-EN.pdf on February 12, 2021.

202 Hargreaves, A., Shirley, D., Wangia, S., Bacon, C., & D'Angelo, M. (2018). *Leading from the middle: Spreading learning, well-being, and identity across Ontario.* Toronto, Canada: Council of Ontario Directors of Education. Accessed at http://ccsli.ca/downloads/2018-Leading_From_the_Middle _Final-EN.pdf on February 12, 2021.

203 Hargreaves, A., Shirley, D., Wangia, S., Bacon, C., & D'Angelo, M. (2018). *Leading from the middle: Spreading learning, well-being, and identity across Ontario.* Toronto, Canada: Council of Ontario Directors of Education.

Accessed at http://ccsli.ca/downloads/2018-Leading_From_the_Middle _Final-EN.pdf on February 12, 2021.

204 Hargreaves, A., Shirley, D., Wangia, S., Bacon, C., & D'Angelo, M. (2018). *Leading from the middle: Spreading learning, well-being, and identity across Ontario.* Toronto, Canada: Council of Ontario Directors of Education. Accessed at http://ccsli.ca/downloads/2018-Leading_From_the_Middle _Final-EN.pdf on February 12, 2021.

205 Brown, J. (2013). *Flat Stanley: His original adventure!* New York: HarperCollins.

206 Hargreaves, A., Shirley, D., Wangia, S., Bacon, C., & D'Angelo, M. (2018). *Leading from the middle: Spreading learning, well-being, and identity across Ontario.* Toronto, Canada: Council of Ontario Directors of Education. Accessed at http://ccsli.ca/downloads/2018-Leading_From_the_Middle _Final-EN.pdf on February 12, 2021.

207 Hargreaves, A., Shirley, D., Wangia, S., Bacon, C., & D'Angelo, M. (2018). *Leading from the middle: Spreading learning, well-being, and identity across Ontario.* Toronto, Canada: Council of Ontario Directors of Education. Accessed at http://ccsli.ca/downloads/2018-Leading_From_the_Middle _Final-EN.pdf on February 12, 2021.

208 Gambino, L. (2019, March 7). *REDress exhibit highlights epidemic of missing and murdered Indigenous women.* Accessed at www.theguardian.com/world /2019/mar/07/redress-exhibit-dc-missing-and-murdered-indigenous-women on December 3, 2020.

209 Dewey, J. (1916). *Democracy and education.* New York: Free Press; Montessori, M. (1972). *The secret of childhood.* New York: Ballantine. (Original work published 1936); Freire, P. (1970). *Pedagogy of the oppressed.* New York: Continuum.

210 Hargreaves, A., & O'Connor, M. T. (2018). *Collaborative professionalism: When teaching together means learning for all.* Thousand Oaks, CA: Corwin, pp. 71–88.

211 Rincón-Gallardo, S. (2019). *Liberating learning: Educational change as social movement.* New York: Routledge.

212 Organisation for Economic Co-operation and Development. (2019). *OECD future of education and skills 2030: Conceptual learning framework— conceptual note—attitudes and values.* Paris: Author. Accessed at www.oecd .org/draft/pj54mx23oh/teaching-and-learning/learning/attitudes-and-values /Attitudes%20and%20Values%20for%202030.pdf on December 3, 2020.

213 Fullan, M., Quinn, J., & McEachen, J. (2018). *Deep learning: Engage the world change the world.* Thousand Oaks, CA: Corwin, p. xv.

214 Fullan, M., Quinn, J., & McEachen, J. (2018). *Deep learning: Engage the world change the world.* Thousand Oaks, CA: Corwin, p. xvii.

215 Fullan, M., Quinn, J., & McEachen, J. (2018). *Deep learning: Engage the world change the world.* Thousand Oaks, CA: Corwin, p. xvii.

216 All preceding quotes are from Fullan, M., Quinn, J., & McEachen, J. (2018). *Deep learning: Engage the world change the world.* Thousand Oaks, CA: Corwin, p. 9.

217 Darling-Hammond, L., & Oakes, J. (2019). *Preparing teachers for deeper learning.* Cambridge, MA: Harvard Education Press, pp. 13–14.

218 Fullan, M., Quinn, J., & McEachen, J. (2018). *Deep learning: Engage the world change the world.* Thousand Oaks, CA: Corwin.

219 Dickson, B. (2019). What is deep learning? *PC Magazine.* Accessed at www .pcmag.com/news/what-is-deep-learning on March 24, 2021; Schmidhuber, J. (2015). Deep learning in neural networks: An overview. *Neural Networks, 61,* 85–117. Accessed at www.sciencedirect.com/science/article/abs/pii /S0893608014002135?via%3Dihub on March 24, 2021.

220 Marton, F., & Säljö, R. (1976). On qualitative differences in learning: I— Outcome and process. *British Journal of Educational Psychology, 46*(1), 4–11.

221 Entwistle, N. (2000, November). *Promoting deep learning through teaching and assessment: Conceptual frameworks and educational contexts.* Paper presented at the ESRC Teaching and Learning Research Programme, Leicester, United Kingdom. Accessed at www.leeds.ac.uk/educol/documents /00003220.htm on December 3, 2020.

222 Hargreaves, D. (2006). *A new shape for schooling?* London: Specialist Schools and Academies Trust; Sims, E. (2006). *Deep learning—1.* London: Specialist Schools and Academies Trust.

223 See the discussion on this research in Sims, E. (2006). *Deep learning—1.* London: Specialist Schools and Academies Trust, p. 3.

224 Egan, K. (1979). *Educational development.* Oxford, England: Oxford University Press.

225 Egan, K. (2010). *Learning in depth: A simple innovation that can transform schooling.* Chicago: University of Chicago Press.

226 Egan, K. (2010). *Learning in depth: A simple innovation that can transform schooling.* Chicago: University of Chicago Press, p. 23.

227 Egan, K. (2010). *Learning in depth: A simple innovation that can transform schooling.* Chicago: University of Chicago Press, p. 33.

228 Gardner, H. (1999). *The disciplined mind: What all students should understand.* New York: Simon & Schuster.

229 Alphonso, C., & Stone, L. (2020, March 3). Ontario backs down on high-school class sizes, online courses, in bid to restart talks with teachers. *The Globe and Mail.* Accessed at www.theglobeandmail.com/canada/article -ontario-backs-down-on-high-school-class-sizes-online-courses-in-bid on March 24, 2021.

230 Bubb, S., & Jones, M. (2020). Learning from the COVID-19 home-schooling experience: Listening to pupils, parents/carers and teachers. *Improving Schools, 23*(3), 209–222, p. 215.

231 Bubb, S., & Jones, M. (2020). Learning from the COVID-19 home-schooling experience: Listening to pupils, parents/carers and teachers. *Improving Schools, 23*(3), 209–222, p. 216.

232 Martin-Barbero, S. (2020, July 21). COVID-19 has accelerated the digital transformation of higher education. *World Economic Forum.* Accessed at www.weforum.org/agenda/2020/07/covid-19-digital-transformation-higher -education/ on March 24, 2021; Braverman, L. R. (2020, October 14). The digital transformation in higher education and its aftereffects. *The Evolllution.* Accessed at https://evolllution.com/managing-institution

/operations_efficiency/the-digital-transformation-in-higher-education-and
-its-aftereffects/ on March 24, 2021.

233 Boston College Lynch School of Education and Human Development.
(n.d.). *Master of education (M.Ed.) in global perspectives: Teaching,
curriculum, and learning environments.* Accessed at www.bc.edu/content
/bc-web/schools/lynch-school/sites/lynch-school-online-programs/online
-masters-in-education-programs/masters-global-perspectives.html on
December 8, 2020.

234 Hagerman, M. S., & Kellam, H. (2020). *Learning to teach online: An open
educational resource for pre-service teachers.* Accessed at http://onlineteaching.
ca on March 14, 2021.

235 Hagerman, M. S., & Kellam, H. (2020). *Learning to teach online: An open
educational resource for pre-service teachers.* Accessed at http://onlineteaching.
ca on March 14, 2021.

236 Hagerman, M. S., & Kellam, H. (2020). *Learning to teach online: An open
educational resource for pre-service teachers.* Accessed at http://onlineteaching
.ca on March 14, 2021.

237 Hagerman, M. S., & Kellam, H. (2020). *Learning to teach online: An open
educational resource for pre-service teachers.* Accessed at http://onlineteaching
.ca on March 14, 2021.

238 Hagerman, M. S., & Kellam, H. (2020). *Learning to teach online: An open
educational resource for pre-service teachers.* Accessed at http://onlineteaching.
ca on March 14, 2021.

239 Dynarski, S. (2018, January 19). Online courses are harming the students
who need the most help. *New York Times.* Accessed at www.nytimes.com
/2018/01/19/business/online-courses-are-harming-the-students-who-need
-the-most-help.html on December 3, 2020.

240 Dynarski, S. (2018, January 19). Online courses are harming the students
who need the most help. *New York Times.* Accessed at www.nytimes.com
/2018/01/19/business/online-courses-are-harming-the-students-who-need
-the-most-help.html on December 3, 2020.

241 Herhalt, C. (2021, February 24). Students report more anxiety, teachers say
COVID-19 safety protocols lacking at TDSB: Survey. *CP24 News.* Accessed
at www.cp24.com/news/students-report-more-anxiety-teachers-say-covid
-19-safety-protocols-lacking-at-tdsb-survey-1.5321868 on March 24, 2021.

242 Stelitano, L., Doan, S., Woo, A., Diliberti, M. K., Kaufman, J. H., &
Henry, D. (2020). *The digital divide and COVID-19: Teachers' perceptions
of inequities in students' internet access and participation in remote learning.*
Santa Monica, CA: RAND Corporation.

243 Miliband, D. (2004). *Personalised learning: Building a new relationship
with schools.* London: DCSF Publications. Accessed at http://publications
.teachernet.gov.uk on December 3, 2020.

244 Zhao, Y. (2018). *Reach for greatness: Personalizable education for all children.*
Thousand Oaks, CA: Corwin.

245 Hargreaves, D. (2006). *A new shape for schooling?* London: Specialist Schools
and Academies Trust.

246 Wexler, N. (2018, April 19). *Mark Zuckerberg's plan to "personalize" learning
rests on shaky ground.* Accessed at www.forbes.com/sites/nataliewexler

/2018/04/19/mark-zuckerbergs-plan-to-personalize-learning-rests-on-shaky -ground/#4c2a5a263bfe on December 3, 2020.

247 Pane, J. F., Steiner, E. D., Baird, M. D., Hamilton, L. S., & Pane, J. D. (2017). *Informing progress: Insights on personalized learning implementation and effects.* Santa Monica, CA: RAND.

248 Christensen, C. M., Horn, M. B., & Staker, H. (2015). *Blended: Using disruptive innovation to improve schools.* San Francisco: Jossey-Bass.

249 Christensen, C. M., Horn, M. B., & Johnson, C. W. (2016). *Disrupting class: How disruptive innovation will change the way the world learns* (Expanded ed.). New York: McGraw-Hill.

250 Christensen, C. M. (1997). *The innovator's dilemma: When new technologies cause great firms to fail.* New York: Collins.

251 Surowiecki, J. (2013, September 3). Where Nokia went wrong. *The New Yorker.* Accessed at www.newyorker.com/business/currency/where-nokia -went-wrong on March 24, 2021.

252 Christensen, C. M., Horn, M. B., & Johnson, C. W. (2008). *Disrupting class: How disruptive innovation will change the way the world learns.* New York: McGraw-Hill.

253 Ravitch, D. (2020). *Slaying Goliath: The passionate resistance to privatization and the fight to save America's public schools.* New York: Knopf, p. 6.

254 Ravitch, D. (2020). *Slaying Goliath: The passionate resistance to privatization and the fight to save America's public schools.* New York: Knopf, p. 6.

255 Malloy, J. (2014). *Exciting celebration of "Transforming Learning Everywhere"* [Blog post]. Accessed at https://johnmalloy.ca/2014/11/05/exciting-celebration-of-transforming-learning-everywhere/ on March 24, 2021.

256 Malloy, J. (2014). *Exciting celebration of "Transforming Learning Everywhere"* [Blog post]. Accessed at https://johnmalloy.ca/2014/11/05/exciting-celebration -of-transforming-learning-everywhere/ on March 24, 2021.

257 Malloy, J. (2014). *Transforming learning everywhere.* Hamilton, Canada: Hamilton Wentworth District School Board. Accessed at http://www .hwdsb.on.ca/about/innovation/transforming-learning-everywhere/our-thinking/ on March 24, 2021.

258 Owston, R., Wideman, H., Thumlert, K., & Malhotra, T. (2016). *Transforming learning everywhere: A study of the second year of implementation.* Toronto, Canada: York University. Accessed at http:// www.ontariodirectors.ca/CODE_TLE/Executive%20Summary%20 ENGLISH%20final%20rev%20FINAL-AODA.PDF on December 8, 2020.

259 Thumlert, K., Owston, R., & Malhotra, T. (2018). Transforming school culture through inquiry-driven learning and iPads. *Journal of Professional Capital and Community*, *3*(2), 79–96. Accessed at https://doi.org/10.1108 /JPCC-09-2017-0020 on December 3, 2020.

260 Owston, R., Wideman, H., Thumlert, K., & Malhotra, T. (2016). *Transforming learning everywhere: A study of the second year of implementation.* Toronto, Canada: York University, p. 20. Accessed at

http://www.ontariodirectors.ca/CODE_TLE/Executive%20Summary%20 ENGLISH%20final%20rev%20FINAL-AODA.PDF on March 14, 2021.

261 University of Ottawa. (2020, August 21). *CHENINE—Change, Engagement and Innovation in Education: A Canadian collaboratory.* Accessed at https:// education.uottawa.ca/en/news/chenine-change-engagement-and-innovation -education-canadian-collaboratory on December 8, 2020.

262 The text of the CHENINE Charter that follows is reproduced and adapted from the CHENINE Center that Andy established and leads as its director. The co-creators of the charter are Amal Boultif, Megan Cotnam-Kappel, Phyllis Dalley, Michelle Hagerman, Jess Whitley, and Joel Westheimer. Visit https://chenine.ca/en/about/ to read the complete version of the charter.

263 Parmar, B. (2020, October 12). Screen time is as addictive as junk food— how do we wean children off? *The Guardian.* Accessed at www.theguardian .com/commentisfree/2020/oct/12/screen-time-addictive-social-media -addiction on December 3, 2020.

264 Isaacson, W. (2017). *Leonardo da Vinci.* New York: Simon & Schuster.

265 Herrmann, D. (1999). *Helen Keller: A life.* Chicago: University of Chicago Press.

266 Wiseman, E. (2018, December 16). Nadiya Hussain: *"This is more than a job—it's important to be out there."* Accessed at www.theguardian.com /food/2018/dec/16/nadiya-hussain-bake-off-winner-this-is-more-than-a-job on December 3, 2020.

267 Robinson, K., & Aronica, L. (2009). *The element: How finding your passion changes everything.* New York: Penguin.

268 Robinson, K. (2006). *Do schools kill creativity?* [Video file]. Accessed at www.ted.com/talks/sir_ken_robinson_do_schools_kill_creativity?language =en on December 3, 2020.

269 Andy counts himself as a prime example of this, as he reports in his memoir, Hargreaves, A. (2020). *Moving: A memoir of education and social mobility.* Bloomington, IN: Solution Tree Press.

270 Hargreaves, A., Boyle, A., & Harris, A. (2014). *Uplifting leadership.* Hoboken, NJ: Wiley.

271 Hargreaves, A., & Harris, A. (2011). *Performance beyond expectations.* Nottingham, England: National College for School Leadership.

272 Hargreaves, A., & Harris, A. (2014). *Performance beyond expectations.* Nottingham, England: National College for School Leadership, p. 54.

273 Kagan, S. (1994). *Cooperative learning.* San Clemente, CA: Kagan Cooperative Learning.

274 Orwell, G. (1970). *A collection of essays.* Boston, MA: Houghton Mifflin Harcourt, p. 316.

275 Darwin, C. (1872). *The expression of the emotions in man and animals.* London: John Murray.

276   Sahlberg, P., & Doyle, W. (2019). *Let the children play: How more play will save our schools and help our children thrive.* New York: Oxford University Press, p. 325.

277   Yogman, M., Garner, A., Hutchinson, J., Hirsh-Pasek, K., & Golinkoff, R. M. (2018). The power of play: A pediatric role in enhancing development in young children. *Pediatrics, 142*(3). Accessed at https://pediatrics .aappublications.org/content/142/3/e20182058 on December 8, 2020.

278   Dewey, J. (1916). *Democracy and education.* New York: Free Press.

279   Lucas, B., & Spencer, E. (2017). *Teaching creative thinking: Developing learners who generate ideas and can think critically.* Carmarthen, Wales: Crown House Publishing.

280   Lucas, B., & Spencer, E. (2017). *Teaching creative thinking: Developing learners who generate ideas and can think critically.* Carmarthen, Wales: Crown House Publishing, p. 17.

281   Altman, L. K. (1982, September 14). The tumultuous discovery of insulin: Finally, hidden story is told. *New York Times.* Accessed at www.nytimes .com/1982/09/14/science/the-tumultuous-discovery-of-insulin-finally -hidden-story-is-told.html on December 3, 2020.

282   Hargreaves, A., Boyle, A., & Harris, A. (2014). *Uplifting leadership.* Hoboken, NJ: Wiley.

283   Disengage. (n.d.). In *Merriam-Webster's online dictionary.* Accessed at www .merriam-webster.com/dictionary/disengage on December 9, 2020.

284   Disengagement. (n.d.). In *Oxford English Dictionary online.* Accessed at www.lexico.com/definition/disengagement on December 9, 2020.

285   Van der Loo, L. (2020). *As the world burns: The new generation of activists and the landmark legal fight against climate change.* Portland, OR: Timber.

286   McKenna, L. (2015, April 9). *What happens when students boycott a standardized test?* Accessed at www.theatlantic.com/education/archive /2015/04/what-happens-when-students-boycott-a-standardized-test/390087 on December 3, 2020.

287   Lowery, W. (2017). *They can't kill us all: The story of the struggle for Black lives.* New York: Back Bay Books.

288   Chamorro-Premuzic, T. (2020, March 9). *How to work with someone who's disengaged.* Accessed at https://hbr.org/2020/03/how-to-work-with-someone -whos-disengaged on December 3, 2020.

289   Chamorro-Premuzic, T. (2020, March 9). *How to work with someone who's disengaged.* Accessed at https://hbr.org/2020/03/how-to-work-with-someone -whos-disengaged on December 3, 2020.

290   Kinder, M. (2020). *Essential but undervalued: Millions of health care workers aren't getting the pay or respect they deserve in the COVID-19 pandemic.* Washington, DC: Brookings Institution. Accessed at www.brookings.edu /research/essential-but-undervalued-millions-of-health-care-workers-arent -getting-the-pay-or-respect-they-deserve-in-the-covid-19-pandemic/ on March 24, 2021.

291   Gerth, H. H., & Mills, C. W. (1946). *From Max Weber: Essays in sociology.* Oxford, England: Oxford University Press, p. 214.

292 Gerth, H. H., & Mills, C. W. (1946). *From Max Weber: Essays in sociology.* Oxford, England: Oxford University Press, p. 215.

293 Weber, M. (1958). *The Protestant ethic and the spirit of capitalism.* New York: Scribner, p. 181.

294 Weber, M. (1958). *The Protestant ethic and the spirit of capitalism.* New York: Scribner, p. 182.

295 Tyack, D., & Tobin, W. (1994). The "grammar" of schooling: Why has it been so hard to change? *American Educational Research Journal, 31*(3), 453–479. Accessed at www.jstor.org/stable/1163222 on October 8, 2020.

296 Katz, M. B. (1975). *Class, bureaucracy, and schools: The illusion of educational change in America.* New York: Praeger.

297 Weber, M. (1978). *Economy and society: An outline of interpretive sociology.* Berkeley, CA: University of California Press, p. 1000.

298 Lee, M., & Larson, R. (2000). The Korean 'examination hell': Long hours of studying, distress, and depression. *Journal of Youth and Adolescence, 29,* 249–271. Accessed at https://doi.org/10.1023/A:1005160717081 on March 24, 2021; Dah-Sol, G. (2019, October 23). Why Korean students are obsessed with university admission. *Asia Times.* Accessed at https://asiatimes.com/2019/10/why-korean-students-are-obsessed-with-the-university-admission/ on March 24, 2021.

299 Bassock, D., Lapham, S., & Rorem, A. (2016). Is kindergarten the new first grade? *AERA Open, 1*(4), 1–31. Accessed at https://journals.sagepub.com/doi/pdf/10.1177/2332858415616358 on March 24, 2021.

300 Callahan, R. E. (1962). *Education and the cult of efficiency: A study of the social forces that have shaped the administration of public schools.* Chicago: University of Chicago Press.

301 Strauss, V. (2020, June 21). *It looks like the beginning of the end of America's obsession with standardized tests.* Accessed at www.washingtonpost.com/education/2020/06/21/it-looks-like-beginning-end-americas-obsession-with-student-standardized-tests/ on December 3, 2020.

302 Marx, K. (1967). *Writings of the young Marx on philosophy and society* (L. D. Easton & K. H. Guddat, Trans.). Garden City, NY: Anchor. (Original work published 1844)

303 Alienation. (n.d.). In *Merriam-Webster's online dictionary.* Accessed at www.merriam-webster.com/dictionary/alienation on December 3, 2020.

304 Marx, K. (1967). *Writings of the young Marx on philosophy and society* (L. D. Easton & K. H. Guddat, Trans.). Garden City, NY: Anchor. (Original work published 1844), p. 292.

305 Shantz, A., Alfes, K., Bailey, C., & Soane, E. (2015). Drivers and outcomes of work alienation: Reviving a concept. *Journal of Management Inquiry, 24*(4), 382–393.

306 Goldthorpe, J. H., Lockwood, D., Bechhofer, F., & Platt, J. (1968). *The affluent worker: Political attitudes and behavior.* New York: Cambridge University Press.

307 Gallup. (2017). *State of the American workplace.* Accessed at https://quality incentivecompany.com/wp-content/uploads/2017/02/SOAW-2017.pdf on March 24, 2021, p. 2.

308 Shantz, A., Alfes, K., Bailey, C., & Soane, E. (2015). Drivers and outcomes of work alienation: Reviving a concept. *Journal of Management Inquiry, 24*(4), 382–393.

309 Anyon, J. (1980). Social class and the hidden curriculum of work. *Journal of Education, 162*(1), 67–92.

310 Anyon, J. (1980). Social class and the hidden curriculum of work. *Journal of Education, 162*(1), 67–92, p. 79.

311 Anyon, J. (1980). Social class and the hidden curriculum of work. *Journal of Education, 162*(1), 67–92, p. 79.

312 Anyon, J. (1980). Social class and the hidden curriculum of work. *Journal of Education, 162*(1), 67–92, p. 73.

313 Golann, J. W., & Torres, A. C. (2020). Do no-excuses disciplinary strategies promote success? *Journal of Urban Affairs, 42*(4), 617–633; Pondiscio, R. (2019). *How the other half learns: Equality, excellence, and the battle over school choice.* New York: Avery.

314 Shirley, D., & MacDonald, E. (2017). *The mindful teacher* (2nd ed.). New York: Teachers College Press.

315 Shirley, D., & MacDonald, E. (2017). *The mindful teacher* (2nd ed.). New York: Teachers College Press.

316 Anomie. (2020). In *Encyclopaedia Britannica.* Accessed at www.britannica .com/topic/anomie on December 9, 2020.

317 Durkheim, E. (1951). *Suicide: A study in sociology* (J. Spaulding & G. Simpson, Trans.). New York: Free Press. (Original work published 1897)

318 Brown, P., & Rans, R. (1985). Material girl [Recorded by Madonna]. On *Like a virgin* [CD]. New York: Sire.

319 Collins, S. (2009). *The hunger games.* New York: Scholastic Press.

320 Winterson, J. (2009). *The stone gods.* Boston, MA: Houghton Mifflin Harcourt.

321 Durkheim, E. (1951). *Suicide: A study in sociology* (J. Spaulding & G. Simpson, Trans.). New York: Free Press. (Original work published 1897), p. 257.

322 Collins, J. (2009). *How the mighty fall: And why some companies never give in.* New York: HarperCollins, pp. 45–64.

323 Durkheim, E. (1951). *Suicide: A study in sociology* (J. Spaulding & G. Simpson, Trans.). New York: Free Press. (Original work published 1897), p. 257.

324 American Psychiatric Association. (2013). *Diagnostic and statistical manual of mental disorders* (5th ed.). Washington, DC: American Psychiatric Publishing.

325 Twenge, J. M., & Campbell, W. K. (2009). *The narcissism epidemic: Living in the age of entitlement.* New York: Atria.

326 Twenge, J. M., & Campbell, W. K. (2009). *The narcissism epidemic: Living in the age of entitlement.* New York: Atria, p. 30.

327 Twenge, J. M., & Campbell, W. K. (2009). *The narcissism epidemic: Living in the age of entitlement.* New York: Atria, p. 77.

328 Durkheim, E. (1961). *Moral education: A study in the theory and application of the sociology of education* (1st ed.). (E. K. Wilson & H. Schnurer, Trans.). New York: Free Press. (Original work published 1925)

329 Durkheim, E. (1961). *Moral education: A study in the theory and application of the sociology of education* (1st ed.). (E. K. Wilson & H. Schnurer, Trans.). New York: Free Press. (Original work published 1925), p. 80.

330 Durkheim, E. (1961). *Moral education: A study in the theory and application of the sociology of education* (1st ed.). (E. K. Wilson & H. Schnurer, Trans.). New York: Free Press. (Original work published 1925), p. 235.

331 Durkheim, E. (1951). *Suicide: A study in sociology* (J. Spaulding & G. Simpson, Trans.). New York: Free Press. (Original work published 1897), p. 110.

332 Hargreaves, A., & Shirley, D. (in press). *Well-being and socio-emotional learning: How to build everyone back better.* Alexandria, VA: Association for Supervision and Curriculum Development.

333 Shirley, D. (1997). *Community organizing for urban school reform.* Austin: University of Texas Press; Putnam, R. D. (2000). *Bowling alone: The collapse and revival of American community.* New York: Simon & Schuster; Warren, M. (2001). *Dry bones rattling: Community building to revitalize American democracy.* Princeton, NJ: Princeton University Press.

334 Carney, T. P. (2019). *Alienated America: Why some places thrive while others collapse.* New York: HarperCollins; Cass, O. (2018). *The once and future worker: A vision for the renewal of work in America.* New York: Encounter.

335 Reich, R. B. (2020). *The system: Who rigged it, how we fix it.* New York: Knopf, p. 125.

336 Blustein, D. L. (2019). *The importance of work in an age of uncertainty: The eroding work experience in America.* New York: Oxford University Press, p. 42.

337 Joseph, K. (1974). *Speech at Edgbaston.* Accessed at www.margaretthatcher .org/document/101830 on December 3, 2020.

338 Herrnstein, R. J., & Murray, C. (1994). *The bell curve: Intelligence and class structure in American life.* New York: Free Press, p. 204.

339 Murray, C. (2013). *Coming apart: The state of white America, 1960–2010.* New York: Crown Forum.

340 Murray, C. (2013). *Coming apart: The state of white America, 1960–2010.* New York: Crown Forum, p. 362.

341 Vance, J. D. (2016). *Hillbilly elegy: A memoir of a family and culture in crisis.* New York: HarperCollins.

342 Vance, J. D. (2016). *Hillbilly elegy: A memoir of a family and culture in crisis.* New York: HarperCollins, p. 146.

343 Vance, J. D. (2016). *Hillbilly elegy: A memoir of a family and culture in crisis.* New York: HarperCollins, p. 146.

344 Wilkinson, R., & Pickett, K. (2018). *The inner level: How more equal societies reduce stress, restore sanity, and improve everyone's well-being.* New York: Penguin.

345 Sahlberg, P., & Walker, T. D. (2021). *In teachers we trust: The Finnish way to world-class schools.* New York: Norton.

346 Waller, W. (1932). *The sociology of teaching.* New York: Wiley, p. 10.

347 Waller, W. (1932). *The sociology of teaching.* New York: Wiley, pp. 195–196.

348 Waller, W. (1932). *The sociology of teaching.* New York: Wiley, pp. 195–196.

349 Waller, W. (1932). *The sociology of teaching.* New York: Wiley, p. 196.

350 Holt, J. (1964). *How children fail.* London: Penguin; Holt, J. (1967). *How children learn.* London: Penguin.

351 Tyack, D., & Tobin, W. (1994). The "grammar" of schooling: Why has it been so hard to change? *American Educational Research Journal, 31*(3), 453–479. Accessed at www.jstor.org/stable/1163222 on October 8, 2020.

352 Dahl, R. A. (1958). A critique of the ruling-elite model. *The American Political Science Review, 52*(2), 463–469, quote from p. 466.

353 Bachrach, P., & Baratz, M. S. (1962). Two faces of power. *The American Political Science Review, 56*(4), 947–952, p. 948.

354 Lukes, S. (1974). *Power: A radical view.* London: Macmillan.

355 Three examples are, first, the publication in 1971 of Italian Marxist Antonio Gramsci's 1929 *Prison Notebooks* and the resulting prominence of his concept of *hegemony*—rule through ideas and language of the powerful that become accepted as mere common sense. See Gramsci, A., Hoare, Q., & Nowell-Smith, G. (1971). *Selections from the prison notebooks of Antonio Gramsci.* New York: International Publishers. Second, in 1977, French philosopher Michel Foucault launched theories of power associated with all-encompassing state surveillance in Foucault, M. (1977). *Discipline and punish: The birth of the prison.* New York: Pantheon Books. Last, feminist theorists later dissolved the distinction between personal and political issues in understandings of identity, autonomy, and agency. See, for instance, Barclay, L. (2000). Autonomy and the social self. In N. Stoljar & C. Mackenzie (Eds.), *Relational autonomy: Feminist perspectives on autonomy, agency, and the social self* (pp. 52–71). New York: Oxford University Press.

356 Lukes, S. (2005). *Power: A radical view* (2nd ed.). Basingstoke, England: Palgrave Macmillan, p. 26.

357 Lukes, S. (2005). *Power: A radical view* (2nd ed.). Basingstoke, England: Palgrave Macmillan, p. 27.

358 Lukes, S. (2005). *Power: A radical view* (2nd ed.). Basingstoke, England: Palgrave Macmillan, p. 28.

359 Lukes, S. (2005). *Power: A radical view* (2nd ed.). Basingstoke, England: Palgrave Macmillan, p. 109.

360 Lukes, S. (2005). *Power: A radical view* (2nd ed.). Basingstoke, England: Palgrave Macmillan, p. 84.

361 Fielding, M. (2001). Students as radical agents of change. *Journal of Educational Change, 2*, 123–141, p. 124.

362 These examples come from Hargreaves, A., Shirley, D., Wangia, S., Bacon, C., & D'Angelo, M. (2018). *Leading from the middle: Spreading learning, well-being, and identity across Ontario.* Toronto, Canada: Council of Ontario Directors of Education. Accessed at http://ccsli.ca/downloads/2018-Leading _From_the_Middle_Final-EN.pdf on February 12, 2021.

363 Sahlberg, P., & Walker, T. D. (2021). *In teachers we trust: The Finnish way to world-class schools.* New York: Norton, p. 107.

364 Sahlberg, P., & Walker, T. D. (2021). *In teachers we trust: The Finnish way to world-class schools.* New York: Norton, p. 107.

365 Sahlberg, P., & Walker, T. D. (2021). *In teachers we trust: The Finnish way to world-class schools.* New York: Norton, p. 107.

366 Atchley, P. (2018). *Distraction is literally killing us* [Video file]. Accessed at www.ted.com/talks/paul_atchley_distraction_is_literally_killing_us_paul _atchley_tedxyouth_kc on December 3, 2020.

367 Abbott, T. (2020, February 11). America's love affair with their phones. *Reviews.org.* Accessed at www.reviews.org/mobile/cell-phone-addiction on March 24, 2021.

368 Cho, V. (2016). Organizational problem solving around digital distraction. *Journal of Professional Capital and Community, 1*(2), 145–158, p. 151.

369 Cho, V. (2016). Organizational problem solving around digital distraction. *Journal of Professional Capital and Community, 1*(2), 145–158, p. 151.

370 Cho, V. (2016). Organizational problem solving around digital distraction. *Journal of Professional Capital and Community, 1*(2), 145–158, p. 154.

371 Fullan, M., Quinn, J., & McEachen, J. (2018). *Deep learning: Engage the world change the world.* Thousand Oaks, CA: Corwin, pp. 80–82.

372 Fullan, M., Quinn, J., & McEachen, J. (2018). *Deep learning: Engage the world change the world.* Thousand Oaks, CA: Corwin, p. 61.

373 Many quotes in this and following sections are taken from our original interview transcripts with teachers and staff in the Consortium, and have not been published previously. Some of the quotes can be found in our original report for CODE: Hargreaves, A., Shirley, D., Wangia, S., Bacon, C., & D'Angelo, M. (2018). *Leading from the middle: Spreading learning, well-being, and identity across Ontario.* Toronto, Canada: Council of Ontario Directors of Education. Accessed at http://ccsli.ca/downloads/2018 -Leading_From_the_Middle_Final-EN.pdf on February 12, 2021.

374 Turkle, S. (2015). *Reclaiming conversation: The power of talk in a digital age.* New York: Penguin, p. 55.

375 Turkle, S. (2015). *Reclaiming conversation: The power of talk in a digital age.* New York: Penguin, p. 55.

376 Turkle, S. (2015). *Reclaiming conversation: The power of talk in a digital age.* New York: Penguin, p. 55.

377 Organisation for Economic Co-operation and Development. (2019). *TALIS 2018 results: Teachers and school leaders as lifelong learners* (Vol. 1). Paris:

Author. Accessed at https://doi.org/10.1787/1d0bc92a-en on December 3, 2020.

378   Ledsom, A. (2019, August 30). *The mobile phone ban in French schools, one year on. Would it work elsewhere?* Accessed at www.forbes.com/sites /alexledsom/2019/08/30/the-mobile-phone-ban-in-french-schools-one-year -on-would-it-work-elsewhere/#a4fe6255e705 on December 3, 2020.

379   Taylor, R. (1986). A kind of magic [Recorded by Queen]. On *A kind of magic* [Vinyl record]. Los Angeles, CA: EMI/Capitol Records.

380   Koretz, D. (2017). *The testing charade: Pretending to make schools better.* Chicago: University of Chicago Press.

381   Koretz, D. (2017). *The testing charade: Pretending to make schools better.* Chicago: University of Chicago Press, p. 178.

382   Koretz, D. (2017). *The testing charade: Pretending to make schools better.* Chicago: University of Chicago Press, pp. 182, 186.

383   Koretz, D. (2017). *The testing charade: Pretending to make schools better.* Chicago: University of Chicago Press, p. 192.

384   Nichols, S. L., & Berliner, D. C. (2007). *Collateral damage: How high-stakes testing corrupts America's schools.* Cambridge, MA: Harvard Education Press; Zhao, Y. (2018). *What works may hurt—Side effects in education.* New York: Teachers College Press; Tymms, P. (2004). Are standards rising in English primary schools? *British Educational Research Journal, 30*(4), 477–494; Rothstein, R. (2014, February 14). *A strong precedent for a better accountability system.* Washington, DC: Economic Policy Institute. Accessed at www.epi .org/blog/strong-precedent-accountability-system/ on March 24, 2021; Hargreaves, A. (2003). *Teaching in the knowledge society: Education in the age of insecurity.* New York: Teachers College Press; Ravitch, D. (2021, February 21). What you need to know about standardized testing. *Washington Post.* Accessed at www.washingtonpost.com/education/2021/02/01/need-to-know -about-standardized-testing/ on March 24, 2021.

385   Tucker, M. (2020, June 26). *COVID-19 and our schools: The real challenge.* Accessed at https://ncee.org/2020/06/covid-19-and-our-schools-the-real -challenge/ on March 24, 2021; Finn, C. E. (2020, November 25). How badly has the pandemic hurt K-12 learning? Let state testing in the spring tell us. *Washington Post.* Accessed at www.washingtonpost.com /opinions/2020/11/25/how-badly-has-pandemic-hurt-k-12-learning -let-state-testing-spring-tell-us/ on March 24, 2021; Washington Post Editorial Board. (2021, January 8). Why we shouldn't abandon student testing this spring. *Washington Post.* Accessed at www.washingtonpost .com/opinions/why-we-shouldnt-abandon-student-testing-this- spring/2021/01/08/839eb860-4ed4-11eb-83e3-322644d82356_story.html on March 24, 2021.

386   Campbell, D. T. (1975). Assessing the impact of planned social change. In G. M. Lyons (Ed.), *Social research and public policies: The Dartmouth/OECD conference.* Hanover, NH: Public Affairs Center, Dartmouth College, p. 35.

387   Hargreaves, A. (2020). Large-scale assessments and their effects: The case of mid-stakes tests in Ontario. *Journal of Educational Change, 21,* 393–420. Accessed at https://doi.org/10.1007/s10833-020-09380-5 on December 3, 2020.

388 Lee, J., & Kang, C. (2019). A litmus test of school accountability policy effects in Korea: Cross-validating high-stakes test results for academic excellence and equity. *Asia Pacific Journal of Education, 39*(4), 517–531.

389 Ontario Ministry of Education. (2014). *Achieving excellence: A renewed vision for education in Ontario.* Toronto, Canada: Queen's Printer for Ontario. Accessed at www.edu.gov.on.ca/eng/about/great.html on December 3, 2020.

390 Hargreaves, A., Shirley, D., Wangia, S., Bacon, C., & D'Angelo, M. (2018). *Leading from the middle: Spreading learning, well-being, and identity across Ontario.* Toronto, Canada: Council of Ontario Directors of Education. Accessed at http://ccsli.ca/downloads/2018-Leading_From_the_Middle _Final-EN.pdf on February 12, 2021.

391 Hargreaves, A., Shirley, D., Wangia, S., Bacon, C., & D'Angelo, M. (2018). *Leading from the middle: Spreading learning, well-being, and identity across Ontario.* Toronto, Canada: Council of Ontario Directors of Education. Accessed at http://ccsli.ca/downloads/2018-Leading_From_the_Middle _Final-EN.pdf on February 12, 2021.

392 Hargreaves, A., Shirley, D., Wangia, S., Bacon, C., & D'Angelo, M. (2018). *Leading from the middle: Spreading learning, well-being, and identity across Ontario.* Toronto, Canada: Council of Ontario Directors of Education. Accessed at http://ccsli.ca/downloads/2018-Leading_From_the_Middle _Final-EN.pdf on February 12, 2021.

393 Hargreaves, A. (2020). Large-scale assessments and their effects: The case of mid-stakes tests in Ontario. *Journal of Educational Change, 21*, 393–420. Accessed at https://doi.org/10.1007/s10833-020-09380-5 on February 12, 2021.

394 Hargreaves, A. (2020). Large-scale assessments and their effects: The case of mid-stakes tests in Ontario. *Journal of Educational Change, 21*, 393–420. Accessed at https://doi.org/10.1007/s10833-020-09380-5 on December 3, 2020.

395 Hargreaves, A. (2020). Large-scale assessments and their effects: The case of mid-stakes tests in Ontario. *Journal of Educational Change, 21*, 393–420. Accessed at https://doi.org/10.1007/s10833-020-09380-5 on February 12, 2021.

396 Hargreaves, A., Shirley, D., Wangia, S., Bacon, C., & D'Angelo, M. (2018). *Leading from the middle: Spreading learning, well-being, and identity across Ontario.* Toronto, Canada: Council of Ontario Directors of Education. Accessed at http://ccsli.ca/downloads/2018-Leading_From_the_Middle _Final-EN.pdf on February 12, 2021.

397 Hargreaves, A. (2020). Large-scale assessments and their effects: The case of mid-stakes tests in Ontario. *Journal of Educational Change, 21*, 393–420. Accessed at https://doi.org/10.1007/s10833-020-09380-5 on December 3, 2020.

398 Hargreaves, A., Shirley, D., Wangia, S., Bacon, C., & D'Angelo, M. (2018). *Leading from the middle: Spreading learning, well-being, and identity across Ontario.* Toronto, Canada: Council of Ontario Directors of Education. Accessed at http://ccsli.ca/downloads/2018-Leading_From_the_Middle _Final-EN.pdf on February 12, 2021.

399 New Pedagogies for Deep Learning. (2019). *Homepage—New Pedagogies for Deep Learning*. Accessed at www.npdl.global on December 9, 2020.

400 Hill, P. W., & Crévola, C. A. (1999). Key features of a whole-school, design approach to literacy teaching in schools. *Australian Journal of Learning Difficulties, 4*(3), 5–11.

401 Hargreaves, A. (2020). Large-scale assessments and their effects: The case of mid-stakes tests in Ontario. *Journal of Educational Change, 21*, 393–420. Accessed at https://doi.org/10.1007/s10833-020-09380-5 on December 3, 2020.

402 Hargreaves, A. (2020). Large-scale assessments and their effects: The case of mid-stakes tests in Ontario. *Journal of Educational Change, 21*, 393–420. Accessed at https://doi.org/10.1007/s10833-020-09380-5 on February 12, 2021; Hargreaves, A., Shirley, D., Wangia, S., Bacon, C., & D'Angelo, M. (2018). *Leading from the middle: Spreading learning, well-being, and identity across Ontario*. Toronto, Canada: Council of Ontario Directors of Education. Accessed at http://ccsli.ca/downloads/2018-Leading_From_the _Middle_Final-EN.pdf on February 12, 2021.

403 Hargreaves, A., Shirley, D., Wangia, S., Bacon, C., & D'Angelo, M. (2018). *Leading from the middle: Spreading learning, well-being, and identity across Ontario*. Toronto, Canada: Council of Ontario Directors of Education. Accessed at http://ccsli.ca/downloads/2018-Leading_From_the_Middle _Final-EN.pdf on February 12, 2021.

404 Hargreaves, A., Shirley, D., Wangia, S., Bacon, C., & D'Angelo, M. (2018). *Leading from the middle: Spreading learning, well-being, and identity across Ontario*. Toronto, Canada: Council of Ontario Directors of Education. Accessed at http://ccsli.ca/downloads/2018-Leading_From_the_Middle _Final-EN.pdf on February 12, 2021.

405 Hargreaves, A. (2020). Large-scale assessments and their effects: The case of mid-stakes tests in Ontario. *Journal of Educational Change, 21*, 393–420. Accessed at https://doi.org/10.1007/s10833-020-09380-5 on February 12, 2021.

406 Hargreaves, A. (2020). Large-scale assessments and their effects: The case of mid-stakes tests in Ontario. *Journal of Educational Change, 21*, 393–420. Accessed at https://doi.org/10.1007/s10833-020-09380-5 on February 12, 2021.

407 Campbell, C., Clinton, J., Fullan, M., Hargreaves, A., James, C., & Longboat, K. D. (2018). *Ontario: A learning province*. Toronto, Canada: Queens Printer.

408 Campbell, C., Clinton, J., Fullan, M., Hargreaves, A., James, C., & Longboat, K. D. (2018). *Ontario: A learning province*. Toronto, Canada: Queens Printer, p. 12.

409 McGaw, B., Louden, W., & Wyatt-Smith, C. (2020). *NAPLAN Review Final Report*. Australia: State of New South Wales, State of Queensland, State of Victoria, and Australian Capital Territory.

410 Bolton, R. (2020, August 30). Education critics should focus on the message, not the messenger. *Australian Financial Review*. Accessed at www.afr.com /work-and-careers/education/education-critics-should-focus-on-the-message -not-the-messenger-20200830-p55qms on March 24, 2021.

411 Fullan, M. (2021, February). The right drivers for whole system success. *CSE Leading Education Series #1*. Melbourne, Australia: Centre for Strategic Education. Accessed at https://michaelfullan.ca/wp-content/uploads/2021/03/Fullan-CSE-Leading-Education-Series-01-2021R2-compressed.pdf on March 24, 2021.

412 Article 29 Data Protection Working Party of the European Union. (2013). *Opinion 03/2013 on purpose limitation*. Accessed at https://ec.europa.eu/justice/article-29/documentation/opinion-recommendation/files/2013/wp203_en.pdf on December 9, 2020.

413 Scottish Government Learning Directorate. (2019, August 30). *National standardised assessments in Scotland: Purpose and use*. Accessed at www.gov.scot/publications/scottish-national-standardised-assessments-purpose-and-use/ on December 3, 2020.

414 Sahlberg, P. (2011). The fourth way of Finland. *Journal of Educational Change, 12*(2), 173–185. Accessed at https://pasisahlberg.com/wp-content/uploads/2013/01/The-Fourth-Way-of-Filand-JEC-2011.pdf on December 9, 2020.

415 Marris, P. (1974). *Loss and change*. New York: Pantheon Books.

416 Shulman, L. S. (2005, February 6–8). *The signature pedagogies of the professions of law, medicine, engineering, and the clergy: Potential lessons for the education of teachers*. Paper presented at the Math Science Partnerships (MSP) workshop, Irvine, California.

417 Wiliam, D. (2017). *Embedded formative assessment* (2nd ed.). Bloomington, IN: Solution Tree Press. Also look at Wiliam's website for relevant video material at www.dylanwiliam.org/Dylan_Wiliams_website/Welcome.html.

418 Hargreaves, A., & O'Connor, M. T. (2018). *Collaborative professionalism: When teaching together means learning for all*. Thousand Oaks, CA: Corwin, chapter 3.

419 Specialist Schools and Academies Trust. (2011, December 20). *Professor Dylan Wiliam at the Schools Network Annual Conference* [Video file]. Accessed at www.youtube.com/watch?v=wKLo15A80lI on March 24, 2021.

420 TeacherToolkit.co.uk. [@teachertoolkit]. (n.d.). *Tweets and replies* [Twitter profile]. Accessed at https://twitter.com/TeacherToolkit on December 9, 2020.

421 McGill, R. (2021). *Mark. Plan. Teach. 2.0.* London: Bloomsbury Press.

422 Ravitch, D. (2020). *Slaying Goliath: The passionate resistance to privatization and the fight to save America's public schools*. New York: Knopf.

423 Carr, P. J., & Kefalas, M. J. (2009). *Hollowing out the middle: The rural brain drain and what it means for America*. Boston, MA: Beacon Press; Wood, R. E. (2008). *Survival of rural America: Small victories and bitter harvests*. Lawrence, KS: University Press of Kansas.

424 Hargreaves, A., & Fullan, M. (2012). *Professional capital: Transforming teaching in every school*. New York: Teachers College Press.

425 Kyzyma, I. (2018). Rural-urban disparity in poverty persistence. *Focus, 34*(3), 13–19.

426 Mackey, D. (2016, February 17). Rural by choice. *The Daily Yonder*. Accessed at https://dailyyonder.com/rural-by-choice-glenns-ferry-idaho/2016/02/17 on March 24, 2021.

427 Biesta, G. J. J. (2013). *The beautiful risk of education*. Boulder, CO: Paradigm.

428 Biesta, G. J. J. (2013). *The beautiful risk of education*. Boulder, CO: Paradigm, p. 124.

429 Siskin, L. S., & Little, J. W. (1995). *The subjects in question: Departmental organization and the high school*. New York: Teachers College Press; Hargreaves, A. (1994). *Changing teachers, changing times: Teachers' work and culture in the postmodern age*. New York: Teachers College Press.

430 Sachar, L. (1998). *Holes*. New York: Yearling.

431 Wortham, S. (2006). *Learning identity: The joint emergence of social identification and academic learning*. New York: Cambridge University Press.

432 Hargreaves, A., Parsley, D., & Cox, E. K. (2015). Designing rural school improvement networks: Aspirations and actualities. *Peabody Journal of Education, 2*(90), 306–321; Johnston, C., Kim, M. J., Martin, K., Martin, M., Shirley, D., & Spriggs, C. (2018). Rural teachers forging new bonds—and new solutions. *Educational Leadership, 76*(3), 56–62.

433 Primus, V. (2009, May/June). Songs for hard times. *Harvard Magazine*. Accessed at https://harvardmagazine.com/2009/05/song-hard-times on March 24, 2021.

434 Hobbs, T. D. (2019, April 19). *Three decades of school shootings: An analysis*. Accessed at www.wsj.com/graphics/school-shooters-similarities/ on December 3, 2020.

435 Christakis, E. (2020, December). *School wasn't so great before COVID, either*. Accessed at www.theatlantic.com/magazine/archive/2020/12/school -wasnt-so-great-before-covid-either/616923/ on December 3, 2020.

436 O'Connor, M. (2017). *Everybody knows everybody? Investigating rural secondary students' language choices in response to audience across argument writing experiences*. Unpublished doctoral dissertation, Boston College, Newton, MA.

437 Dewey, J. (1921). *Democracy and education*. New York: Macmillan, p. 101.

438 Sizer, T. R. (1984). *Horace's compromise: The dilemma of the American high school*. New York: Houghton Mifflin.

439 These quotes and the others in this paragraph can be located at Coalition of Essential Schools. (n.d.). *Common principles*. Accessed at http://essential schools.org/common-principles/ on December 9, 2020.

440 Biden, J. (2020, October 22). Remarks made in the final U.S. presidential debate with Donald Trump, as reported in Millbank, D. (2020). The only thing worse for Trump than an unwatchable debate is a watchable one. *Washington Post*.

441 Westheimer, J. (2015). *What kind of citizen? Educating our children for the common good*. New York: Teachers College Press.

442 See also Fullan, M. (2021, February). *The right drivers for whole system success*. Melbourne, Australia: Centre for Strategic Education.

Index

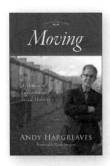

Moving
Andy Hargreaves
Social mobility—the chance, through education, to achieve greater success than one's parents—is a compelling issue of our time. Beginning in 1950s northern England, this revealing memoir links Andy Hargreaves's experiences of social mobility to today's challenges of inequity and immobility.
BKF953

Loving What They Learn
Alexander McNeece
Deep learning and high engagement are possible for all students, regardless of subject, grade, or previous experience. With *Loving What They Learn*, you will discover how to quantifiably measure students' needs, help strengthen their academic self-concept, and increase their self-efficacy.
BKF917

Fifty Strategies to Boost Cognitive Engagement
Rebecca Stobaugh
Transform your classroom from one of passive knowledge consumption to one of active engagement. In this well-researched book, Rebecca Stobaugh shares fifty strategies for building a thinking culture that emphasizes essential 21st century skills—from critical thinking and problem solving to teamwork and creativity.
BKF894

Personalized Deeper Learning
James A. Bellanca
Foster deeper learning with two templates—one for students, the other for teachers—that increase student agency and learning transfer within critical skill sets. Any teacher—regardless of grade, existing curriculum, or student load—can adapt, scale, and sustain these powerful personalized learning plans.
BKF975

Solution Tree | Press

a division of
Solution Tree

Visit SolutionTree.com or call 800.733.6786 to order.

Wait! Your professional development journey doesn't have to end with the last pages of this book.

We realize improving student learning doesn't happen overnight. And your school or district shouldn't be left to puzzle out all the details of this process alone.

No matter where you are on the journey, we're committed to helping you get to the next stage.

Take advantage of everything from **custom workshops** to **keynote presentations** and **interactive web and video conferencing**. We can even help you develop an action plan tailored to fit your specific needs.

Let's get the conversation started.

Call 888.763.9045 today.

SolutionTree.com

A BJ Vinson Mystery

No good deed goes unpunished, as investigator BJ Vinson is about to discover.

Writer John Pierce Belhaven was murdered before he could reveal the name of another killer—one connected to the biggest scandal to rock Albuquerque in years. Two of the city's most prominent citizens—Barron Voxlightner and Dr. Walther Stabler—vanished in 2004, along with fifty million dollars looted from Voxlightner Precious Metals Recovery Corp. It only makes sense that poking into that disappearance cost Belhaven his life.

But BJ isn't so sure.

He's agreed to help novice detective Roy Guerra reopen the old case—which the wealthy and influential Voxlightner family doesn't want dredged up. But Belhaven was part of their family, and that connection could've led to his murder. Or did the sixty-year-old author die because of a sordid sexual affair?

DON TRAVIS is a man totally captivated by his adopted state of New Mexico. Each of his seven BJ Vinson mystery novels features some region of the state as prominently as it does his protagonist, a gay, former Marine ex-cop turned confidential investigator. Don never made it to the Marines (three years in the Army was all he managed) and certainly didn't join the Albuquerque Police Department. He thought he was a paint artist for a while, but ditched that for writing a few years back. A loner, he fulfills his social needs by attending SouthWest Writers meetings and teaching Wordwrights, a weekly writing class at the North Domingo Baca Multigenerational Center in Albuquerque.

Facebook: Don Travis
Twitter: @dontravis3
Website: dontravis.com

FOR **MORE** OF THE **BEST GAY ROMANCE**